D1520492

BEYOND HEGEMONY

Manchester University Press

For Diana, Luca and Francis

Darrow Schecter

BEYOND HEGEMONY

Towards a new philosophy
of political legitimacy

Manchester University Press
Manchester and New York

distributed exclusively in the USA by Palgrave

Copyright © Darrow Schecter 2005

The right of Darrow Schecter to be identified as the author of this work has been asserted by him in accordance with the Copyright, Designs and Patents Act 1988.

Published by Manchester University Press
Oxford Road, Manchester M13 9NR, UK
and Room 400, 175 Fifth Avenue, New York, NY 10010, USA
www.manchesteruniversitypress.co.uk

Distributed exclusively in the USA by
Palgrave, 175 Fifth Avenue, New York,
NY 10010, USA

Distributed exclusively in Canada by
UBC Press, University of British Columbia, 2029 West Mall,
Vancouver, BC, Canada V6T 1Z2

British Library Cataloguing-in-Publication Data
A catalogue record for this book is available from the British Library

Library of Congress Cataloging-in-Publication Data applied for

ISBN   0 7190 6088 5 *hardback*
EAN   978 0 7190 6088 5

First published 2005

14 13 12 11 10 09 08 07 06 05   10 9 8 7 6 5 4 3 2 1

Typeset by
Action Publishing Technology Ltd, Gloucester
Printed in Great Britain
by CPI, Bath

Contents

Acknowledgements

I have been lucky to discuss the ideas in this book with people in different fields, many of whom have helped me clarify my thoughts on the complex issue of political legitimacy. I accept sole responsibility for any flaws, oversights and related shortcomings, and would like to take this opportunity to say a couple of words of thanks.

Over the past few years I have had the pleasure of working with a number of very gifted undergraduate, MA, and doctoral students at the University of Sussex, a number of whose ideas have significantly improved the text which follows. Amongst the undergraduates I would especially like to thank Simon Parkyn and Will Woodward. Several students on the Sussex MA degrees in Social and Political Thought (SPT) and Critical Theory have been passionate and inspiring. Thanks to Ben Day, Michael Heyman, Vincent Leysen, Charles Masquelier, Christopher Reade, Matt Robinson and Sam Thomas. At the doctoral level I would like to thank Tim Black and Catherine Hollis for their insights, and to congratulate Arianna Bove and Erik Empson. Learning together with Chris Wyatt has been a brilliant experience that I will not forget.

Colleagues at the University of Sussex, some of whom have just arrived and others who are leaving, read draft chapters and have been remarkably generous with their time and comments. I am indebted to Andrew Chitty, Gordon Finlayson (welcome), Eric Jacobson (good luck), Kathryn MacVarish, Luke Martell, Stephen Robinson, Neil Stammers, Daniel Steuer, Céline Surprenant and Michael Underhill for their suggestions. Edith Meredith and Karin Owen's great administrative work made things much easier in the day-to-day struggle with bureaucracy. This is probably also the right place to say that Steve Brown, Andrew Chitty, William Outhwaite and Richard Whatmore continue to make postgraduate study at Sussex an exercise in academic excellence. The fine work done on the MA and DPhil programmes in SPT and Intellectual History in recent years owes a great deal to their talent and dedication.

Colleagues at other universities have been supportive in different ways. Thanks to Richard Bellamy, Jean Demer Piac, Jeremy Lester, David McClellan, Drew Milne, Alan Norrie, Stuart Toddington and especially to Fabio Vighi. It has been very enjoyable working with Tony Mason and Lucy Nicholson at Manchester University Press, and I look forward to new projects with them in the future.

Without the aid of Hildegard Göbel, Werner Göbel, Fareba Lotfie and Amy West, which came in the form of infinite patience and good humour, I would still be writing. Many thanks!

Acknowledgements

Fernand Avila, Gary Barber, Costantino Ciervo, Mike Evans, Giovanni Ghiandoni, Richard Mogg, Patrizia Luzi, Mand Ryaïra, Jarret Schecter and my parents have helped me in ways I never anticipated but hope to reciprocate some day.

The best ideas in this book stem from my discussions with Chris Thornhill, and I dare say that he has got a better handle on them than I do.

This book is dedicated to Diana, Luca and Francis for reasons they already know, and I am slowly beginning to understand.

D.S.

Introduction

SINCE the recent consolidation of what is often referred to as the linguistic turn of social and political thought and the related rise to academic and cultural prominence of postmodernism, it would appear that the modernist aspiration to elaborate an updated version of the Enlightenment has failed. Many observers regard the collapse of Soviet state socialism in 1989–90 and the subsequent globalisation of both capitalism and anti-capitalist protest movements as symptomatic of the irreversibility of the modernist capitulation to postmodernism in economics, politics, international relations, art and philosophy. According to this line of interpretation, the term modernism indicates a circumscribed historical period marked by attempts to appropriate the philosophical and scientific ideals of the Enlightenment and French Revolution for utopian experiments in politics and aesthetics within the framework defined by the emergence of nation-states and the rise of industrial capitalism. Examples of the modernist attempt to combine radical politics and aesthetics in Europe include early Bolshevism in Russia, futurism in Italy and surrealism in France and Spain. As these examples suggest, modernism is characterised by the links between reason, the imagination and the possibility of revolution suggested by the events of 1789 and 1917. By contrast, postmodernism emerges with the rise of the new left and new social movements following the student and worker revolts in Paris and Strasbourg in 1968, and is characterised by the ascendance of the combined forces of the media, communication, the advance of marketing techniques and the democratisation of consumer choice. Whilst many modernist and postmodernist thinkers regard reason and technology to be forces for progress, postmodernists generally decouple reason and technology from grand-scale visions of political alternatives to liberal democracy and capitalism. Utopia remains but is articulated in more fragmented and small-scale versions such as those realised in alternative lifestyles and identities, self-ironic literary satire and movement politics. Supporters and opponents of the very notion of postmodernism seem to agree that, whatever postmodernism means, it suggests something about a vaguely post-political cultural form in which the grand narratives of modernist politics have been jettisoned for the more modest claims of individuals in their search for intra-personal dialogue and understanding.[1] Manifestations of this change can be seen in the shift from the universal claims of Enlightenment rationality commonly ascribed to Rousseau and Marx to the more textual and interpretative orientation exemplified in theories of communicative action, deconstruction and pragmatism. The political programme implied by the transition from Enlightenment reason aiming at knowledge to communicative reason aiming at understanding is that language and language games offer an interactive and humanist perspective on the possibility of solving conflict and reaching consensus on fundamental issues that is appropriate for politics after the fall of metaphysics and the demise of traditional idealism associated with thinkers like Kant and Hegel.[2] Theorists of communicative action are likely to oppose this juxtaposition by insisting that communication and understanding are in fact instances of post-metaphysical knowledge that emerge in dialogue, and as such, communicative and pragmatic reason mark an epistemological step beyond the dogmatic and solipsistic premises of the philosophy of consciousness developed by the thinkers of traditional idealism. There is thus a series of elective affinities uniting contemporary liberal and democratic notions of freedom of expression, value-neutral inquiry in the arts and sciences, suspicion of metaphysics and the defence of individual liberty, on the one hand, with the emphasis on the diversity of individual experience, the plurality of local contexts, and the impossibility of foreseeing the outcomes of open dialogue that characterises the writings of the theorists of postmodernism and the linguistic turn, on the other.

Construed in these terms, it appears that the illiberal and undemocratic features of particular modernist movements such as state socialism and futurism can be traced back to the Enlightenment notion of the perfectibility of humanity through reason, which is used by political fanatics to impose systems of illegitimate rule on populations that never wanted to pursue such integral visions of the good of all or the general will in the first place. Against the excesses of the radical modernist interpretation of Enlightenment, the liberal democratic interpretation of the Enlightenment which has in effect prevailed to date and is rearticulated in different ways by postmodernists and theorists of communicative action stresses the danger of any political project aiming to establish the legitimate good for all of humankind. Instead, the state must remain neutral with regard to competing claims of what constitutes the good life, and thus limit its interventions in the private affairs of citizens to those actions that can be squared with the universal postulates of legality. In defence of this position it can be claimed that it is the liberal democratic freedoms of assembly and expression that are the first casualties whenever an attempt is made to entrust the state with the task of deciding what is good for the citizenry. Through the legal enforcement of a free press, freedom of communication, and free exchange of goods and information, the citizenry can decide these things for themselves. From the liberal democratic perspective, the ideals of the Enlightenment are thus best preserved through free institutions which do not attempt to impose a metaphysical and tyrannical vision of political legitimacy. Neutral and objective law is the foundation of liberal democratic legitimacy – not extra-legal conceptions of the legitimate good. Extra-legal conceptions of the good are moreover irrational or in any case private and purely subjective. Hence liberal democratic

Introduction

Enlightenment requires that reason indicate the boundaries of legitimate state intervention, but more important, it requires that the claims of reason and legitimacy stop with the delineation of those boundaries. These are epistemological and political boundaries beyond which reason becomes irrational and states become illegitimate. Political legitimacy that limits itself to legitimate intervention and enforcement of a form of law that is itself neutral with regard to competing conceptions of legitimacy is the indispensable *precondition* of freedom. Liberal democratic epistemology proceeds from a starting point which is also a conclusion: liberals know what the preconditions of liberty are from a perspective that is *already* emancipated from illegitimate political intrusion into the naturally legitimate private sphere of interpersonal interaction and economic exchange. It is from this already emancipated position that the difference between the practice of legitimate law enforcement and the illegitimate abuse of law is ascertainable.

One of the central tasks of the current book is to analyse this circularity in liberal argument with a view to radicalising its premises rather than simply deconstructing it. Hence the book offers amongst other things an immanent critique of liberalism rather than an immanent reparation of liberal ideas or an attack on liberalism from supposedly post-liberal political positions. It will be seen that an immanent critique of liberal epistemology leads to a re-examination of the question of the *conditions* of political legitimacy. Liberalism regards this question as an epistemological and political question centrally concerned with law. When the question of the conditions of political legitimacy is radicalised in terms of its premises and conclusions, liberalism is undermined without undermining the possibility of a non-instrumental praxis of law which mediates between humanity and nature in a way that produces knowledge rather than the fabricated consensus characteristic of hegemony. This book attempts to challenge the liberal democratic interpretation of the Enlightenment without advocating a return to metaphysical conceptions of the good or the establishment of a dictatorial order necessary to impose any such political programme. To this extent it seeks to provide the philosophical and political impetus for a relaunching of the Enlightenment project and the centrality of reason and law involved in that project. This may sound like an attempt to re-consolidate the bases of the liberal world-view in the face of contemporary socio-political realities, but it is not. It will be useful for the reader if I state at the outset that the present study is guided by the idea that the path beyond liberalism and liberal democratic versions of the Enlightenment starts with an examination of the fundamental tenets underpinning the juridical bases of liberal epistemology. The book seeks to provide this examination in a way that challenges the assumptions of liberal democrats, postmodernists and advocates of the linguistic turn in social and political thought. What is attempted is a reconfiguration of reason, legality and legitimacy which breaks decisively both with the liberal democratic understanding of the mediated relation between those terms and with authoritarian projects to establish extra-legal legitimacy. In this context, the first questions that may arise include: why focus on reason, legality and legitimacy as the best way to mount a critique of liberal democracy, postmodernism and recent social and political thought, and how does this critique indicate an alternative to radical modernist and liberal democratic conceptions of Enlightenment?

Despite the many problems with liberalism which will be explored here, there is as yet no credible theory of politics capable of envisaging the contours of a legitimate political order outside the mediations of reason and law, i.e. outside the epistemological and political boundaries which are theorised with particular rigour in the liberal tradition from Kant to the present. The reasons why this is so will be examined in chapter 1. Moreover, political projects aiming to adjust the boundaries of liberal conceptions of reason and law as a way of moving from liberal legitimacy to democratic legitimacy fail in supposedly post-liberal and post-metaphysical democratic humanist theory and practice. The reasons for this failure will be explained in detail in chapter 2 by way of an analysis of state socialism and new social movements. Albeit in very different ways, state social-ism and new social movements attempt to move beyond the limited legitimacy of liberal democratic forms of legality. The failure of various attempts to steer a non-authoritarian and non-paternalistic (or politically correct) path beyond liberal theory and practice has a long history. A pivotal moment in the critique of liberal legality is found in the works of the early Marx, in which he distin-guishes between the political emancipation secured by the French Revolution and a form of human emancipation to be realised in a coming revolution. With hindsight it is clear that the libertarian revolution Marx was thinking of did not come to fruition in the former USSR, but what remains unclear is how it might be possible to break the boundaries of liberal democratic legality associated with political emancipation without embracing state socialist despotism, social democratic reformism, academic irrelevance or sheer political marginality. From the Bolsheviks to the new social movements, it appears to a great number of Marx's interpreters that the trick to moving beyond liberalism is to move beyond liberal law or law full stop. This is true but it is also in an important sense absolutely false. It will be argued here that it is false if what is meant by this is the determination to temper or soften liberal conceptions of reason and law with more humanistic and democratic conceptions of the legitimate good based on the experiences of social classes and minority groups which are oppressed by political emancipation in its liberal democratic instantiation. It may seem like a very unusual line of interpretation, but Marx himself warns against this notion of democratisation in *On the Jewish Question* (1843). Arguing in a polemical vein with Bruno Bauer, Marx observes that the project to define political eman-cipation in opposition to racial exclusion remains locked within the humanist parameters of the liberal democratic interpretation of the Enlightenment. Without denying or dismissing the real discrimination against Jews in his day (and foreshadowing a look ahead to new social movements today without dismissing discrimination against women, blacks, gays, indigenous peoples, religious minorities and ethnic-linguistic regionalist movements) Marx explains why the enfranchisement of the Jews amounts to their integration within a political order that does not address a more radical question in the literal sense of going to the root of a problem. The latter concerns the relation between collective humanity and nature considered independently, at least in the first instance, from ethnic origin and other particular anthropological notions of group identity and political loyalty. For Marx, the relation between collective humanity and nature is mediated by (1) the intellectual, sensuous and imaginative labour that transforms nature into the objects, tools and resources which make human transcendence of need possible, as well as (2) the legal property relations which structure the labour process and the ownership and distribution of its fruits. In this context the mediating processes and movements denoted by the terms humanity, nature, labour, transformation, objects, transcendence, need and legal property relations are of central importance for Marx as well as for the argument developed in the present study. He is correct in thinking that there can be no decisive move beyond the legal boundaries of political emancipation without a radical change in the work conditions and property relations which structure the labour process in liberal democratic states. But although Marx goes to the root by seizing upon the centrality of the instances of mediation between humanity and nature, he does not analyse all the implications of his own insights in nearly enough detail. The reasons why and the implications will become clear in chapters 2–5.

Marx's non-socialist opponents consistently raise the point that there is more to the mediation of humanity and nature than labour, however broadly conceived by Marx, and also more to that mediation than the laws codifying property relations. This can be reformulated as the twin claim that there is more going on in civil society than labour–capital relations, and more going on in the state than law. A recurrent claim made by postmodernists and proponents of the linguistic turn is that because of the ability of humans to communicate with each other, make collective decisions, settle disputes, etc., the humanity–nature relation has to be grasped dialogically rather than in the solipsistic fashion that Marx uses. Marx confuses humanity with labouring humanity when in fact he should be considering humans in their speaking and acting capacity as political beings with individual histories situated in the most variegated contexts and communities. It is said that Marx forgets that this key dimension of the human condition is already underscored by Aristotle in the *Politics* and the *Nicomachean Ethics*. A number of contemporary Aristotelians and communitarians argue that rhetorical subterfuge and oral virtuosity are political virtues which capture something about the essentially human capacity for action and expression that sets humans apart from other forms of natural life such as plants and animals. Postmodernists add that the ambiguities and figurative masks enlisted in literary expression so adeptly employed by Nietzsche indicate that the modernist quest for metaphysical truth and meaning in history must cede place to the reality of rhetorical device and the multiple interpretability of dramatic performance. Moreover, Arendt, Habermas and a range of other thinkers suggest that Marx's methodological monism is explainable in terms of the residual idealism he inherited from Kant and especially from Hegel. In his aspiration to use Hegel's dialectical method whilst turning Hegel upside down in order to convert philosophical idealism into historical materialism, Marx allegedly reduces the richness of the social fabric to the economy in a manner analogous to Hegel's attempt to secure absolute knowledge by collapsing the individual terms of the subject–object and humanity–nature dichotomies in the overarching unity of what Hegel calls spirit. On this account Marx cancels and preserves Hegel's dogmatism in a kind of materialist metaphysics. He is wont to misconstrue the humanity–nature dialogue as a monologue of working human-ity directed at silent nature, and in the process ignore that humanity enters into dialogue with other humanity in a series of learning processes structured by language and speech and capable of taking a myriad of different possible turns. The problem with such interpretations is not so much that they are caricatures, since there are passages in Marx that can be read in the way advocated by his critics. But it is in any case erroneous to ascribe positivist monocausality to Marx since, as stated, Marx regards the humanity–nature relation to be medi-ated by socio-political and legal institutions. What interests him is not monocausal *essence*, but rather the institutional *forms* through which that medi-ation between humanity and nature achieves an intelligible and knowledge-yielding institutional profile. One can raise many subtle objections concerning areas where Marx is one-sided and where he seems to have gone wrong. Much of contemporary social and political thought indicates that it is relatively easy to do this and lose sight of the simple point that there is no real freedom in the form of transcendence of need and socio-politically created necessity without a form of economy that guarantees a stable material existence for all citizens. Whilst *laissez-faire* supply-side economics palpably cannot guar-antee this, it is becoming clear that welfare state and Keynesian economics are also incapable of doing this to the extent that they are being systematically dismantled as part of the ongoing expansion of a globalised economy regulated by capitalist relations of production. These relations have ruptured the political integrity of the sovereignty of individual nation-states to such an extent that many citizens in Europe and the rest of the world are increasingly likely to regard national elections as symbolic exercises necessary for the legitimation of political and economic decisions that have already been taken elsewhere in places like New York, Washington, London, Paris, Strasbourg, Brussels, Frankfurt and Milan. It is a truism to say that if there is a collective decision to revolutionise legality and overturn the existing relations of production this will entail speech and dialogue; it is rather more cynical and politically strategic to suggest that the reason why this decision has not yet happened and will not happen is because of the irreducibility of speech and dialogue to the instrumental dimension of labour.

Although he never says as much, the young Marx intimates that liberal thinking about reason, law and politics is most radical precisely in those instances in which the liberal vision is ostensibly most anti-democratic and most anti-humanist in the sense implied by the standpoint adopted in 1843. The reasons why this is so will become clear in the discussion to follow in subsequent chapters, but they can nonetheless be briefly sketched in this introduction. Marx attempts to think the humanity–nature relation in a way that places him in an unsuspected proximity with certain liberal thinkers such as Kant. This proximity constitutes a simultaneous distance from pragmatic, communicative action, linguistic, communitarian, postmodernist, new social movement and other democratic humanist critiques of liberalism. The latter generally seek to retain the juridical understanding of the relation between knowledge and freedom in liberals like Kant and the early Rawls, and to then broaden that juridical base of political legitimacy by including ostensibly wider, non-juridical considerations on the specificity of what is essentially human drawn from Aristotle and to a lesser extent Hegel. These include speech and communication, the struggle for recognition, considerations of 'the political', the politics of friendship, friend–enemy relations, community, ambiguities in the definition of gender and other perspectives addressing what are construed as instances of lived experience escaping the violence of juridical formality. In admittedly very divergent degrees of admixture, and however updated and modified to suit current socio-political realities they may be, Kantian legal epistemology and Aristotelian anthropology define the parameters of virtually all of contemporary social and political thought in the mainstream and on the margins alike. At the risk of great simplification, one could say that mainstream and marginal perspectives outside of anarchist circles generally seek to retain the idea of the rule of law or *Rechtsstaat*, and then widen and temper the formality of law with the informality and local and historical dimensions of individual and group identity/particularity. Taken together, one is generally looking at instances of formal juridical essence coupled with instances of non-juridical plural essence. Though the latter component is now known to students and the public as sociology and anthropology rather than Aristotelian philosophy, the fact remains that much of the social and political thought that has been presented as radical since 1968 actually has an ancient lineage. Moreover, little of this thought is radical in the sense suggested by Marx's early writings. In contrast to the latter, the advocates of the democratic humanist perspective insist that (1) humanity enters into dialogue with other humanity and (2) it is impossible to understand socio-political institutional forms independently of ethnic and other particular anthropological notions of human identity, origin and aspiration. It will be demonstrated in chapter 1 and at various junctures throughout this book that Kant's juridical epistemology is different from liberal democratic humanist epistemology and politics in one decisive respect that links Kant with Marx rather than Rawls. Apart from his writings on the public sphere, Kant is interested in the conditions of the possibility of experience, knowledge and freedom. The key to discerning those conditions is to be found in the mediation between humanity and nature. For Kant that mediation is rational and legal. It is not in the first instance interpersonal, communicative, interactive, politically agonistic or identity-creating. Kant intimates that reason and law are not subjective attributes of the human 'anthropos', but rather instances of mediation between humanity and the world. Insofar Kant is in agreement with Marx. Well before Nietzsche, Freud, Heidegger and Lacan, Kant decentres the epistemological subject by stripping it of essential attributes. It is thus misleading to dismiss idealism as metaphysical, since Kant is already a post-metaphysical and post-anthropological thinker for whom the mediation of humanity and nature is a knowledge-creating process in which humanity is both united and separated from nature by reason and law. Kant forfeits the immensity of this discovery in those moments in his thinking when he tries to square this discovery of idealist philosophy with his political commitment to liberal notions of individual autonomy and negative freedom; insofar he is at loggerheads with Marx. Those are moments in which he shifts the idealist argument acknowledging the more than exclusively subjective dimension of law and reason to the anthropological argument that humanity gives itself laws and is rational when it does so. Kant uncovers the link between humanist metaphysics and anthropology, and discerns that the move beyond them is to be sought in reason and law. When he intuits that this takes him beyond the premises of liberalism, however, he retreats to anthropological and metaphysical notions of human essence that close humanity off from the processes of mediation and contact with the world. Reason and law become instrumental devices in the struggle of the autonomous individual subject pitted against nature in antagonistic isolation. The implications of this instrumentalisation of reason are a major concern of critical theory and important for the argument developed here. Hence a quick introductory word of explanation is in order.

As the aforementioned indicates, there is a moment in philosophical idealism that is post-metaphysical, potentially post-anthropological and post-liberal in a distinctly non-humanist way without embracing Heidegger's ontological post-humanism or the post-humanist systems-theoretical approach to legality and legitimacy associated with people like Niklas Luhmann (1928–98). That epistemological moment will be traced at different stages in the unfolding of the central arguments of *Beyond Hegemony*. It is a rational and legal moment which suggests that a form of post-humanist idealism is the key to the possibility of non-instrumental knowledge, but that this possibility is lost if the law and rationality, as the bases of Enlightenment, are abandoned to the instrumental project of individual survival pursued through the strategies of class domination. That particularly antagonistic form of securing the means of survival is inimical to the discovery of non-instrumental knowledge necessary to satisfy the conditions of legitimate law, that is, of political legitimacy understood and practised in epistemological rather than hegemonic terms. It is in this sense that it is Marx and not Rawls or other neo-liberals who takes the baton from Kant. In chapter 3 it will be seen why there is no plausible way to shore up liberalism in its traditional and contemporary guises for reasons that have to do with law, legitimacy, class domination and instrumental reason. In chapters 4–5 it will become clear why the best way to move beyond Kant, liberalism and sociologically informed versions of Aristotelianism is via Marx, and further, that the best way to rediscover what Marx's thought represents in terms of the possibility of legitimate law beyond state socialist Leninism, social democracy and academic hagiography is via the combined efforts of legal theory and critical theory. The project sketched in the following chapters does not at all intend to rescue Marx from ignominious association with state socialism in order to preserve the intellectual prestige of Marxism: that would be a rather conservative academic exercise. It is rather to help renew and continue the trajectory of critical theory and politics that moves from Kant to Marx and then dramatically stagnates in the state socialist regimes in Eastern Europe and Cuba, on the one hand, and which has been unable to decisively break with liberalism in the West, on the other. The term critical theory as it is used in this book refers in the main to the body of ideas expounded in the writings of the philosophers and legal theorists affiliated with the Institute of Social Research founded in Frankfurt in 1930 by K. A. Gerlach, subsequently taken over by Max Horkheimer, and widely known today as the Frankfurt School.[3] The arguments deployed in the search for an epistemological conception of political legitimacy in *Beyond Hegemony* are indebted to and informed by the founding members of the first generation of Frankfurt School theorists, and particularly by the ideas of T. W. Adorno. There is no space in this introduction or in the chapters that follow to provide a detailed critical commentary on the origins of critical theory, the Institute of Social Research or the ideas of the individual theorists. Their ideas guide the present study and are noted and referenced where appropriate. But the ideas of Adorno, Horkheimer, Benjamin, Marcuse and others are not treated systematically at any stage: they must be borne in mind as useful background material. For a very thorough introduction, interested readers should consult Rolf Wiggershaus's critical study, *The Frankfurt School* (1994).[4] One might say that the original intention of the first generation is to steer a path beyond positivism, functionalism and traditional idealism through wide-ranging interdisciplinary research extending from legal theory and political economy to sociology and aesthetics. One of the sources of inspiration for *Beyond Hegemony* is the goal of redressing the virtual theoretical silence that seems to have reigned between the legal theorists Franz Neumann (1900–54) and Otto Kirchheimer (1905–72) and the other theorists connected with the Institute.

The attempt to re-evaluate Marx beyond state socialist Leninism, social democracy and academic preservation or simplistic critique is attempted by the present author in *Radical Theories: Paths Beyond Marxism and Social Democracy* (1994). That study is followed by *Sovereign States or Political Communities? Civil Society and Contemporary Politics* (2000). In order to situate the approach taken in the following chapters, it is helpful to mention what is attempted in the two preceding works. *Radical Theories* outlines the contours of an entirely feasible non-statist socialist economy that differs quite notably from the Soviet and social democratic systems. To this extent, it defends a libertarian socialist alternative to state socialism and social democracy which is elaborated on the basis of the ideas of Marx, a number of syndicalist and anarchist movements, and especially the ideas of G. D. H. Cole (1889–1959). *Sovereign States* attempts to locate and analyse instances of non-statist politics that exist in contemporary civil societies and which could eventually flourish given the economy sketched in *Radical Theories*. The present study can be seen amongst other things as an implicit critique of the argument developed in *Sovereign States* insofar as that book deploys a version of democratic humanist anthropology of the kind that is criticised in chapter 2 of the current book. In *Sovereign States* the public sphere, community and recognition are cited as examples of non-statist politics in which a form of human freedom which is essentially political is able to assert itself against instances of instrumental reason at work in the economy in general and in the capitalist economy in particular. As such, the book tries to argue for a kind of Marx–Arendt synthesis which brings together Marx's critique of political economy and Arendt's Aristotelian defence of republican politics. That synthesis as formulated by this author fails for reasons which will become clear in chapter 2 and subsequent chapters. The critique of the metaphysics of sovereignty in that book is nonetheless valid and is useful to bear in mind for what follows. Yet the critique of metaphysics cannot stop with sovereignty – that critique must address the larger question of democratic humanism and its relation to liberalism. Seen from the perspective of *Beyond Hegemony*, the previous book presents an account of informal, non-statist democratic legitimacy without any sustained theoretical critique of law, liberalism or traditional idealism. One can look at Foucault's care of the self, Derrida's politics of friendship, the various accounts of the politics of recognition, or any one of myriad possible alternative forms of informal extra-legal legitimacy. A close inspection of

Introduction

these theories reveals that a theory of *a legitimate form of law*, combined with a theory of non-instrumental reason, is considerably more radical in Marx's sense and more elucidating in an Enlightenment sense than celebrating what is excluded or marginalised by *legal forms of legitimacy*. This distinction will attain clarity in successive stages. What remains from *Radical Theories* is the theory of libertarian socialism which is re-articulated in chapters 4 and 5 of the present study, whilst what remains of *Sovereign States* is the critique of the metaphysics of sovereignty. Those arguments now need to be brought together in order to develop the theory of a legitimate form of law that is offered here.

There are thus four principal sources informing the present study. They are critical theory, legal theory, a radically modified form of idealism and libertarian socialism. It will be seen that the version of critical idealism elaborated here in response to ostensibly post-metaphysical post-idealism incorporates elements of the Kantian insistence on the conditioned nature of experience, knowledge and freedom with elements of Hegel's theory of objective spirit and the notion that the real is rational. Both these dimensions of idealism will be explained in relation to the overall argument concerning the formulation of a legitimate form of law. At first glance it looks as if Kant presents the world of existing institutions with a series of *a priori* moral prescriptions about reason and law which are hopelessly formal and abstract, whilst Hegel's historicism seems to rescue reason and law from abstraction only by completely eradicating the difference between what is and what ought to be. This is to misconstrue Kant as a theologian and Hegel as a positivist sociologist. It will be explained why both interpretations are wrong and what is missed by overlooking the juridical and transcendental character of Hegel's thinking as well as the sociological implications of Kant's thought that are carried forward by Marx. The links between (1) the libertarian socialist alternative to Soviet state socialism and social democracy in *Radical Theories* and (2) the political possibilities suggested by legal theory are discussed in chapters 4 and 5 without re-rehearsing the more intricate and practical details of Cole's proposals in favour of non-statist social-ism. Instead, libertarian socialism is analysed as the most appropriate kind of economy implied by critical idealism and a legitimate form of legality. The unsuspected proximity between certain dimensions in Kant and certain dimen-sions in Marx (and, by extension, in Cole and libertarian socialism in general) alluded to in this introduction is a juridical proximity which addresses property relations and the conditions of transcendence in relation to the possibility of freedom from necessity and knowledge. What Kant in his theory of practical reason and in writings on the public sphere (chapter 1) regards as a prerequisite of legitimate law is revisited by Marx from a post-Hegelian standpoint as a valid injunction. But validity here for Marx is not *a priori* in Kant's sense of practical reason. Validity concerns the creation of the socio-political institutions which would make an epistemological and juridical condition more than an eternally posited epistemological *limit*, that is, more than ideology. Marx discovers that only a radical change in the legal relations governing humanity's transformation of nature in order to transcend dumb dependence on nature for all citizens can ensure that the conditioned nature of experience and knowledge can be explored in an epistemological dimension addressing questions of freedom rather than in an instrumental dimension addressing questions of functional stability and crisis management. That is, the liberal democratic freedoms of the press, assembly and contractual exchange cannot ensure the fulfilment of the conditions of legitimate law, any more than public-sphere deliberation by itself can guarantee that law is epistemologically valid rather than merely politically effective. The re-articulation of the Enlightenment project pursued in the following chapters re-evaluates the importance of this discovery and draws out its most significant implications.

Notes

1 The notion of the postmodern as symptomatic of the end of the grand narratives of modernism has become a standard interpretation since the publication of Jean-François Lyotard, *La Condition postmoderne* (*The Postmodern Condition*), Paris, Minuit, 1979. The fact that so many of the questions taken up by postmodernists and post-structuralists are recurrent themes in the writings of modernists makes it impossible to insist on the categorical separation of these terms. For example, many post-structuralist writers such as Michel Foucault celebrate the perspectival pluralism and anti-metaphysical vitalism they find in the writings of Friedrich Nietzsche. In terms of the period of his life and the central concerns of his work, however, Nietzsche is clearly a modernist.
2 Ludwig Wittgenstein's theory of language occupies a central place in this evolution from metaphysics and idealism to post-metaphysics and pragmatism. For an introduction to the major ideas of the author of the *Tractatus* (1921), see David Pears, *Wittgenstein*, London, Fontana, 1971.
3 The Institute was forced into American exile during the National Socialist dictatorship (1933–45) and re-established in Frankfurt after the Second World War. It still exists today, albeit with the rather drastically modified political agenda associated with the second generation of critical theorists such as Jürgen Habermas, under the direction of Axel Honneth.
4 See too the very informative and extremely competent introductions provided by David Held, *Introduction to Critical Theory: Horkheimer to Habermas*, London, Hutchinson, 1980, Raymond Geuss, *The Idea of a Critical Theory*, Cambridge, Cambridge University Press, 1981, Joan Always, *Critical Theory and Political Possibilities: Conceptions of Emancipatory Politics in the Works of Horkheimer, Adorno, Marcuse, and Habermas*, Boston MA, Greenwood Press, 1995, and Diana Coole, *Negativity and Politics: Dionysus and Dialectics from Kant to Poststructuralism*, London, Routledge, 2000. These are four of the best exegetical works on the Frankfurt School and critical theory available in English.

Chapter 1

Liberalism and discourses of legality: limiting human agency in the name of negative liberty

THIS chapter seeks to shed some light on a somewhat contradictory situation. The priority of legality over legitimacy which lies at the heart of liberalism from Kant to the present is both the source of liberalism's critical power and its crucial weakness. This separation is the source of liberalism's critical power insofar as it provides the adherents of the doctrine with the possibility of insisting on formal and legal conceptions of freedom and justice against various populist notions on the political right and left of an extra-legal conception of communitarian well-being which is ostensibly bridled by legal formality. The strategies of such discourses of legitimacy will be examined in chapter 2. For now it might simply be observed that contemporary discourses of legitimacy tend in various ways to stress a communicative or agonistic or expressive dimension of human action which is frustrated by the formalism necessary to secure a set of universal principles equally applicable to all citizens. For defenders of legitimacy, the price exacted for legal universality is too high – citizens can be legally equal only in negative terms of non-infringement. The almost exclusive concern with negative forms of liberty in liberalism serves to undermine more fundamental, non-contractual, positive ties which bind citizens in political communities. Moreover, in the history of political thought, and especially with Kant, legality appears to be closely wedded to an idealist and deeply individualist notion of human subjectivity which, despite Kant's critique of metaphysics in the *Critique of Pure Reason*, is still too metaphysically reified and static to do justice to the plural and transient dimensions of existence and being. Thus discourses of legitimacy seek to move beyond the historical insensitivity implicit in the timeless conceptions of human nature and subjectivity characteristic of liberal forms of idealism, in order to embrace more worldly and open visions of human essence and possibility. Against such (arguably equally) arbitrary versions of legitimacy, liberal legality seems to have the great advantage of neutrality and of allowing individuals to choose their allegiances as they see fit. That is, against the more or less authoritarian/paternalistic implications of different versions of positive liberty toward which discourses of legitimacy in widely different degrees tend, liberalism protects all individuals by guaranteeing a universally enforceable form of negative liberty which they can exercise in accordance with their own individual will. Advocates of liberalism insist on the priority of legality over the forced acceptance of one of the variously contestable forms of legitimacy. They also insist on the distinction between theory and practice as the only alternative to 'forcing people to be free'.[1] In this chapter it will be shown that despite these real advantages *vis-à-vis* the discourses of legitimacy, liberalism is not neutral with respect to different visions of legitimacy. If liberalism's great strength seems to be its ability to dispense with authoritarian versions of legitimacy, it nonetheless must show that legality is in and of itself legitimate. The argument in this book is that legality is not in and of itself legitimate, and that, moreover, legality as form (non-discriminatory universality) requires more anti-authoritarianism than even liberalism can deliver. Below it will be explained why this is so, beginning with a very brief recapitulation of some of the main points of convergence in Kant's philosophy between political liberalism, the liberal priority of legality over legitimacy, and the cognitive status of privately organised interests in liberal thought and practice. The evolution of liberal thought never completely severs its ties with its Kantian base, which is why he serves here as the paradigm philosopher of the liberal project. There are a number of reasons for choosing Kant as the first key representative of modern liberalism. Kant sets out the political and philosophical components of the liberal project in terms of law and epistemology in a way that contemporary liberals may choose to disagree with but cannot ignore. Like Locke before him, Kant is a philosopher of knowledge who draws out the political and legal implications of epistemological questions. The subsequent political alliance of liberalism with *laissez-faire* economics associated with more recent thinkers such as Hayek and Friedman should not deflect attention away from this fundamental point: liberalism articulates a world-view which attempts to ask epistemological questions about the limits of knowledge at the same time that it asks political questions about the limits of the legitimacy of the state. Both of these questions converge in a series of inquiries about the legislative capacity of rational humanity which is at the centre of Kant's philosophical investigations. There are obviously very close links between liberalism and the Enlightenment, and if there is an Enlightenment philosopher of liberalism, it is Kant.[2]

The philosophical origins of modern liberalism: Kant and beyond

Kants's theory of practical reason outlines the *a priori* faculties through which humans are free. Humans are free when they elevate themselves above the mechanical causality operative in nature and operating on the objects of experience, and they achieve this when they reflexively unify themselves with reason. The key faculty in this act of transcendence of mechanical causality is the

rational will, which is the same for all reasonable beings and is an essential defi-
nitional component of being human. Fundamental to the rational will as human
essence in Kant's terms is the corresponding idea that the rational will is a legislating will.[3] In their political existence as citizens, humans give concrete
expression to their freedom in the form of laws. Law is the form in which eleva-
tion above the mechanical causality at work in nature makes a realisation of the
human essence of freedom as adherence to reason in a supra-sensible world of
free will possible. Individual autonomy from the forces in the world external to
human purpose is thus realised in those rational laws that humans will for themselves – submission to this kind of law is freedom rather than submission to
heteronomous authority. But contrary to theorists of the discourses of legitimacy, who insist in various ways that the real is rational or at least in the process
of becoming rational, Kant never says that liberty and positive law are more or
less the same thing. He argues instead that positive law is not legitimate unless
it conforms to the maxims furnished by the practical reason of a morally
autonomous transcendental subject with a rational will capable of synthetic
knowledge of the phenomena of experience. In the first instance synthesis refers
to the mediated unity of sensuous intuition and conceptual understanding that
is realised in the act of knowledge.[4] This is a subject freed from economic necessity through property ownership and/or the lucrative exercise of a profession
(women and non-professional workers are excluded) and in control of their
non-rational impulses through the exercise of reason. In *An Answer to the
Question: What is Enlightenment?* Kant maintains that, above and beyond
autonomous individuals, it is really only a reasoning public, individually
endowed with economic self-sufficiency and rational self-control, that can exert
a political pressure for positive law to become ethical.[5] In this context, morality
is virtually synonymous with private morality and a property-based version of
natural rights. As a philosophical justification of ascendant liberalism, this
means a morality which has its social foundations in the institutions of private
property, exchange, marriage and the inviolability of individual conscience,
none of which can be infringed upon by public authority that is to be considered legitimate. Hence in Kant's writings one can identify the solid fusion of a
private ethic of individual economic success and ownership, inviolability of
conscience, and legality as the form in which human freedom is enacted. This
fusion becomes a hallmark of early liberalism's confident assault on political
absolutism, which is at the same time a declaration of epistemological and
juridical independence from the subaltern classes in the process of rapid formation with the rise and spread of industrialisation. One can also identify a priority
of legality before legitimacy with a number of significant political implications
which will be examined below.[6]

Instead of inquiring about the primacy of mind or matter as virtually all of
the philosophers before him do, Kant raises a prior epistemological question

with important political and anthropological implications: how is human experience itself possible? In so doing, he develops the idea of the unified consciousness of a transcendental subject which synthesises the two forms of sensible intuition (space and time) with the twelve categories of the understanding (substance, causality, reciprocity, possibility, existence, necessity, unity, plurality, totality, reality, negation, limitation).[7] This synthesis enables the objects of perception to become objects of possible experience, thus liberating philosophy from the empiricist–rationalist debate about the primacy of mind or matter. The Kantian question concerning how experience itself is possible raises a more fundamental question central to Kant's philosophy, i.e. what makes humanity possible? Because he rejects any first cause that is deducible from experience (which is also why belief in God is not a matter of experience or reason), his questioning leads him to inquire about *the conditions* of the possibility of humanity. For Kant these conditions are *a priori*, transcendental-deductive, rational, formal and legal. Despite the post-metaphysical implications of his critique of pure reason (he sounds out the limits of reasonable thought, beyond which thought lapses into metaphysical speculation with authoritarian political implications), Kant remains at least in part faithful to a political-philosophical tradition that regards the conditions of knowledge and legality to be prior to and constitutive of human experience in general and of human freedom in particular. But he is determined to articulate the delimitation of the boundaries of what is humanly knowable and politically possible in a secular and liberal idiom. He limits human agency, and, by extension, political legitimacy, to those actions that conform to legal form. Whereas many subsequent theorists of legitimacy tend to make a direct appeal to the validity of direct human experience and unmediated post-metaphysical agency, Kant's critical philosophy both affirms and limits human agency through the media of rationality and legality. He affirms human autonomy insofar as his defence of law is not an argument in favour of theological law or an apology of church or geopolitical military power. Law is rational and not an arbitrary matter of human happiness, faith, special need, extraordinary desire or communication. Thus formal–legal epistemology in Kant places drastic limitations on the capacity of authority to satisfy the demands for legitimacy captured in extra-legal demands for happiness, satisfaction of need, etc. Kant separates matters of faith, need, happiness, work and communication from matters of reason, and attributes rationality and the capacity of (collective) self-legislation to humankind rather than to the top of an ecclesiastical hierarchy or a political caste. The subversive dimension of Kant's epistemology with regard to the absolutist order of his day is the insistence that the conditions of possible experience are the same for all human beings. The form of that universality is legal, and as such, legality in Kant can be interpreted as both the condition of the possibility of objects of experience, whose existence is governed by laws, and the condition of the possibility of humanity, whose freedom is enacted in rational self-legislation.

Whereas the concept of essence would normally be contrasted with form as the content contained or framed by it, Kant's liberal version of idealism achieves what might seem like the paradoxical result of a formal theory of human essence. In refraining from a positive definition of freedom, and simultaneously insisting on the primacy of legality over legitimacy, Kant defends a formal conception of human essence that never discloses what that essence is. It is difficult to overestimate the political import of this position, since it signals the emergence of a liberal world-view which makes a substantial claim about what reason is at the same time that it imagines to know what constitutes the essence of humanity. That essence is juridical and rational for Kant and for virtually all post-Kantian liberals who regard themselves to be building on the work of the Enlightenment philosophers. Kant leaves matters at that, in the conviction that a more than negative conception of freedom is likely to mean a positively determined, i.e. dogmatic, conception of freedom that is bound to result in political tyranny. From a liberal Enlightenment perspective, the epistemological end of metaphysics in terms of the critique of pure reason and unmediated knowledge – an acknowledgement of the limits of reason – is synonymous with the demise of political despotism and authoritarian government. Similarly, an attempt to make issues of legitimacy the form and content of legality would be tantamount to the abolition or at least dilution of legality in the name of some group or person's arbitrary definition of the substantive bases of legitimate order. Hence to attempt to bend legal formality to meet the infinitely varied extra-legal demands of happiness is to lurch from the objective rationality of legal discourse to the irrationality of arbitrary wish-fulfilment. A central claim underpinning this line of liberal argument exemplified by Kant is that there is a way to reconcile the claims of freedom with those of authority in a non-arbitrary, i.e. in a just and objective, manner that is equally binding upon all citizens. The binding nature of the arrangement stems from the formal–legal–objective triad that impedes any personal usurpation of political power at the same time that it guarantees supra-personal neutrality. It heralds the institutionalisation of an historically new kind of politics that outlaws abuse and corruption at the same time that it defines the boundaries of what can be rationally known. In so doing, these formal–legal conditions provide the objective framework within which humans can achieve autonomy from the mechanical causality of the natural world and from their own irrationality. In addition, they become truly human in an uncompromisingly individual way. Kant attempts to demonstrate that any attempt to fuse legality (theory) with legitimacy (practice) in the struggle to overcome the metaphysical separation between what ought to be and what is must result in a coerced reconciliation of the ideal (rational) and the real (actual). Coerced reconciliation is in this context not really reconciliation at all, but an ideological apology for the exercise of power. This means that, despite Kant's critique of metaphysics, he retains the dichotomies operative in earlier, more overtly theological interpretations of this-worldliness and other-worldliness. In the face of the continued exercise of power and the distortion of social and political reality resulting from power relations, the liberal separation of legality and legitimacy theorised with philosophical rigour by Kant and adopted by many subsequent liberal thinkers has the political integrity of occupying, at least potentially, a critical position with regard to the institutions of coerced reconciliation. Insofar as these institutions manifestly do not conform to the stringent criteria of legal rationality separating juridical notions of universality from tradition, privilege and mere functional efficiency (with the exception of some of Mill's followers, liberal thought from Kant to Rawls is outspokenly anti-utilitarian), any and all institutions are susceptible to critique. This holds true as long as liberals insist on the distinction between rational law, arbitrary decree and executive discretion, and continue to ask critical questions about the relation between human freedom and legal form.

By contrast, discourses of legitimacy are compelled, in various degrees, to sanction instances of coerced reconciliation as the desirable consequence of what their proponents take to be a triumph over metaphysics. Framed in these terms, metaphysics impedes humanity from full flourishing by positing the existence of formal-objective conditions external to the individual subject to which human agency must bend – hence Nietzsche's idea that the death of God also marks the liberation of humankind from the metaphysical in its religious, epistemological and legal guises, thus preparing the ground for a fully terrestrial philosophy of existence. Here the metaphysical is synonymous with the limiting of the human, whilst the post-metaphysical represents the overcoming of the distinctions between legality–legitimacy, ethics–politics, theory–practice and is–ought in the already existing institutions of human societies. Few thinkers embracing post-metaphysical epistemological stances would argue that these antinomies are completely resolved in existing institutions. Indeed, much of contemporary social and political thought is marked by generally awkward attempts to balance Kantian positions with more communicative ones found in Aristotle and pragmatism, in some instances, or with some version of systems theory, in other instances. Since Kant's position on property excluding women and salaried workers from the public sphere is no longer reconcilable with political stability under conditions of universal suffrage, and since this stability depends not only on liberal notions of law but on democratic notions of equality and welfare, it is generally accepted by mainstream theorists that there is no plausible return to the priority of legal form over the plurality of legitimate practices. But within the terms of contemporary theory, these arguments are by and large played out with a strategic eye to questions of social integration and the best possible means of ensuring stability (leaving open the possibility of an authoritarian solution), rather than arguments about how the epistemological dimension of legality might be re-conceptualised in the light of contemporary socio-economic realities. The great strengths of the liberal position, at least in terms of theoretical principles, are (1) not to be committed to any particular conception of the good, and (2) to remain steadfast in the conviction that every coerced reconciliation of private and public, state and civil society, theory and practice, legitimacy and law, and of ethics and politics, amounts to ideological sleight of hand. It also amounts to a justification of a quasi-voluntarist usurpation of political power by individuals or groups. As suggested above, the liberal position also affords the individual thinker and citizen a vantage point from which to criticise the institutions of coerced reconciliation independently from either the pressure of mobilised popular opinion or considerations of functional stability, i.e. to criticise from a legal-philosophical rather than from a politically opportunist position.[8]

In addition to the remarkable rigour of a number of thinkers in the liberal tradition and the apparent superiority of arguments in favour of legality in the legality–legitimacy debate, it would seem further that history is on the side of the kind of theory and practice which resists the fusion of the spheres demarcated as separate in liberal theory. From a liberal perspective, the authoritarian character of so-called totalitarian societies of the twentieth century can be explained in terms of attempts to catapult beyond legal formality to more immediate forms of identification between individual and state. Contemporary liberals often argue that these projects have been attempted in terms of social class and community in state socialism, nation and community in fascism, or as religion and community in the new 'fundamentalisms'. All of these instances of political authoritarianism make use of legal systems. The alleged superiority of specifically liberal, and by extension liberal democratic/liberal republican discourses of legality, resides in the fact that liberal legal form does not constitute an instance of coerced reconciliation between one group's (class, race, religious, etc.) conception of the good with the rest of society. Liberal legal anthropology does not appear at first glance to posit an immediate identity between individual and polity based on the supposed primacy of a non-legal or pre-legal anthropological ascription such as labour, language, ethnicity or religious faith and, indeed, claims that it is neutral with regard to these and other extra-legal essences. The problem of political authoritarianism thus looks like it is traceable to the specification of one arbitrarily chosen essence at the expense of a more legal-universal conception of humanity, which can be imposed upon universal humanity only through coercion. The fury of class, race and religious vengeance seems to be held in check by the non-essentialist formalism of liberal law, which entails among other things the safeguarding of tolerance for all non-violent opinions and interests, as well as enforcement of the right to non-infringement guaranteed by the protection of privacy and the gains of acquisition.

Yet if it is the great merit of liberal democratic theory to distinguish between legality–legitimacy and ethics–politics, etc., these distinctions are nonetheless untenable in their liberal formulation. They are untenable not because they are metaphysical, however, but because they are articulated within an ideological framework conflating the pursuit of private interests with the pursuit of 'natural' interests and the exercise of reason. This is an important point to bear in mind in establishing what is unconvincing about contemporary critique which assails liberal idealism as residually metaphysical, though without really questioning the legal bases of the liberal order.[9] Here the word 'natural' suggests the spontaneous coexistence and harmony characteristic of the liberal version of the state of nature. In this way the legal, private-ethical and individualist discourses of negative liberty acquire an apparent self-evident objectivity against the seemingly arbitrary claims of legitimacy, politics and public interests characteristic of positive conceptions of liberty. The aforementioned dichotomies in liberal thought are *potentially* truthful insofar as they resist the logic of coerced reconciliation. They become ideological as soon as they individualise and privatise the separations as being somehow unconditionally natural, rational or ontological. Phrased slightly differently, the critical distance between the real and the rational afforded by the distinctions typically deployed in negative conceptions of liberty – and generally disparaged since 1945 as metaphysical by opponents of liberalism and idealism – is a potentially truthful distance which, when invoked to consolidate the hegemony of private interests, forfeits its potential truth content.[10] This suggests that there is a potentially truthful moment in liberalism that points beyond liberalism, and that this moment is at least in part contained in the possibility of critique *vis-à-vis* existing institutions which is promised, if to date only very inadequately delivered, in law. The ambiguity of law in this context is that it holds out the possibility of Enlightenment and the possibility of moving beyond tradition, privilege, random discrimination, etc. Yet as the work of Weber and Foucault signals, unless the discourses of legality are fully freed from arbitrary and decisionist elements, the law becomes an even more effective means of domination than the more transparently brutal conduct sanctioned by tradition and privilege.[11] This is an acute problem in modern industrial legal systems, where it becomes extremely difficult to disentangle the political rights of public citizens, bureaucratic systemic imperatives, and notions of rationality and efficiency which are tightly interwoven with the organised pursuit of private interests. Important for the argument to be developed in this book, however, is that what is doubtful about the specifically liberal separation of public–private and ethics–politics does not necessarily point *directly* to the desideratum of extra-legal forms of legitimate power, or a simple elimination of those separations, any more than the critiques of liberal forms of idealism necessarily point directly to some form of unmediated (i.e. metaphysical) materialism of the kind that is often mistakenly imputed to Marx.[12] The fact remains that when confronted with the numerous genres of publicly organised oppression found throughout history, the anonymous, rights-endowed private person of liberal inspiration will always seem to represent an at least potentially truthful moment against artificially constructed forms of community, oppressive political power and corruption. The writings of Locke, Mill and Tocqueville as well as those of more recent liberal theorists such as Aron, Berlin and the early Rawls defend this position with persuasive clarity and conviction.

Because of the authoritarian and often mendacious character of virtually all forms of legitimacy ever known, liberalism has had the great strategic advantage of being able to pose as the opponent of power and coerced reconciliation between the individual and public authority. In recent history, the critical force of this legacy seems to have been strengthened further by the experience of state socialism and other anti-liberal theories which have turned out to be decidedly authoritarian in practice. Indeed, it could be argued that common to state socialism, fascism and the new religious fundamentalisms is an attempt to impose a direct identification between individual and polity by making the issue of legitimacy a 'who' question. That is, instead of the anonymous, rights-endowed private legal subject of liberal theory, the public *legitimation subject* is directly identified, so that the state is constructed as a workers' state, an organic ethnic-national community, a Jewish state, an Islamic state, etc.[13] The coerced integration of individual and state thus achieved can be analysed as an authoritarian step beyond the legal forms of integration which guarantee individual liberty, in the direction of more paternalistic forms which unjustifiably curb it in order to secure greatly increased levels of legitimacy. These are observable in two guises. The first is the directly authoritarian manner of the 1920s and 1930s. The second can be seen in the more 'acceptable' one approved of by much of contemporary theory stressing community, communication and recognition. In the latter, specific forms of participation in public life are invoked as instances of non-systemic action which complement and complete the limited forms of legitimacy confined within the supposedly narrow domains of law. As will be seen in chapter 2, the attempted transposition of legality into legality–legitimacy constitutes a crisis both for liberal conceptions of legality as well as the variously invoked concepts of extra-legal legitimacy.[14] Without anticipating the argument of the next chapter in too much detail here, it should be briefly explained why this might be the case.

On the one hand, universal suffrage and democratic-popular demands for legitimacy have helped to create a political reality in which liberal legal form is no longer plausible as the sole prerequisite of legitimacy. (Thankfully, there is no going back to restricted forms of suffrage.) On the other hand, the discourses of legitimacy have made the subject of legitimacy in varying degrees a rather doubtfully constructed collective 'who' (the people, the workers, etc., in openly authoritarian versions, and the participants of discussion, communitarians, etc., in more acceptable, contemporary versions). One result of this attempted trans-position of legality into an amalgam of formal legality tempered by humanist conceptions of legitimacy is that the conditions of the possibility of humanity become historically realised forms of existing humanity itself and no longer at least in part objectively external to individuals and groups. The solipsistic, and indeed narcissistic, implications of this step and its epistemological conse-quences are fairly evident. From a consistently liberal-philosophical standpoint insisting on the priority of the right over the good (legality), the voluntarist selection of a particular *subject* of legitimation or *legitimating action* (like assumed communication or imputed community) necessarily gives rise to coer-cive forms of reconciliation and integration between those who rule in the name of the legitimate subject group or action, on the one hand, and the rest of society, on the other. Thus the following questions immediately arise: might a consistently liberal state of law or *Rechtsstaat* actually be relaunched to obviate such coerced identifications and allow more freely chosen, contractual forms of interaction between citizens as well as genuinely transparent forms of mediation between citizens and public authority? Is the barely concealed antagonism char-acteristic of régimes that identify the 'who' of legitimation minimised in régimes where there is no publicly identified legitimation group/source? One might best proceed bearing in mind that the organisation and handling of questions of economic and other forms of necessity through private ownership, contractual relations and market-based forms of (now extensively state-regulated) compet-itive enterprise have proven historically to be neither free from force nor efficient in satisfying human need. While this remains a contested subject, the perhaps not so banal fact that one now speaks of the 'two-thirds' world provides striking evidence in support of this claim. Even less contestable is the claim that within modern societies with liberal democratic political institutions, material privation and massive inequality linked with private ownership and market rela-tions have given rise to social antagonism and an extensive array of legitimacy-related demands which have irretrievably shattered the early liberal theorisation of purely legal forms of legitimacy. One can either reject these demands as incompatible with purely legal forms of legitimacy such as those found in Kant and Hans Kelsen (1881–73)[15] or one can critically analyse the historical and theoretical reasons why the individual pursuit of privately owned wealth does not result in the aggregate good of all or the best possible allocation of material resources.[16] Moreover, the privatisation of conflict is not a genuine step beyond 'who-based', i.e. voluntarist/decisionist, conceptions of legitimacy or essentialist conceptions of humanity. Both of these issues will be discussed below. For now it is important to signal that insisting on the separation or crit-ical distance between social and political institutions that exist at any given historical moment, on the one hand, and criteria informing a discussion of different possible forms of rationality, on the other, is not necessarily an obscure manoeuvre or a form of liberal idealist or metaphysical ideology. Indeed, the antinomies deployed in liberal thought are not immediately false, unless one believes in either pure legitimacy in the completely successful union of theory and practice making legality redundant, or one believes in 100 per cent operative functionalism, in which the normative questions related to those antinomies are obviated in a totality of mutually reinforcing subsystems.[17] But that critical distance is not automatically created through economic exchange or the institution of contracts 'freely' entered into, the results of which have given rise to precisely those legitimacy-related demands which seem to impugn the plausibility of legal neutrality. Nor is it arrived at by way of an 'ideal speech situation' which would leave existing forms of economy and state unchanged, or for that matter by way of hybrid combinations which satisfy both privately organised interests and considerations of political stability. It is also not some kind of original condition or position to which we can return simply by way of a thought experiment.

Like the negative–positive liberty debates and the debates on natural–positive law, the legality–legitimacy debates are in important respects misleading in terms of ascertaining what is at stake in political theory and practice. A question of central importance that is for the most part overlooked in these discussions concerns the *conditions* under which non-coercive reconciliation between citizens is possible. In the rest of this book it is demonstrated why this means a non-instrumental mediation between humanity and nature, or, if one prefers, a reconciliation between humanity and nature, bearing in mind that humanity is both part of and distinct from nature for reasons which will be elaborated. For now it is important to stress the centrality of the humanity–nature relation in contradistinction to every attempt at a supposedly direct reconciliation between humanity and other humanity through dialogue, recognition, re-appropriation of the products of labour, state intervention in the economy and economic redistribution, etc.[18] Stated in this way, reason and Enlightenment are not the ready-made tools of a transcendental subject or some preordained, historically emerging subject. Reason might be better theorised as what is allowed to appear and become operative in a non-instrumental mediating capacity in the humanity–nature relation when the basis of legislation consists of non-antagonistic forms of knowledge, i.e. knowledge that is not an instrumental or strategic response to institutionalised scarcity and danger. It will be explained in later chapters why non-instrumental knowledge is Kantian in one precise sense: it is synthetic and it has conditions. It will also be seen how it is possible to establish that there are forms of non-antagonistic knowledge in societies characterised by acute socio-political antagonism, and why law offers the key to a political transition from an antagonistic society relying mainly on instrumental reason to a reconciled society in which reason is not juxtaposed with needs and values. For the moment it might be mentioned that the reconciliation of humanity and other humanity – conflict resolution – is at the centre of the legality–legitimacy and negative–positive liberty debates. But in the search for a direct mediation between the different parts of divided humanity without posing the question of a possible reconciliation of humanity and nature, these debates have tended to spiral inconclusively in endless circles around the primacy of either the individual (rights and liberty) or the state (political authority). As indicated above, framing the question of liberty in terms of the boundaries of legitimate interference in individual liberty will almost inevitably seem to vindicate private orientations toward the economy, state, public goods, etc., i.e. negative liberty.[19] Where collective solutions seem mendacious or simply coercive, privacy in the form of ownership and non-interference will inevitably seem like rationality, or at least optimal strategy, or both. Privacy and negative liberty, sanctioned through liberal discourses of legality, are thus able to pose as the absent truth of free individuals in their struggle against the existing lie of public authority. As long as public authority continues to represent an instance of coerced reconciliation, and therefore in a real sense a lie, there will be cultural bridges between the philosophical heights of deconstruction (Nietzsche and Derrida) and the banality of tax evasion (Stirner): if citizens are not really members of a political community to which they owe allegiance because it serves them all on an equal basis, there are no compelling reasons to submit to the claims of authority in either theory or taxes.

By way of summary of the main ideas of this section, it should be noted that in discussing Kant and the potentially critical dimensions of liberal political theory in this chapter, reference has been made to an idealist tradition of posing the question of the conditions of the possibility of humanity as an epistemological question. In the idealist tradition this question is prior to the anthropological-political question of the direct reconciliation of a divided humanity with itself through dialogue or other means. It is seen how in the case of Kant, these conditions are transcendental-deductive, rational, formal and, most important for the purposes of this chapter, legal. It is also suggested that the transposition of legality into legitimacy constitutes a crisis for liberal conceptions of legality and for attempts to alloy strictly legal conceptions of legitimacy with extra-legal sources of legitimation. Whilst chapter 2 deals with the parameters of the legitimacy crisis, this chapter is centrally concerned with discourses of legality. The argument thus far has pointed to a number of ambiguities inherent in the primacy of legality in liberal legal thought and the concomitant dichotomies attendant on legal primacy within a liberal framework. It has been suggested that these dichotomies might be powerfully critical of political domination – potentially far more incisive than direct appeals to extra-legal forms of legitimacy – and yet untenable in their liberal formulation. It is now possible to explore some of those ambiguities in greater detail, starting with the privatisation, through the institution of contract and civil law, of the 'who' question of legitimacy in ostensibly neutral régimes of liberal legality. As stated, liberal theory owes a substantial part of its political ballast to a series of dichotomies directly related to the central question of legality and legitimacy. These dichotomies potentially serve as a wedge against ideological arguments conflating existing social and political institutions with the successful realisation of the regulative ideas that inspire actual practice. It was noted that there is a moment in liberal thought that is always at least to some extent at odds with liberal practice. This moment is the foundation of liberalism's critical power as well as a potentially destabilising moment for liberalism itself, i.e. an instance that suggests how the realisation of certain liberal ideas is prevented by actually existing liberal institutions. The separation of ethics and politics, for example, in contrast to the notion of the ethico-political found in thinkers like Gramsci and Gentile and the rapprochement of ethics and politics in Hegelian *Sittlichkeit*, can be invoked to work as an ethical force for the reform of actually existing political institutions. This pressure is dissolved if existing socio-political institutions are declared to be already ethical or in an inexorable process of becoming ethical. To forfeit this critical moment in liberal theory and practice would be tantamount to a capitulation to the institutions of coerced reconciliation. In taking this step liberalism would be liable to the same charge of an authoritarian usurpation of legality which it has so effectively deployed against virtually all of its feudal-aristocratic, supposedly totalitarian and fundamentalist opponents. Since movements such as communism have tended to be much more sensitive to issues of legitimacy than those of legality, they have always been open to the charge of authoritarianism which liberalism, both in theory and as a political movement, has been able to elude. But as an historically operative political movement, however, liberalism has restabilised itself through a series of strategic compromises rather than a process of self-imposed reforms. Some of these compromises have been quite clearly authoritarian, whilst others have been rather pragmatic and populist, as illustrated by the examples of Keynesianism and corporatism. It is clear that liberal dichotomies have not destabilised liberalism by giving rise to projects to reform social and political institutions in an effort to create credible forms of legal universality against tradition, domination and privilege. Had it been destabilised in this manner, liberalism would have been compelled to overthrow itself in the sense just alluded to, i.e. in the project of honourably failing to fully realise liberal ideas of freedom, justice and equality. On closer inspection it seems that the aforementioned dichotomies in their liberal formulation are not really articulated in a battle with organised political power or the tyranny of the majority, nor do they constitute the absent truth suppressed by the lie of publicly coerced reconciliation. The fact is that far from overthrowing itself because of the discrepancies between ethics and politics, theory and practice, etc., liberalism has established itself hegemonically by setting the parameters of legitimate political debate without being directly in power as an identifiable 'who' of legitimation. How has this been possible?

Tracing the evolution of liberal epistemology and politics: the return of metaphysics and the demise of the public sphere

Prior to the period of liberal hegemony, when feudal forms of domination maintained urban and rural working populations in conditions of direct dependence on their masters, the battle for political authority was contested in a system of antagonistic pluralism. The monarch, vassals, corporations, guilds and clergy, each with their own statutes, privileges and traditions, were among the most prominent competitors in this struggle. As a political form, monarchy was eventually able to assert itself as a recognised central authority. This movement is charted at the philosophical level by the theorists of absolute monarchy such as Bodin, Spinoza, Pufendorf and, perhaps most famously, by Hobbes. Monarchies across Europe proceeded to curb the autonomy of the corporations, guilds and ecclesiastical powers with a unified system of law and administration. Privileges were transformed into an increasingly systematic array of codes regulating rights and obligations. In this manner it was also possible to create a system of norms regulating contract and introducing predictable forms of economic competition. This standardisation and contractual regulation of property and exchange helped create propitious conditions for calculation and investment decisions. It was in other words instrumental in securing the legal and cultural conditions for the emergence of capitalism as the prevailing modern economic system of production. In contrast to hierarchical forms of feudal domination characterised by a vertical chain of command, the emerging system of contractual agreement entered into by mutually consenting parties seemed to offer a model of horizontal reciprocity between equals. The process of centralisation undermining feudalism and concentrating public authority in the monarchy, along with the subjection of the special privileges of intermediary bodies to the increasingly unified norms of the state, reached a climax with the events of 1789 in France. The new state brought into existence by the Jacobins had the task of carrying forward the process of administrative centralisation and legal standardisation that the French monarchy, and subsequently other European monarchies, could no longer guarantee. In curbing the power of intermediary institutions such as guilds and corporations, the emerging modern state responded to the demands of the ascendant liberal bourgeoisie and created the conditions for its further expansion in its quest to definitively succeed the aristocracy. In this quest the bourgeoisie made use first of the monarchy, and then the modern state, in the context of post-1789 France and elsewhere.[20]

For the liberal bourgeoisie, however, the modern state represented an ambivalent ensemble of institutions. On the one hand, this form of central authority was highly efficient in subduing the vestiges of antagonistic feudal pluralism. On the other hand, the modern state was also a potential threat, especially insofar as it could fiscally overburden the motors of the new economy through the taxation necessary to finance the maintenance of armies, bureaucracies and a myriad of other operations. An ancient system of payments based on loyalties and codes of honour was being replaced with the foundations of the tax system needed to provide central government with a stable source of revenue. Through excessive public spending of money secured by heavy taxation of private economic interests, the modern state threatened to jeopardise the success of administrative centralisation smoothing the way for economic rationalisation.[21] Thus the unequivocally centralist ideas of the apologists of absolute monarchy such as Bodin and Hobbes were succeeded by a much more ambivalent attitude toward central authority after the French Revolution. This uneasiness appears in the writings of liberals like Mill and Tocqueville in the nineteenth century. It is an uneasiness that becomes a strident abjuration of the state in the twentieth century in the polemical tones of Hayek, Friedman and Nozick. The financial and manufacturing interests accompanying ascendant liberalism needed a state that would suppress aristocratic whim and economic stagnation, and provide reliable conditions for investment and growth. But they also needed a considerable degree of flexibility and reliable guarantees of non-intervention from the state where these were necessary for economic expansion. Thus from the perspective of the interests driving the emerging economy, it was (and remains) necessary, in a manner of speaking, to bring the state in (to protect ownership) and simultaneously keep it out (in order not to infringe too much upon the prerogatives of private ownership). In concrete historical terms, these contradictory imperatives have given rise to a range of state forms, none of which corresponds to classical notions of liberal legality or the implementation of the right before the good.[22]

If one considers the attempt to juggle the twin imperatives of securing state intervention in economic matters when necessary (fascism, Keynesianism and corporatist Fordism), on the one hand, and having the option to reimpose a retrenchment of state management of the economy when necessary (neo-liberal post-Fordism/flexible specialisation), on the other, it becomes clear that in practice the dichotomies which characterise liberal thought are not centrally concerned with a critique of the institutions of coerced reconciliation in the name of the individual liberty of *all* individuals. As such, the liberal democratic state fails to make good on the Enlightenment goal of replacing the arbitrary exercise of power and privilege characteristic of feudal-aristocratic regimes with the supposedly universal norms of the state of law. As will be shown, this is because the dichotomies serve in both theory and practice to institute a legal form of legitimacy rather than a legitimate form of legality. Liberal theorists claim to distinguish theory and praxis, politics and ethics, state and civil society, etc., in the name of individual liberty and protection from the arbitrary exercise of unaccountable power. Yet as a political movement liberalism does not really depend on their separation – on the contrary. In having to bring the state in and to simultaneously keep it out, the tenability of those separations is undermined. However, the untenability of liberal dichotomies does not mean that public and private or state and civil society are fused in liberal democratic regimes, nor that such a fusion would resolve the legality–legitimacy problem in favour of total legitimacy, i.e. as the withering away of the state or some such vision of the spontaneously organised 'administration of things'. It is thus fair to ask what is going on in such régimes, if it is neither fusion of the right (ethics, private law) and the good (politics, legitimacy) nor the separation of the right and the good. Rather than being a question of private versus public, ethics versus politics, theory versus practice, etc., what is more fundamentally at stake is the role of reason and law in mediating the relations between humanity and nature. Kant is correct to argue that law and reason mediate between humanity and nature in ways which create the conditions for experience and knowledge. Hence the decisive question becomes: what kind of law and what kind of reason are being enlisted in the pursuit of what kind of knowledge? In legal systems respecting private ownership of property and the means of production, citizens secure the means of their survival and possible transcendence of scarcity in labour processes which are hierarchically structured, and in which the fruits of the collective labour process are not equally shared because of private appropriation of collectively produced wealth.[23] Over time, the hierarchical structuring of the work process tends to ossify the division of labour operative in the different sectors of the economy. This ossification results in an entrenched fragmentation of tasks institutionalised as the division of labour. For most individuals the division of labour militates against a global understanding of the processes that regulate human interaction with the natural world. As a result, these processes seem to acquire their own mysterious laws that have more to do with ideological notions of merit, good luck and destiny than they do with the science of economics or principles of reason. This seems clear given the fact that, by revolutionising property relations, science and reason could be applied in the collective endeavour to best organise, in a planned interaction with the natural world, the satisfaction of human needs and the scientific investigation of the world without ideological manipulation. Antagonistically structured property relations distort scientific investigation of the structure of mediations constituting the world at the same time that they institutionalise inequalities concerning access to the means of survival. Such inequalities shackle politics to the struggle for survival, thus undermining the possibility of creating the institutional bases of a form of political liberty beyond naturalistic/mechanical causality. At first glance, this would suggest that the private appropriation of collectively produced wealth should be replaced by collective appropriation of collectively produced wealth, i.e. by public ownership. Yet as the experience of state social-ism in the former Soviet Union and elsewhere illustrates, it is possible to implement forms of collective ownership without drastically altering the divi-sion of labour or modifying highly instrumental forms of reason. Hence in terms of the possibility of transcending necessity without that transcendence boomeranging in the spectre of political authoritarianism, the specific forms of collective ownership and control that are instituted are as crucial as the modal-ities of reason that are adopted. There is an extensive secondary literature on communist forms of Fordism and hierarchical management in Soviet, Chinese, Cuban and other communist workshops. Historical research suggests that widening ownership from private to public does not automatically push legality beyond its formal limits to legitimacy – if by legitimacy is meant a legitimate form of legality rather than merely hegemony or consensus. Nor does the widening of the purview of legality, either through public ownership or univer-sal suffrage, immediately produce uncoerced reconciliation between citizens. Thus there is no continuum from theory to practice in liberalism or commu-nism, or indeed in politics generally, which also means that there is no automatic continuum from legality to legitimacy. This point will be taken up in detail in chapter 2, and is an important point to keep in mind for the chapters to come.[24]

In the discussion of Kant earlier in this chapter, it was seen that Kant's philoso-phy is in important respects already post-metaphysical in that it specifies the conditions of objectivity in conceptual form rather than identifying the essential primacy of either mind or matter. In this context, if metaphysics is centrally concerned with unmediated essences and unconditional first causes, the post-metaphysical is marked by the reality of the conceptual mediation between subject and object. The post-metaphysical is thus also critically idealist, since attempts to forge a direct epistemological link with the real are retreats to primitive empiri-cism/materialism, on the one hand, or solipsistic rationalism, on the other. For Kant, knowledge is mediated by the forms through which knowledge is transmit-ted; the difference between forms of knowledge and pure knowledge itself is unfortunately unbridgeable. Attempts to attain unmediated knowledge are meta-physical in the negative, speculative sense suggested by the notion of 'pure reason'.[25] In political terms, this epistemological humility is translated into a defence of legal form against any essential notion of the legitimate human good, and the concomitant suspicion that there is a strong link between metaphysical speculation and political despotism. It is suggested above that the primacy of law and form over legitimacy and essence in Kant quietly becomes an apology of freedom of conscience, non-infringement and, most important, the rights of private property, i.e. of liberal values and a liberal conception of individual, competitive liberty. Thus in Kant, as in many liberal thinkers, ostensible epistemological humility is coupled with a distinctly individualist and normative version of human freedom which cannot be defended as neutrality in the face of different conceptions of the good life. In dispensing with an identifiable legitimation subject whilst retaining legitimacy in the form of anonymous legality, liberalism does not respect the sanctity of the theoretical dichotomies it is legally empowered to enforce. Liberalism gets closer to transcending metaphysical essence than any other existing political doctrine in theory as well as in practice, which is part of the reason why it continues to be such a compelling intellectual and practical force in the world. But it stops well short of a full transition to a political form free from symbolic and real violence. This is because liberal democratic states privatise unitary essence at the individual level (autonomy) at the same time that they collectivise unitary essence at the state level (sovereignty).[26] It is this step in the liberal argument that is being called into question here, whilst at the same time trying to explore what a radicalisation of the Kantian defence of Enlightenment law and rational epistemology might mean in terms of freedom and the transcendence of necessity. Citizens and philosophers may choose to argue in a consistently post-metaphysical vein due to the epistemological and political discovery of the objectivity of form. But this does not sanction conflating the legally regulated pursuit of private interests with non-coercive politics, as liberals generally do.[27] Nor does it compel them to accept existing socio-political institutions and the existing dichotomy between private ethics and public politics. A different interpretation of objectivity and of mediating form could outline a different set of property rights and imply different conceptions of legality, transcendence and freedom as a consequence.

In relation to questions of objectivity and knowledge, Kant shows that the primacy of the external world versus the primacy of mind is a falsely posed question of essences. It is the form of objectivity, and conversely, the objectivity of form, that counts for humans, not the essence of the object (the thing in itself).[28] Similarly, the question of legality versus legitimacy is falsely posed. After the Enlightenment, it is the form of legality that counts for citizens of a world in which a return to hierarchically ordained political privilege, mythology and the rule of tradition is not reconcilable with scientific rationality. A legal form of legitimacy suggests that legitimacy is the real truth or essence behind the apparently fortuitous outputs of the legal system. This essentialist understanding of legitimacy provides the basis of the notion of sovereignty, i.e. that there is a unitary general will beyond the will of all, making the disagreements of a plurality of wills reconcilable. Keeping this in mind, a central argument of this book is that the critique of metaphysics directed at idealism is misplaced in important respects. That critique generally attempts to demonstrate that the root of epistemological and political problems is to be sought in the supposedly metaphysical and solipsistic premises of idealist reason, which needs to be converted into an interpersonal, variously formulated communicative type of reason or an impersonal theory of systemic integration. The argument here is that there are moments of truth in idealism (and particularly liberal idealism insofar that it is wary of any immediate theory–praxis fusion) that insist on the reality of conceptual form over metaphysical essence. Given the right form, these moments are potentially anti-hierarchical and anti-authoritarian and carry radical epistemological and political implications. Hence it is wrong to simply dismiss liberal forms of idealism as metaphysical, as many Marxists and would-be post-metaphysical theorists of communication do. The preceding discussion of liberal and idealist dichotomies implies that whilst those dichotomies are not false, especially as they offer a potential political-epistemological resistance against coerced reconciliation, they become ideological and false when they are used to legitimise the validity of private property or when they are invoked as timeless natural or ontological truths about the impossibility of new forms of political mediation between humanity and nature. To oversimplify the matter for a moment, it might be argued that in being wary of instances of coerced reconciliation, certain thinkers in the liberal-idealist tradition such as Kant and Croce express something profound with a false argument. They are right to point out that it is epistemologically false and politically oppressive to legitimise existing institutions with the status of being the successful embodiment of theory, but wrong to confer permanent epistemological or political validity on what the same state recognises, through legality, to be private or contractual modes of conduct. The latter can also be coercive, though obviously in different ways. Liberalism does not solve the problem of political coercion. But neither does it call upon citizens to applaud various forms of institutionalised coercion as realised democracy, the ethical state, communism, community, *Dasein*, successful communication or agonistic recognition. There is thus great epistemological promise in the possibility of retaining philosophical liberalism's theoretical distance from existing forms of domination if this distance can be maintained without endorsing the exploitative social relations enforced by civil law or absconding into aesthetic or pseudo-philosophical flight. One of the issues to be explored in the following chapters is the possibility that an epistemologically stringent critique of metaphysics could be brought to bear on the discourses of legality which buttress legal forms of legitimacy culminating in sovereignty conceived as a collective instantiation of individual autonomy. This would entail a critique of sovereignty in all of its many guises, including those implied by the examples just cited, but most importantly it would furnish a devastating critique of sovereignty in its currently hegemonic liberal democratic form. It has been suggested throughout this chapter why the critique of liberal discourses of legality is especially important. Liberal idealism typified by thinkers such as Kant and Croce is unique in that it offers a stringent epistemological and political critique of coerced reconciliation. Yet liberalism unconditionally dismisses the possibility of uncoerced reconciliation of theory and practice, subject and object, legality and legitimacy, etc., thereby forgetting its own epistemological discovery of the mediated, synthetic and conditional quality of knowledge, experience and, by extension, of politics. The discoveries of liberal idealism need to be deepened and explored further rather than jettisoned, ignored or, as generally happens in contemporary liberal democracies, dogmatically preserved in their original articulation.[29]

This attempt at unconditional preservation can be observed in the speculative attempts to re-imagine the original state of nature or what Rawls takes to be the original position of humanity prior to the law, i.e. in attempts to reproduce an ahistorical but somehow credible account of the origins of the state. There are two discrepant explanations about the rational origins of liberal democracies, in contrast to the theological origins of the states of gods and monarchs, and the dogmatic origins of the various kinds of non-liberal dictatorship. At times one encounters the argument that, regardless of the outcomes in the fields of social action regulated by private law, citizens must accept their political institutions as their collective (as opposed to competing-individual) creation. These institutions constitute the necessary condition for the very possibility of the competitive private individual. They are free to attempt to modify those outcomes through the *Rechtsstaat*, but the *Rechtsstaat* is, in its de-personalised objectivity, non-negotiable and beyond the scope of private ends. Indeed, attempts to make subjective and privately motivated incursions into this formal objectivity are by definition corrupt and illegal. At other times, however, one encounters a slightly different argument, namely, that the right to property and the universal validity of contract precede the state. In this version, property and contract are merely given formal sanction by the state, which is created on the basis of the free individual. According to this second argument, public political authority was established when sundry private individuals made an admittedly fictive collective agreement to leave the state of nature, in order to found a collective body to protect their natural rights in individual person and property. In many instances, liberal and liberal democratic thinking combines various elements of both of these arguments in an unstable mix of natural and positive law to account for the grounds of political obligation. In their diverse articulations, they constitute the basis of the liberal legal anthropology that stands at the centre of liberal discourses of legality and legal forms of legitimacy in modern industrial democracies. Hence this particular state form is always there as a necessary precondition in the first instance, and always there as an intrusive threat in the second, potentially overstepping its minimal role of guaranteeing natural rights of person and property. From *laissez-faire* to authoritarian populism/fascism, and from there to Keynesianism and neo-liberalism, this state can be justified as legitimate in its interventionist moments, and defended as equally legitimate when it is rolled back.[30] The adoption of *legal measures* to bring the state in or scale back its sphere of jurisdiction clearly indicates that at present law is not neutral nor does it instantiate the right before the good. It is in large measure an instrument in the struggle for hegemony. There are a number of possible responses to this dilemma. A conformist option consists in the insistence that these problems with the contemporary practice of law do exist, but there is simply no alternative to the liberal democratic *Rechtsstaat*. This is an example of the will to dogmatic preservation in spite of the glaring reality that the social structure of advanced industrial societies has been completely transformed since the original articulation of the liberal idea. One finds this tendency in a great deal of communicative action theory, systems theory, civil society theory and theories of 'the political'. An alternative response to the crisis in liberal democratic legality is to reject legality altogether. Recent years have witnessed a proliferation of non-liberal versions of the will to power and the will to pleasure. Examples include Negri and Hardt's 'multitude' and the bio-political schizoid nomadism of people like Deleuze and Guattari. These four theorists identify instances of extra-legal legitimacy based on a creative reading of Marx in the first instance and very original readings of Nietzsche and Foucault in the second. Extra-legal legitimacy is potentially attributable to a limitless range of ostensibly post-liberal political subjectivities, as the work of Bhabha, Butler and Zizek confirms. Yet if the foregoing analysis of the promise and ambiguity of liberalism is correct, there is little point in dogmatic preservation or the exaltation of alternative subjectivities to liberal subjectivity. The point is that it is possible to transcend subjectivity in its existing form altogether, but such transcendence has two conditions. These conditions will be outlined in the next chapter and cannot be elaborated upon at this stage in the argument. Working toward a conclusion to this chapter, one might say that the critique of instrumental reason offered by critical theory needs to be broadened into a critique of instrumental law. This would constitute a preliminary step toward a theory of a legitimate form of legality capable of clearly indicating the metaphysical dimensions and violent implications of all legal forms of legitimacy.

Instrumental legal interventions in the reorganisation of economic and social relations are generally upheld as rational and legitimate by the defenders of liberal democratic polities. There will of course be disagreements amongst some members of the political class and economic élites about when it is necessary and rational to curb public spending for the sake of a strong currency and to stimulate private investment, and when it is rational and necessary to increase public spending to create jobs and stimulate consumer demand. These disagreements are likely to be vociferous in periods of transition such as the current construction of the financial and political institutions of the European Union. But within the constellation of options open within a democratic-liberal framework, there is overarching agreement that reason is employed in the successful (and at times not so successful) legal mediation between the strategic demands of organised private interests and the public demands of the citizen body. The legitimacy of such régimes stands and falls with the claim that the divisive logic of strategy and calculation pervading the private sphere of competing individuals is discursively mediated by the collective reasoning of the citizens of the public sphere. When it becomes clear that the parameters of the public reason of citizens are fundamentally congruent with the logic of strategy and calculation of competing groups and individuals, it is no longer convincing to argue that citizenship is a sphere of rational deliberation or equality, since strategy and competition are enlisted to secure advantages rather than to guarantee equality or reach substantive agreement. These features of the system crystallise in particular historical moments such as Weimar, the corporatism of the 1970s and globalisation today. In these moments a legitimacy crisis ensues, compelling the state to modify or enforce the outcomes of the various processes regulated by private law. The economic processes regulated by private law provide the material base for the financing of state operations. That is, since the state is dependent on tax revenue for its very existence, it must somehow reconcile citizens to the reality of structural inequality in the economy, on the one hand, and the subordination of political institutions to the instrumental rationality that sustains that structural inequality, on the other. That is to say, legitimacy becomes a matter of degrees of functional *success* and integration rather than non-instrumental mediation through public deliberation. This is a staggering normative defeat for liberal democracy, since the legitimacy of liberal democratic polities is supposedly based on the substitution of universally accepted norms (the rights of expression, assembly and participation are the same for all) for the vagaries of power politics in all its various guises. It might be countered that the non-egalitarian consequences ensuing from the institutionalisation of a negative concept of liberty are held in check by more democratic aspirations to community and positive liberty enacted as welfare and equality. In this manner, liberal democratic governments seem to do justice to the requirement to satisfy liberal as well as democratic aspirations – it is a legitimate rather than just a legal political form. But if the issue is really functional success and integration, where functional success and integration can at any time assume a democratic-authoritarian/populist form, what one really means by politics in liberal democratic régimes is the continual construction and reconstruction of an elastic form of hegemonic consensus. Under such conditions it is clear that the public sphere and the communicative dimension of the life-world are largely ideological constructions. In sum, it can be said that liberalism offers a critique of coerced reconciliation based on a theoretical defence of a series of dichotomies, the individual terms of which are in reality mediated coercively. In addition, liberalism offers a theory of political legitimacy based on a moment of unanimous consensus in the state of nature, whilst in practice liberal democratic polities are continually obliged to reorganise and manipulate the bases of mobilised popular consent in order to gain support for private decisions that have already been made or are being planned. In keeping with the general line of argument pursued in this chapter, it is nonetheless possible to trace a utopian moment in the liberal critique of coerced reconciliation and the theory of unanimous consensus that points well beyond the liberal democratic state without catapulting toward political authoritarianism, political correctness or celebrations of extra-legal legitimacy. It is possible to analyse this moment by briefly returning to the liberal project of investing law with a cognitive dimension that would make it more than an instrument for adjudicating conflict or a code for balancing the steering imperatives of autonomous social systems. This will be done by way of a brief look at the Kantian idea of the public sphere.

Two conditions inform Kant's ideas of a critical public mediating between morally autonomous individuals and the positive laws enacted by public political authority. First, the individuals making up the public sphere are endowed with a rational will that is independent of all empirically existing institutions and independent of individual experience. He holds that in order for the will to unify itself with reason, it must constitute itself in abstraction from emotions, impulses, drives and needs that one might associate with legitimate need and expression in a more contemporary context. His point is that everyone has different needs and a different concept of happiness. In order for the will to attain the standpoint of autonomous reason, these demands, legitimate or not, must be left at home – only a highly paternalistic state can satisfy people's private longings. Second, the critical debate of an assembly of rational wills must take place in a sphere of freedom, not in a workplace or laboratory where a chain of command to solve tasks efficiently is more appropriate than an assembly of equals. Kant openly excludes women, children and salaried workers from the public sphere and political participation because of their lack of autonomy. They are emotionally and economically dependent, which means that if given the chance to express their views, they will directly address the question of their dependence by embracing an authoritarian politics of legitimate need and happiness rather than a juridical politics of freedom and rational cognition. If this happens, law is deprived of its epistemological dimension at the same time that the possibility of the transcendence of natural necessity and mechanical causality is lost. Hence the public sphere is not operative in order to make people happy or secure. University professors, government administrators and other economically independent élites occupy the public sphere in order to collectively formulate principles of public reason. These discursively redeemed principles directly confront the representatives of public authority with ethically informed universal claims that the latter cannot ignore. In this way the bourgeois public sphere is capable of definitively undermining Hobbes's claim that authority, not truth, is the source of law.[31]

But what would happen should the state refuse to adjust the content of law-making to the truths of discursive rationality? A legitimacy crisis ensues. From the perspective of critical theory and legal theory adopted in this book, the promise of modern legal rationality is that this is not in the first instance a legitimacy crisis concerning the distribution of wealth, status, security or other phenomena that can be administratively or technically attended to with the aid of institutionalised forms of instrumental reason. It is a crisis of reason in relation to the epistemological legitimacy of law. When forms of law are out of step with the cognitive content of reason, law forfeits the epistemological dimension that separates modern law from other more or less hegemonic models of public authority such as diktat, charisma, privilege and tradition that characterise the pre-Enlightenment past. Kant believes that as the process of Enlightenment takes its course toward increasingly perfect forms of knowledge, substantive rationality and legal formality will harmonise to the extent that populist forms of legitimacy, civil disobedience and revolution will become superfluous. In other words, where law is underwritten by the cognitive truths furnished by humanity's synthetic encounter with reason, politics ceases to be the domain of power, privilege and ideological mendacity. The long-term prospect is that humanity will no longer need to live in fear of arbitrary forms of legitimacy or random accounts of destiny that have served despotisms throughout the ages. Yet the restrictions on suffrage operative in Kant's day have been abolished long ago, and with them the social structure which at least in principle allowed the bourgeois public sphere to satisfy the conditions of an epistemologically based practice of legislation. Two responses predominate in the contemporary politics and society of Western states. The first is that the promise of a form of legitimacy based to a significant degree on epistemological criteria represents an irretrievably lost opportunity. As such, legitimacy is now mainly a pragmatic issue of functional and systemic stability. This means that the heroic epoch of liberalism is gone and the epistemological dimension of legality has to be diluted in order to accommodate legitimate demands for at least minimum levels of wealth, happiness, security, welfare, recognition, status, justice, equality and entertainment. The second response is that structures of communicative action anchored in the life-world and civil society transmit knowledge that exercises a cognitive pressure on the legal system in the same way that the participants in the public sphere did so in the past, with the difference that this now happens on a democratic basis without restrictive access. Both responses are inadequate for reasons which are clear from the discussion in this chapter. The response that is worked out over the course of the following chapters explains why the juxtaposition of rational legal knowledge with irrational legitimate need is the reified product of an instrumental practice of legality informed by an instrumental conception of rationality. Demands for happiness and various forms of recognition are potentially legitimate in an epistemological sense, though not within the framework in which they are currently aggregated. The epistemological content of these demands is undermined when articulated and represented as movements for inclusion within a juridical framework which retains the liberal dismissal of sensuous and aesthetic rationality, but which now treats them as administrative problems in need of regulation. This is a framework within which they are distorted, marginalised or ignored. In order to liberate legitimate knowledge from legal oppression without forfeiting the epistemological dimension of legality, the relations between legality and legitimacy have to be reconsidered in the light of a reconceptualisation of the conditional, synthetic and mediated quality of the relations between humanity and nature.

Notes

1 The priority of legality over legitimacy is formulated by John Rawls as the priority of the right before the good in *A Theory of Justice*, Cambridge MA, Harvard University Press, 1971, and in 'Justice as Fairness: Political not Metaphysical', *Philosophy and Public Affairs*, 14 (summer 1985), p. 224. Rawls develops the ideas of the 1985 article into an elaborate defence of what he refers to as post-metaphysical liberalism in *Political Liberalism*, New York, Columbia University Press, 1993. During the course of the evolution of his work, Rawls never abandons his philosophical and political commitment to the priority of the right, which is to say that he retains a Kantian view of legality despite the abjuration of metaphysics in his writings of the 1980s and 1990s.

2 Moreover, the flaws in Kant's idealism do not alter the fact that his philosophy carries implications that indicate paths well beyond the liberal framework in which they are developed which are quite distinct from the neo-liberal interpretations which have dominated since the publication of *A Theory of Justice*. For instance, there is a clear trajectory from Kant to Hegel to Marx which has already received extensive commentary. There are also far less well known links between Kant and radical socialist politics, such as those found in the writings of the Austro-Marxists Max Adler and Rudolf Hilferding. Kant's ideas also had a profound impact on the ethical socialism of Herman Cohen (1842–1918) and other theorists of the Marburg school such as Paul Natorp, Friedrich Albert Lange, Karl Vorländer, Rudolf Stammler and Franz Staudinger. Cohen's *Ethik des reinen Willens* (*The Ethics of the Pure Will*, Duncker & Humblot, Berlin, 1904) remains a seminal work of ethical socialism. Readers of German interested in Cohen (1842–1918) and the Marburg school should read the essays collected in Helmut Holzhey (ed.), *Ethischer Sozialismus. Zur politischen Philosophie des Neukantismus*, Frankfurt, Suhrkamp, 1994. Adorno's translated lectures on Kant (*Kant's Critique of Pure Reason*, Stanford CA, Stanford University Press, 2001) indicate that Kantian idealism can be interpreted in ways which provide new impetus to the development of critical theory. Hence it is important for the approach taken in this book to stress that it is possible to move from liberalism, traditional idealism and Enlightenment, on the one hand, to libertarian socialism, radical idealism and the relaunching of the Enlightenment project, on the other. The reasons why this is possible will be elaborated in detail in this chapter and the chapters to come.

3 Kant, *Kritik der praktischen Vernunft* (*The Critique of Practical Reason*, 1787), Stuttgart, Reclam, 1961, pp. 122–3, 189–9. For a detailed exposition of this juridical reading of Kant, see Gilles Deleuze, *La Philosophie critique de Kant* (*Kant's Critical*

Philosophy), Paris, Presses Universitaires de France, 1963, pp. 27–7, 42–8.

4 Kant thus concedes that the act of knowledge is also to a considerable extent an act of the imagination in which the sensuous and the conceptual are synthesised. The epistemological and political implications of a radicalised version of this position will be a central theme in later chapters.

5 Kant, *Beantwortung der Frage: Was ist Aufklärung?* (*An Answer to the Question, What is Enlightenment?*, 1784), in *Schriften zur Anthropologie*, Geschichtsphilosophie, Politik und Pädagogik 1, Frankfurt a. M., Suhrkamp, 1993, pp. 54–7, now contained in Hans Reiss, ed., *Kant: Political Writings*, Cambridge, Cambridge University Press, 1970. The discussion will return to Kant's idea of the public sphere at the end of this chapter.

6 Kant, *Metaphysische Anfangsgründe der Rechtslehre* (*Fundamental Metaphysical Bases of Legal Theory: The Metaphysics of Morals*, Part I, 1785), Hamburg, Meiner, 1986, pp. 55–65, 73–87.

7 Those interested in understanding the basics of Kantian philosophy and acquiring a familiarity with its basic terms should consult Howard Caygill, *A Kant Dictionary*, Oxford, Blackwell, 1995.

8 In his discussions with the Italian Communist Party in the 1950s and 1960s, for example, Norberto Bobbio was able to show convincingly that Italian workers were better advised to struggle for legal reform rather than the overthrow of the state. In those debates he observes that a 'workers' state' calling for the immediate identification of worker and state operates on the premise that the workers can dispense with formal legality in favour of direct political control through the party. This would inevitably result in an authoritarian subordination of individual workers to the designs of the party to remodel society according to the whims of the leadership, as was borne out by the authoritarian turn of the Russian Revolution. By contrast, a stable legal system would prevent any such authoritarian identification of one social actor with the state, and guarantee freedoms of participation, assembly and expression in addition to rights in the workplace. See Bobbio, *Teoria generale della politica*, Turin, Einaudi, 1999, chapter 4. For a very good summary of Bobbio's views on this subject, see *Quale socialismo?*, Turin, Einaudi, 1976 (translated by Polity Press as *Which Socialism?*), and Richard Bellamy, *Modern Italian Social Theory*, Stanford CA, Stanford University Press, 1987, chapter 8.

9 The result is that a lot of contemporary critique which styles itself as post-metaphysical is actually *democratically metaphysical*, i.e. it takes the liberal notion of unmediated essence and gives it a feminist, gay, communicative or similar idiom. This issue will be explored in more detail in chapter 2. Avoiding the problem of humanist essence by simply celebrating infinite contingency and the play of signifiers is banal and does not challenge liberalism whatsoever, despite what some academic theorists say.

10 The idealist philosophies of Hegel and especially the Italian theorist of fascism Giovanni Gentile (1875–1944) indicate that not all idealism is politically liberal. Matters are complicated further by the distinction between idealism and metaphysics. In fact, Gentile sought to purge idealism of metaphysics by insisting on the unity of knowledge, thought and action. See Bellamy, *Modern Italian Social Theory*, chapter 6. Liberal empiricists in the Anglo-American tradition will almost certainly claim to be non-idealist philosophers. Yet, for reasons discussed above, it is difficult not to subscribe at least in part to Kant's argument that all objectivity is mediated by subjectivity, and thus to some extent formal and idealist. In fact, Kant's idealism strives to overcome determinate aspects of metaphysical thought by asking about the condi-

tions of possible experience rather than conjectural first principles which cannot be derived from experience. His philosophy might be characterised as a form of idealism which is critical of metaphysics and yet acutely aware of what the critique of metaphysics might mean in terms of severely limiting the epistemological claims of reason. As suggested above, attempts to provide a crude materialist critique aiming at the wholesale overturning of idealism generally lapse into metaphysics in a pejorative sense, insofar as they ignore the point that all objectivity is mediated by subjectivity. For an interpretation of Kant as a somewhat reluctant anti-metaphysical idealist, see Adorno's Kant lectures published by Stanford University Press in 2001, and Chris Thornhill's review of those lectures in *The Prague Literary Review*, 2 (2004), forthcoming.

11 One could phrase the matter in the spirit of Horkheimer and Adorno's *Dialectic of Enlightenment*: until humanity allows rationality to become fully rational, legal-rational legitimation is potentially more dangerous than previous forms of legitimacy, such as tradition and custom. A mass electorate can opt to sweep tradition and custom away, but it can also dispense with parliamentary institutions altogether. Democracy does not automatically lead to fascism, but fascism is unthinkable without a populist manipulation of the democratic notion of 'the people'. That manipulation is not possible without a mass electorate that is called upon to vote for rational solutions which are in fact mandates for mobilisation.

12 For two very careful interpretations of Marx that have unfortunately been for the most part overlooked and which do not make this mistake, see Alfred Schmidt, *Der Begriff der Natur in der Lehre von Marx* (*Marx's Concept of Nature*), Frankfurt, Europäische Verlaganstalt, 1962, and Michel Henry, *Marx* I, *Une philosophie de réalité*, and *Marx* II, *Une philosophie de l'économie* (*Marx* I, *A Philosophy of Reality*, and *Marx* II, *A Philosophy of the Economy*), Paris, Gallimard, 1976. Both of these outstanding exegetical works have been translated into English.

13 Those who read Hegel closely will object that where one speaks of rights one is of course also speaking of public authority: there are no 'natural' rights without a state that recognises their existence, just as there is no valid contract without a state that renders contract valid. If the distinction between occupation and ownership is legality and hence the state, there are no pre-legal rights or rights in the state of nature. Hence there is no absolute distinction between the private rights of individual citizens, on the one hand, and the existence of public legal authority, on the other – As such it is a misnomer to speak in terms of individual rights against the state – if an individual has rights to privacy and property, it is through the institutions of the state, namely, through law. This holds unless one relies on the completely fictitious device of the state of nature and the concomitant notion of its putative abandonment for the benefits of public goods. The Hegelian objection to natural rights and his critique of the state of nature and of contract are correct. The implications for liberal attempts to derive the origins of the state from contract or other individualist principles are clear. See Hegel, *Grundlinien der Philosophie des Rechts* (*The Philosophy of Right*, 1821), Frankfurt, Suhrkamp, 1986. The implications of Hegel's argument are explored in later chapters of this book.

14 Hence the tremendous interest in recent years in the ideas of Carl Schmitt, whose entire *oeuvre* can be regarded as a sustained interrogation of the relations between legality, legitimacy and politics. See Carl Schmitt, *Legalität und Legitimität* (*Legality and Legitimacy*, 1932), Berlin, Duncker & Humblot, 1993. The crisis of the Weimar Republic (1918–33) can be seen as a case study of the stakes involved in the legality–legitimacy debate. The period is remembered as a period of exceptional

turbulence and political instability. Yet Schmitt's belief that when it comes to sover-
eignty the exception proves the rule is correct, and points well beyond Weimar
constitutional theory and practice. Some of the key debates are found in Otto
Kirchheimer, 'Bemerkungen zu Carl Schmitts *Legalität und Legitimität*' ('Remarks on
Carl Schmitt's *Legality and Legitimacy*'), and 'Strukturwandel des politischen
Kompromisses' ('Changes in the Structure of Political Compromise'), in Wolfgang
Luthhardt (ed.), *Von der Weimarer Republik zum Faschismus. Die Auflösung der
demokratischen Rechtsordnung*, Frankfurt, Suhrkamp, 1976, and Franz Neumann,
'Der Funktionswandel des Gesetzes im Recht der bürgerlichen Gesellschaft' ('The
Change in the Function of Law within the Legal Structure of Bourgeois Civil Society')
and 'Zum Begriff der politischen Freiheit' ('On the Concept of Political Freedom'), in
Herbert Marcuse (ed.), *Demokratischer and autoritärer Staat*, Frankfurt, Fischer,
1986. These essays are available in English in Andrew Arato and Eike Gebhardt (eds),
The Frankfurt School Reader, New York, Continuum, 1982, and William
Scheuermann (ed.), *The Rule of Law under Siege: Selected Essays by Franz Neumann
and Otto Kirchheimer*, Berkeley CA, University of California Press, 1996. For a very
cogent analysis of the main ideas of Weber, Schmitt, Neumann and Kirchheimer on
legality and legitimacy, see Chris Thornhill, *Political Theory in Modern Germany: An
Introduction*, Cambridge, Polity Press, 2000, chapters 1–3. Perhaps it is somewhat
surprising, given Schmitt's political allegiances in the 1930s, that an imaginary
dialogue between Marx and Schmitt might find them agreeing that capitalism undermines democracy. Schmitt opts for the salvaging of democratic legitimacy against
liberalism and, if need be, against legality. Kirchheimer and Neumann argue that
capitalism undermines democracy and legality, neither of which can be forsaken if a
truly uncoerced relation between citizens is to obtain. If liberal democratic parliamentary institutions under capitalism transform legality into a set of decrees, as
Kirchheimer and Neumann suggest, then liberalism must be drastically reformed,
beyond its historical compromises with corporatism and social democracy, in order
to salvage legality. See William E. Scheuerman, *Between the Norm and the Exception:
The Frankfurt School and the Rule of Law*, Cambridge MA, MIT Press, 1994.
15 Readers interested in an analysis of the development of Kelsen's liberal legal positivism in the context of the legality/legitimacy debates in the Weimar Republic should
consult David Dyzenhaus's excellent book, *Legality and Legitimacy: Carl Schmitt,
Hans Kelsen and Herman Heller in Weimar*, Oxford, Oxford University Press, 1997.
Dyzenhaus demonstrates how the ideas of Kant and Kelsen permeate more recent
liberal thinking on law in the works of H. L. A. Hart and Ronald Dworkin.
16 This manner of phrasing the relation between individuals in organised capitalism is
akin to a liberal caricature of liberalism itself. From Marx to Weber to Bourdieu and
beyond, it is clear that in reality one is not speaking about the individual pursuit of
privately owned wealth. Individuals are socialised into constantly changing class
formations in such a way that access to wealth (as well as the related domains of
health, housing and education) is far from a mere question of individual striving or
merit. This is to say nothing about race, gender and other factors which profoundly
alter the competition of legally equal citizens and the institutional structuration of
their 'life chances'.
17 The link between formal epistemology, legal anthropology and the deployment of a
set of dichotomies is not particular to Kant, but pervades liberal thought from the
distinction between public and private spheres to the demarcation of state and civil
society in theorists like Croce, Bobbio and a host of others.
18 Some ontologists might say that, rather than a reconciliation of humanity with

humanity or between humanity with nature, what is really at stake is a reconciliation of humanity and being. Heidegger implicitly argues for a break with idealist metaphysics and the overcoming of reification through *Dasein* as a conscious political response to the project of overcoming reification through the liberation of labour from commodification and private property through communism. Adorno shows that Heidegger's ontology sidesteps the debates between idealism (Kant, Fichte, Schelling and Hegel) and materialism (Feuerbach and Marx) rather than indicating a convincing path beyond that debate or beyond metaphysics generally. Deleuze and Guattari refer to Heiddeger's attempt to do this as a shifting of the subject–object question (ontic) to one concerned with being (ontology), without ever really demonstrating how or where the epistemological step from the ontic to the ontological actually happens. See Adorno, *Negative Dialektik* (*Negative Dialectics*), Part I, and Deleuze and Guattari, *Qu'est-ce que la philosophie?* (*What is Philosophy?*), Paris, Minuit, 1991, pp. 90–1.

19 For related reasons, this is the structural predicament that has evidently become insurmountable for social democracy. Until there is a full-scale, non-statist socialisation of the economy, public spending will always appear to be luxury spending that is tolerated only in periods of economic expansion. The counter-argument, i.e. that governments need well educated, healthy populations in order to be economically competitive, does not stand up to the reality of the crisis of the first Mitterand government in France in the early 1980s and the neo-liberal turn of social democratic governments across Europe in recent years. For a defence of the theoretical coherence and practical viability of non-statist socialism, see Darrow Schecter, *Radical Theories: Paths beyond Marxism and Social Democracy*, Manchester, Manchester University Press, 1994, especially chapter 4, and Chris Wyatt, 'G. D. H Cole: Emancipatory Politics and Organisational Democracy', DPhil, University of Sussex, 2004, forthcoming as a book.

20 Neumann, 'Zum Begriff der politischen Freiheit', pp. 122–3.

21 Rationalisation is used here in the pejorative Weberian sense associated with instrumental reason. In this context it denotes something quite distinct from the idea of reason in a Kantian and Enlightenment sense.

22 One of the first and most eloquent accounts of the difficulties inherent in the attempt to reconcile capitalist forms of economic growth with adequate financing of the modern state is offered by Marx in the *Eighteenth Brumaire*. Here Marx develops an idea that is already implicit in Hegel's critique of contract. Marx illustrates how the economic forces surpassing feudal-absolutist economies need a legal system that guarantees the enforcement of contract and punishes default of payment, i.e. secures the conditions of regulated competition. Thus at one level the modern state is interventionist in ways that safeguard private economic interests. But in order to finance police and military operations, and, to update matters beyond Marx's frame of reference, to assume responsibility for the provision of services in those many areas where the market is clearly deficient, the state is interventionist in ways that are often at odds with private economic interests. In short, private economic interests come into conflict with the same state that those interests nonetheless depend upon for the regulation of a competitive, market-based economy. The outcome, from Marx to Weimar, fascism, globalised post-Fordism and beyond, is crisis and conflict.

23 Attempts to combat these hierarchical tendencies within (and to some extent against) the legal framework of private ownership have been undertaken all over the world, with a wide variety of results. The most well known are associated with the idea of worker self-management and co-ops. For a guide to the theoretical and practical questions involved, see Schecter *Radical Theories*, chapter 5.

24 That no continua of this kind exist is also borne out empirically. Communist regimes attempt to create legitimacy by extending legality to include and encompass the economy. This experiment has produced widespread authoritarianism in practice. The liberal democratic response is equally flawed, albeit in a completely different way. One might say that the problem for liberal democracy first surfaces in dramatic terms with the Weberian attempt to reconcile value-oriented action and goal-oriented action under the same overarching roof of a form of legality bifurcated into private interests and the public good. The only way to make this reconciliation seem plausible is to somehow maintain that private interests and the public good are reconciled in the moment of voting for public officials. Marx shows that this is illusory with his distinction between political emancipation and human emancipation in *On the Jewish Question* (1843), and echoed in the call to overcome the distinction between civil society and state in communism as the answer to the riddle of democracy. Theorising in the guise of the lucid but bad conscience of German liberalism, Weber also knows that a papering over of the public–private split is illusory, but he chooses to ascribe the problem to bureaucratic rationalisation. At one level, Weber's legacy is that of diagnosing the public–private divide as symptomatic of the modern, Western plague of bureaucracy. At another level, however, because he is unwilling to accept what is correct in Marx's analysis, Weber is compelled to embrace charismatic leadership as a solution to the legitimacy crisis in the offing in the nascent Weimar Republic. To summarise the post-Weberian situation in perhaps somewhat grand terms, one might say that failed attempts to coercively reconcile the theory and practice of democracy as communism have given undue credence to the supposedly democratic character of the functional mediation of the spheres/rationalities which are legally separated in liberal-democratic regimes.

25 For a detailed exposition of this dimension of Kant's philosophy, see Robert B. Pippin, *Kant's Theory of Form: An Essay on the Critique of Pure Reason*, New Haven CT, Yale University Press, 1982. Pippin underscores the difficulties in trying to identify Kant as unqualified post-metaphysical philosopher: 'Of course, the difference between such a philosophy and metaphysics often seems to be the whole point of embarking on this transcendental path, but the issue still remains somewhat obscure. It is certainly clear that Kant meant to criticize traditional, dogmatic metaphysics on the questions of God and the freedom and immortality of the soul ... But it is also true that he uses the word "metaphysics" to describe what he himself is doing' (p. 17). It appears that Kant distinguishes between the reality of mediating concepts as form (idealism) and the belief in unmediated access to the content of knowledge (traditional metaphysical essences).

26 For a more detailed critique of the implicitly metaphysical dimensions of the notion of sovereignty, see Darrow Schecter, *Sovereign States or Political Communities? Civil Society and Contemporary Politics*, Manchester, Manchester University Press, 2000, especially chapter 2.

27 This statement needs qualification in that it is not true of the liberalism of L. T. Hobhouse or that of Piero Gobetti and the social and political ideas of the liberal socialists who fought Mussolini in the Action Party and in the pages of their journal *Giustizia e Libertà (Justice and Liberty)*. See Paolo Spriano, *Gramsci e Gobetti (Gramsci and Gobetti)*, Turin, Einaudi, 1977, Piero Gobetti, *On Liberal Revolution*, New Haven CT, Yale University Press, 2000, Carlo Rosselli, *Liberal Socialism*, New Haven CT, Yale University Press, 2001, and Stanislao G. Pugliese, *Carlo Rosselli: Socialist Heretic and Antifascist Exile*, Cambridge MA, Harvard University Press, 1999.

28 Hence the reality of form in lieu of metaphysical essences or first causes counts as a

central criterion as far as post-metaphysical thinking is concerned. Yet there are a variety of ways of making the case for the objectivity of form. One can do so through a re-articulation of a liberal theory of negative freedom and formal equality before the law (Rawls), a partially functionalist separation of system and life-world (Habermas), or a full-blown theory of systemic autonomy and functional integration (Luhmann). Whilst Habermas's communicative functionalism and Luhmann's systems function-alism claim to move theory beyond metaphysics and the philosophy of consciousness, the argument in this book stresses the reality of form in a different way by investigat-ing the possibilities of rethinking the mediation between public and private, theory and practice, etc., in non-functionalist terms and as a project that one can describe as the uncoerced reconciliation of humanity and nature. What is defended is in a very qualified sense an idealist project (see chapter 4) which cannot be dismissed as a simple return to traditional metaphysics.

29 Perhaps Adorno has something broadly similar in mind in his correspondence with Alfred Sohn-Rethel, when he suggests that it might be possible to 'explode idealism from within', rather than attempt to re-establish a naïve, historically outdated form of liberal idealism, embrace a crude form of pragmatism or champion a dogmatic version of Marxist materialism. See Christoph Gödde (ed.), *Theodor W. Adorno und Alfred Sohn-Rethel. Briefwechsel 1936–1969*, Munich, text + kritik, 1991, pp. 152–3.

30 Thus while there is no continuum between theory and practice or legality and legiti-macy, there are liberal democratic discourses of legality that suggest an at least possible continuum between parliamentary democracy and more authoritarian polit-ical state forms. This possibility is signalled by a liberal, Alexis de Tocqueville, in *Democracy in America* (1835), even before Marx's *Eighteenth Brumaire* (1852). See Tocqueville, *De la démocratie en Amérique*, two volumes (1835), Paris, Gallimard, 1978, and Marx, *Der achtzehnte Brumaire des Louis Bonaparte*, in Iring Fetscher (ed.), *Karl Marx und Friedrich Engels. Studienausgabe*, IV, Frankfurt, Fischer, 1990.

31 Kant, *Was ist Aufklärung? (What is Enlightenment?)*, p. 54.

Chapter 2

Democracy and discourses of legitimacy: liberating human agency from liberal legal form

IN chapter 1 it is argued that attempts to institutionalise some essential notion of the truth or political legitimacy are likely to reproduce authoritarian dogma in epistemological inquiry and in politics. It is also suggested that the liberal tradition from Kant to the present is the most consistent in remaining sensitive to the link between non-dogmatic epistemology and non-authoritarian politics. The preservation of this link owes a great deal to the liberal priority of legality over legitimacy, even if this priority is problematic in its liberal articulation. For liberal idealists like Kant, ideas are real and rational in the sense that they articulate concepts that mediate between the knowing subject and the objective world. The mediation process is not so much an obstacle to direct access to the objective world as it is the condition of post-metaphysical objectivity itself. Kantian epistemology holds that humanity does not simply invent the concepts of human understanding – they make themselves known to humanity through investigation. The concepts confer a mediated reality and objectivity upon the chaos of immediate experience. If people attempt to rely directly on experience without the objective form provided by concepts like space and time and the twelve categories of the understanding, then all they really have are subjective impressions instead of knowledge or freedom.[1] Similarly, just as people do not arbitrarily invent the concepts or categories that frame knowledge, they do not invent reason: they are capable of reflexively unifying themselves with reason if they are rational enough to screen out instincts, passions and other forms of need and hope. In most of the liberal discourses of legality considered in chapter 1, reason is posited as the condition of objective experience of the natural world, that is, of science, and, by extension, of objectively binding rules, that is, of legality. In the liberal tradition epistemological concepts and political legality exist as articulate forms of reason that are prior to and constitutive of individual experience. Liberal thinkers thus urge people to refrain from speculating about possible alternative modes of collective and intra-personal experience at the centre of demands for superior forms of legitimacy beyond liberalism. Hence, in liberal thought, political legality is legitimate only insofar as it conforms to the laws of reason. Whilst the limits of reason end with knowledge of the phenomena of experience rather than the things in themselves, the limits of legitimate political intervention in the affairs of an individual end with the authority to enforce freely chosen contractual agreements. If citizens are to be legally equal, they must be able to coexist within political institutions (objective forms mediating between the individual and the state) that do not privilege any particular, subjective account of freedom or equality over others. The objectivity of reason and the objective, non-arbitrary quality of law are said to provide the formal guarantee of this freedom and equality for all citizens within the liberal version of Enlightenment. Liberals are convinced that the limits to knowledge and the limits to human freedom are not negotiable. The limits are bound up with the contradictions and incoherence that befall human beings whenever they attempt to push reason beyond its formal parameters in the search for unmediated knowledge and freedom. Symptomatic of the boundaries of reason are the dichotomies at the heart of liberal thought such as those between legality and legitimacy, theory and practice, and state and civil society. Attempts to break with liberalism in epistemology and law can be characterised as projects to transcend these dichotomies in the pursuit of less reified forms of knowledge and more democratic and pluralist politics. In seeking to establish more democratic and pluralist forms of politics, liberalism's critics seek to break with the legal epistemology and the correspondingly limited forms of legitimacy that the dichotomies entail in practice. Following the discussion in the previous chapter it is now possible to theoretically examine state socialism and the practice of new social movements as paradigm examples of movements which try to transcend liberalism. Although state socialism varies in each country where it has been attempted, just as each new social movement is different, one can nonetheless detect common characteristics which allow one to observe some general tendencies in both phenomena. It will be seen that in analysing the problems pertaining to the two most decisive and important attempts to transcend the liberal dichotomies in practice, it becomes possible to discern two epistemological and legal conditions of a genuinely non-authoritarian alternative to liberalism. These two conditions will serve as the framework for elaborating the contours of this alternative as the argument unfolds in later chapters.

Beyond the liberal dichotomies to legitimate humanity (I) Locating the problem

The dichotomies in liberal epistemology and politics have been a source of frustration for a range of thinkers and activists who are unhappy with the restricted boundaries of cognition and the limits of formal equality and justice that they imply. These limits seem to impose the spectre of an unknowable, metaphysical world which is more real than this world, and an unattainable dimension of positive freedom which exists, but which is inaccessible to humanity in non-authoritarian form. Thus outside of liberal circles the dichotomies are widely construed as anti-humanist and metaphysical, and, as such, in need of humanist and anti-metaphysical correction in the name of greater knowledge and freedom.[2] A typical recourse in this questioning of liberal epistemological and political dichotomies is often sought by appealing to the unity of theory and praxis captured in the Aristotelian notion of *phronesis*.[3] Whether or not explicit mention of Aristotle is made, the Aristotelian ideal of a theoretical–practical unity recurs in various theoretical guises from Aristotle's day to the present. Examples include Hegel's conception of ethical life, Heidegger's theory of *Dasein,* Habermas's theory of communicative action and contemporary communitarian ideas in North America. Moreover, new social movements, partisans of identity politics and other participants in contemporary political activism insist in varying degrees on the direct theory–practice nexus guiding their respective projects. In very different ways, Hegel and those after him attempt to plausibly account for the successful union of the individual terms that are separated in the dichotomies in liberal thinking such as theory and practice. The critics of liberalism since Hegel find this union at work or potentially at work in actually existing institutions and traditions. In the case of Hegel's idealism, the dictum that the real is rational is intended as a challenge to the particular idealist accounts of reason he finds in Kant, Schelling and Fichte. Hegel rejects what he takes to be the Kantian juxtaposition of an *a priori* 'ought' (what 'should' be), on the one hand, with a seemingly irrational and non-ethical 'is' (actually existing institutions), on the other. He regards earthly reality to have a contradictory, antagonistic but nonetheless rational and comprehensible structure. To contrast a rational 'ought' with an irrational 'is' for Hegel is to ban reason from the world and thereby deprive existing institutions of their legitimacy. According to a Hegelian reading, reason is not an external condition of praxis, and theory and praxis are not categorically separable. He implies that any attempted separation of these elements of dialectical idealism attests to residual metaphysical idealism and the problems of the reified consciousness which is incapable of creative intervention in the historical process. Theory and practice are dialectically mediated for Hegel as a form of practical knowledge that unites all citizens of the modern state in an ethical community. Despite their at times clashing individual aims, they are integrated into the all-encompassing legal reality of the family, civil society and state. The latter constitute the bedrock of what he theorises as objective spirit institutionalised in the concrete socio-political forms of 'ethical life' (*Sittlichkeit*) in the *Philosophy of Right* (1821). Though he accords an important place to the Kantian themes of morality and abstract right in the first two parts of that book, for Hegel philosophy is not primarily concerned with endeavouring to deduce a set of *a priori* principles to which

reality is haplessly invited to conform. Like the structure of individual experience charted in Hegel's *Phenomenology of Spirit* (1807), the institutions
embodying Hegel's objective spirit have a rational structure despite apparent
contradictions. It is this earthly, objective reality that constitutes and is constituted by rational individuals in a dialectic marked by ever greater unity as
history progresses. Hegel's critique of Kant thus displaces the juridical bases of
knowledge and experience from the unified consciousness of the private individual to history and the state. Individual action is always informed by the
theoretical content which that rational structure embodies and transmits to
successive generations in the institutions of ethical life. In a philosophical move
which complements Kant's insistence that all objectivity is mediated by subjectivity and which prepares the ground for Marx, Hegel argues that all subjectivity
is mediated by socio-political objectivity, i.e. by the structures of human society
in its objective, institutional forms. For Hegel and Kant the conditions of
knowledge are rational, and all knowledge is mediated through concepts. Yet for
Hegel the knowledge furnished by reason through experience is mediated by an
historical process which constitutes new subjectivities as it yields increasingly
perfected forms of knowledge and freedom. In this context one might say that
Hegel attempts to build an historical dimension into the transcendental structures of idealist consciousness outlined in thinkers like Kant. Rather than
relativising truth in historically changing forms of community in the manner of
Herder (1744–1803, the real forerunner of contemporary communitarianism),
Hegel identifies a temporal dimension in the constitution of knowledge that is
given expression in the Hegelian concept of experience. The concept of experience is systematically expounded in the *Phenomenology* in opposition to an *a
priori*-based account of knowledge. In that work Hegel seeks to reconcile the
Kantian distinction between knowledge and experience in a series of philosophical arguments with important epistemological and political implications.[4]

The epistemological-political rupture between idealism and more ostensibly
worldly, post-metaphysical political philosophies is initiated with Feuerbach
and continues with Marx's materialist attempt to 'stand Hegel on his feet', both
of which prefigure the attempts by state socialism and new social movements to
transcend the limited legitimacy of institutionalised negative liberty. The overturning of idealism into materialism in Marx's early writings is at the same time
intended to be an attack on a particular conception of legality in which public
and political state institutions are separated from the dynamics of property relations and the private and voluntary associations in civil society. In the eyes of
the Young Hegelians and other critics of Hegel's theory of the state, public and
political state institutions are considered in abstraction from the real bases of
material production and the struggle for survival. This is an untenable form of
idealism which, far from showing the rational at work in the actual, gives a
merely idealised account of the functioning of public and political state institu-

tions. For Hegel's critics, it is ideology, not philosophy. This materialist critique of law as ideology marks the start of a more generic critique of the liberal conceptions of juridical epistemology and the just relations between legality and legitimacy. With regard to Hegel and Marx, the precise nature of the civil–political division is an issue of considerable complexity, and for the purpose of clarity it is worth noting that Hegel does not separate civil and political spheres in a liberal fashion. For Hegel, separation of this kind prevents an adequate understanding of objective spirit in the totality of its variegated but nonetheless mediated institutional forms. Without an adequate understanding of the totality as a dynamic set of mediations, consciousness becomes reified. Reified consciousness, in turn, is blocked off from the theoretical-cognitive unity of praxis. When blocked off from praxis, individuals are incapable of moving to a higher level of theoretical-cognitive unity, which means that the objective spirit mediating subjectivity in a given culture (its social and political institutions) ceases to advance the march of knowledge and freedom there. In these conditions individuals experience alienation from the state and from social and political life in general. The link between thought and action is momentarily severed, as individuals fail to recognise that the state is a collective product of mind at work in the world of institutions. Hegel observes that citizens in that culture are then likely to stagnate and even regress into quasi-childlike desires for safety, repetition, approval-seeking and consolation. That particular culture goes into decline, and the forward march of freedom halts until the progressive course of objective spirit in history is eventually taken up by another culture where the theory–praxis nexus is alive and consciousness is unblocked. Hence from the moment of Hegel's critique of Kant, the manner in which the 'unblocking' of consciousness is to be interpreted and undertaken becomes a crucial epistemological issue charged with political consequences. It is the key to a credible critique of the liberal dichotomies as well as a touchstone for questions concerning praxis and legitimacy. Whilst this is obviously pertinent to the state socialist attempt to project beyond liberal democracy, it is also true of new social movements and theories of communicative action. A central concern here is formulating reliable criteria which clearly specify what counts as praxis. Just as one would want convincing criteria to distinguish between a putsch and a revolution, mere talk and communication, etc., it seems clear that just because people militate for social change does not immediately mean that whatever they happen to do counts as the successful union of theory and praxis. One way to show that praxis means more than any kind of activism is by demonstrating that it is closely related to the crucial question of what counts as knowledge. It is possible to analyse the pursuit of knowledge as a series of human interventions in the world in which the sensuous and intellectual transformation of nature by human labour is organised and structured. In what follows in this chapter and in the rest of this book it will be argued that the key to a general comprehension of epistemology entails understanding the relation between humanity and nature, and that the humanity–nature relation is conceptually as well as institutionally mediated by theory (thought in the broadest sense) and praxis (law which registers the transformation of nature in processes which in turn transform humanity). Hegel succeeds in proving that there is a demonstrable dialectic between thought and institutions which is codified in law. Critical theory after Hegel can proceed from this starting point in an attempt to see if the law regulates humanity and nature on the basis of forms of instrumental reason, or if it reconciles them in forms of non-reified knowledge.[5]

Kant does not think it is possible to unblock consciousness without a return to the traditional metaphysics of pure reason or a decline into highly arbitrary accounts of individual experience bereft of universal, cognitive content. In Kant this account of knowledge is closely connected with the distinction between phenomena and the things in themselves, in the first instance, and the distinction between theory and practice in general and legality and legitimacy in particular, in the second instance. Kant implies that attempts to forge unities out of these discrete entities will engender a merely apparent theoretical-cognitive unity which in reality is going to be an instance of coerced reconciliation, i.e. an instance of dogmatism and despotism. Against what he considers to be a reified account of the knowledge process in Kant, Hegel is concerned to show how subject and object are mediated in a process eventually culminating in absolute knowledge, i.e. that there is an epistemological path beyond formal knowledge and the fatality that knowledge is blocked off from the things in themselves. In his social and political philosophy he is concerned to show that the modes of rationality and action pertaining to the respective spheres or moments of objective spirit are successfully mediated through institutions in civil society like the corporation which for Hegel include the associations people enter and leave on a voluntary basis such as trade unions and universities. But he also explicitly maintains that the ends of civil society, such as individual security and the acquisition of individual wealth and private property, cannot be confused with the universal aims of the state. This clearly sets Hegel apart from liberal conceptions of the relation between legality, legitimacy and knowledge. Hegel argues for the reality of absolute knowledge in epistemological terms, and he argues for the reality of more than liberal levels of legitimacy as a result of the socio-political mediations of objective spirit in political terms. Hegel's thought offers the first sustained attempt to show that the project of moving beyond the limits of formal epistemology is closely linked with the parallel project of overcoming the liberal opposition of individual and state which constitutes the crucial limitation of all liberal forms of legitimacy.[6]

In his early writings, Marx attempts to show that Hegel's argument in the *Philosophy of Right* about the superiority of modern forms of freedom stands and falls with his account of the successful mediation of the civil and political spheres. He claims that Hegel is correct to argue dialectically in terms of the totality of mediations against Kant's epistemological-political separations. But he maintains that Hegel is incorrect to suppose that institutions such as the corporation effectively mediate between civil and political spheres: rather than reconciling the conflicting actors of civil society, the state regulates those conflicts through forced compromise and coerced integration from above. Thus Marx's 1843–44 writings address the issue of the dichotomy between citizens' working lives, which are structured by the division of labour and the systematic subordination of creative labour to the laws of surplus value and profit, on the one hand, and their formal political equality, on the other. These arguments are elaborated with tremendous theoretical clarity and insight in *The Critique of Hegel's Philosophy of Right, On the Jewish Question* and the *1844 Paris Manuscripts.* Here too it is important to be clear: Marx is not primarily mounting a moral critique of modern forms of exploitation, nor is he advocating a more successful union of the civil and political spheres than is possible within Hegel's theoretical framework. Marx suggests that régimes that are characterised by this failed mediation are indeed rational in Hegel's sense. The 'real is rational' insofar as it is not a mere aggregate of random events, but rather exhibits the properties of a mediated totality of processes which have a structure and which are developing according to discernible tendencies in society and the economy which are knowable and which can be understood and changed. Although rational, from Marx's perspective this rationality is not rational enough to be legitimate. This is because the legal regulation of human interaction with the natural world through private ownership of land and private control of machines and technology serves to establish an antagonistic relationship between subject and object in epistemology at the same time that it gives rise to a conflictual relation between owners and non-owners of property in politics. This is an ideological relationship which for Marx cannot be remedied in either epistemology or politics by the limited forms of political equality compatible with private ownership.

Marx does acknowledge that despite their tremendous advantages within the hierarchical structures of a privately managed economy, the owners of private property and the means of production are likely to be frustrated in their aims to exercise genuine freedom. Like those individuals who have nothing to sell but their labour power, the socially advantaged are in large measure incapable of realising their species-essence as creative producers – they too are subject to the structural constraints operative in competitive market economies. Nonetheless, Marx sees the primary conflict in modern industrial societies to be the conflict dividing humanity into social classes. The individuals of these classes are alienated from *external nature* to differing degrees by antagonistic property relations. However, humanity is also part of nature, i.e. what could be termed humanity's *internal nature* or, in somewhat unconventional usage, *human nature.*

Humanity is distinct from and yet also part of nature because of humanity's mediated unity with reason discerned with clarity in Kant's account of the synthetic quality of knowledge in which subjective factors enter into relation with objective factors. The question of the division between humanity and humanity's appurtenance to nature, in terms of certain mimetic impulses and a variety of drives and needs that evolve and undergo change in the course of history, is not really central for Marx. For Marx the natural world is generally construed as an external terrain of possibilities to be utilised for human purposes. As such, in the *Grundrisse* and *Capital* Marx lays great emphasis on the modes of production and appropriation in the human struggle to transform the natural world, which is spontaneous with its ravages but not spontaneously generous with its potential fruits, into something more adaptable to human designs.[7] The socio-political repression of humanity's inner nature assumes a crucial role in the work of thinkers like Nietzsche, Freud, Foucault, and in the writings of feminists, identity politics theorists and some new social movement theorists. Marx is more centrally concerned with the struggle between social classes for control of external nature. That struggle assumes an immediate form in the struggle for land as well as a mediated form in the struggle for control of the products created in a labour process which in capitalism is decisively structured by private ownership and control of the means of production.[8] If the transformative dimension of the labour process is restructured by liberating it from the shackles of private ownership, Marx argues, labour will become infinitely more creative and production levels will increase dramatically, thus creating the material abundance necessary to unite a previously divided humanity in a fully legitimate and international democratic political community he calls communism. As Marx suggests in the *German Ideology* (1845–46, written with Engels), material abundance becomes the key condition of uncoerced reconciliation in the form of a society in which people are free to hunt in the morning, fish in the afternoon and criticise in the evening. By implication, he suggests that maximum legitimacy will be attained when the political *form* provided by the institutions of what Hegel calls objective spirit (law in the broadest sense of a form of thought indicating the rational structure of all economic, social and political mediations between humanity and nature) is harmonised with the new material *content* constituted by an end to the struggle of social classes for control of the labour process and its products (collectively organised and executed labour). In his determination to think Feuerbach's materialist humanism through to dialectical materialist conclusions, Marx is lead to the hypothesis that the key to the reconciliation of a divided humanity is to be sought not in the state, or even in the institutions of civil society as a whole, but in political economy. Marx's opponents usually argue that this approach reduces the philosophy of right in the broadest Hegelian sense of an all-encompassing rationality permeating objects and institutions to codes of ownership which can simply be overturned or confiscated by the state. This critique is not completely without justification, and indeed, it is clear that state socialism generally pursues this line of interpretation. Yet it is often overlooked that Marx is in agreement with Hegel insofar as both thinkers consider the rationality of the real to consist in the mediation of humanity and nature which is achieved in labour and law. That is to say that, contrary to a great many interpretations of Marxism, Marx can be analysed as a legal theorist who radicalises the insights of Kant and Hegel. This point will be explored in detail in chapter 4.[9]

In the introduction to the *Grundrisse*, Marx explains that the objectivity of socio-political forms is not best understood in Hegel's idealist terms as the objectively realised manifestation of the ideas of consciousness in the successive moments of their expression, negation and further expression on the way to absolute knowledge. Hegel's dialectical idealism, which posits the objective mediation of all subjectivity, is not materialist enough from the standpoint of dialectical materialism. Materialist objectivity, as distinct from objective spirit, is constituted by the transformation of nature through human labour power which, under capitalism, assumes institutional form in a series of processes that are systematically distorted by the legally sanctioned private appropriation of publicly created wealth. Thus, for Marx, bourgeois legal relations in capitalism regulate humanity's control over the human appropriation of external nature. Private ownership of the means of production institutionalises a form of arbitrary control of external nature which reduces the rational synthesis between subjective and objective factors to techniques of subjective expropriation. What this means can be quickly illustrated with an example. A group of carpenters seek to build and sell furniture, and, like most workers, they have only their own labour to sell in return for wages. This puts the carpenters in a relationship of dependence on one set of people who own the land where wood is available for transformation into furniture. They are also dependent on another set of people (although they could in principle be the same) who own the equipment and tools necessary for that transformation of external nature. The carpenters are removed from control of external nature in the immediate sense that private property excludes them from use of the land where wood grows. They are also excluded from control of nature in a more mediated sense due to the rights of ownership that place the tools necessary for knowledge, production and the further transformation of nature into tools and property in private hands. Whether used for scientific or productive purposes, the carpenters are prevented from access to the tools of knowledge except in the limited sense of being able to work with them under the conditions of wage labour specified by the owners and protected by the laws of the state. The carpenters are separated from external nature in two related senses. They are separated (1) from wood and other raw materials, and (2) from humanly transformed external nature (in the form of manufactured products necessary for the production of furniture) as a result of the private appropriation of the products of the labour process. Marx suggests that abolishing private ownership will guarantee direct access to raw materials as well as the products of the labour process in which nature is transformed by technical and creative work. Direct access to the natural world of this kind becomes the condition of material abundance conducive to the uncoerced reconciliation between a heretofore divided humanity, and as such, conducive to direct legitimacy. What Marx does not consider in enough detail is the possibility that the abolition of antagonistic property relations is a necessary condition for the institutionalisation of a form of democratic legitimacy beyond the limited form offered by liberal democracy, but it is not sufficient. The history of state socialism in the former Soviet Union and state socialist governments elsewhere to be considered in the next section suggests that: (A) if the superseding of antagonistic relations between humanity and external nature (relations between a divided humanity in class terms in senses 1 and 2 above) is not accompanied by (B) the superseding of antagonistic relations between humanity living in society and inner/human nature (understood just for the moment in very broadly Nietzschean/critical theory terms as that dimension of humanity which is itself part of but not reducible to nature because of humanity's synthetic relation to reason and law), people are forced to enter into a logic of conquest, control and fear *vis-à-vis* both outer and inner nature.[10] It will be seen in chapters 3 and 5 that the second possibility (B) is discounted by liberals and thinkers like Freud as unconditionally impossible. A central point to be taken up in those chapters is that the project of realising full democratic legitimacy, i.e. epistemological legitimacy, can best be understood and enacted in non-ideological terms as an epistemological-political process working toward reconciliation with nature in dimension A as well as in dimension B. Reconciliation in this sense offers an alternative to the two forms of instrumental reason operative in liberal democratic institutions. These are regulation or control of external nature by private humanity through private property and the division of labour, and regulation and subordination of human nature by public humanity through political domination and the control apparatuses of the parliamentary democratic state. Reconciliation can be approached in terms of both senses captured by A–B above, each of which delineates a different model of reason and a different praxis of subject–object relations. Though A and B imply different models of subject–object relations, the central question remains that of the mediation between subject and object. Attempts to bypass this issue in the name of a supposedly post-metaphysical third term like being, intersubjectivity, etc., on the one hand, or the spontaneous steering of distinct subsystems, on the other, is to ignore the fact that *the forms of mediation* between subject and object already imply the third term mediating between them – not beyond them. That third term is thought, which assumes theoretical form in concepts and practical form in institutions. It will be seen in chapters 3 and 4 that there is no decisive break with the reality of conceptual form, i.e. with some form of idealism, which is not also a break with the possibility of non-coercive mediation and praxis.[11]

Due to its stringent defence of private property, liberalism flaunts the supposed impossibility of reconciliation of humanity and external nature via law. The private ownership of natural resources such as land as well as the private appropriation of the fruits of the labour process are said to be essential for human freedom. Liberal philosophers such as Kant also flaunt the supposed impossibility of reconciliation between humanity and inner nature (henceforth called human nature). Kant argues that the operations of reason, enacted through the transcendental unity of consciousness, are rational only insofar as they are conducted in abstraction from human needs, drives, impulses, personal experience, etc. In contrast to the two major experiments in democratic legitimacy represented by state socialism and new social movements, briefly considered in the next section, proponents of liberalism can justifiably argue that at least liberals openly acknowledge the conflicts between humanity and nature in both senses captured by A and B above. When taken to task about the openly antagonistic premises of liberal thought, liberalism offers an epistemological-political response which virtually all forms of opposition to liberalism seek to challenge. The liberal response is organised around the legal anthropology triad of reason, knowledge and freedom discussed in chapter 1. It is a response that basically reaffirms two essential tenets. First, there is an admittedly high price for the internal logical consistency of reason and, by extension, a high price for the non-contradictory format of law. But there is no non-authoritarian alternative, short of arbitrary idealisations of supra-legal legitimacy. In order for reason to be rational and not an easily manipulated dogma based on subjective conceptions of the good and happiness, it must abstain from normative prescriptions about the substantive notions of the good, and limit itself to formal consistency. This position complements the epistemological agnosticism which holds that we can have formal knowledge of phenomena, but can never know the noumena, i.e. the things in themselves as essences. Second, since reason must abstain from normative prescriptions about substantive notions of the good, happiness, etc., so too must law. Legality thus precedes legitimacy in liberalism. Legality cannot pronounce directly on questions of legitimacy. But if liberal legal systems cannot resolve the conflicts denoted by A and B, these conflicts can at least be regulated in a way that protects each individual's negative liberty. For liberals this is the most that can be accomplished without lapsing into dogma and despotism. Humanity's antagonistic relation with external nature is remedied within the limits of the possible by conferring on everyone a natural right to acquire and keep property, so that they can maximise their chances of securing a stable material existence for themselves and their family. Hence this antagonistic relation with external *nature* is also one of *social* antagonism in liberalism. This is true in a double sense. The possibility of a democratic form of collective economic organisation in order to secure everyone a stable material existence is discounted as impossible because of natural scarcity, which can best be brought under control through competitive individualism. This possibility is also dismissed because such political forms would inevitably curtail individual freedom by imposing a single vision of the good life on all citizens. But this is only half the story. Not only is it the case that external nature is mean with its fruits – humans are by nature violent and aggressive. As such, human nature can best be kept under control through vigorous policing. Since an uncoerced form of reconciliation between humanity and both external and human nature is deemed impossible and undesirable, law is assigned regulatory functions, and justice becomes largely a matter of punishment. Both internally and externally, nature is posited as a threat and a hostile 'other' with which there is never reconciliation but only the possibility of calculation and control. In early liberalism nature is understood as an essence in abstraction from the economic and political forms in which humanity and nature are socially mediated. The logical consistency of *a priori* theoretical construction is achieved in thinkers in this tradition by blocking out the possible explosion of spontaneity and unpredictability represented by untamed nature in the natural world and humanity. This blocking out of contradictory and unpredictable impulses is widely viewed by liberal thinkers as offering the best strategy for keeping untamed nature at bay economically, as well as enforcing social order politically.[12]

With the gradual passing of restrictions on suffrage and the rise of a mass electorate and mass political parties, this *a priori* conception of liberal legality could not withstand political pressures for democratisation diagnosed by Tocqueville and socio-economic changes in the structure of the bourgeois public sphere analysed by Weber and later Habermas. In Europe, liberalism was compelled in practice to evolve into liberal democracy and social democracy, though not before passing through a period of authoritarian transition in countries like Italy, Germany, Spain, Portugal and Greece. Pressures for democratisation and the transformation of the public sphere have meant that the priority of legality in liberal thought has been compromised by demands for increased legitimacy which cannot be accommodated within the Kantian framework of legality based in practice on comparatively low levels of general literacy and correspondingly high levels of restriction on suffrage enforced through property and income qualifications. The rise of a mass electorate can be analysed in this context in conjunction with the structural transformation of the public sphere. That is, the demise of the bourgeois public sphere, based as it was on an open exchange of information on the part of a highly educated, economically independent, and as a consequence very restricted social stratum, has been accompanied by the rise of mass parties and the rapid transformation of the structure of political legitimation. It is perhaps possible to ascribe epistemological attributes to law during the historical period chronicled by Habermas, in which the public sphere in principle exerts a rational and ethical pressure on positive law and the state. However, as Kant intimates in his political writings and as Habermas later argues in *The Structural Transformation of the Public Sphere* (1962) and *Legitimation Crisis* (1973), this epistemological dimension of legal rationality is forfeited if the genuinely discursive and communicative dimensions of the public sphere are eroded or, as the early Habermas formulates it, colonised by systemic imperatives of the economy and bureaucratic-administrative systems.[13] In this case the public sphere is reduced to a sphere for the production, circulation and exchange of commodities, such that Marx's arguments against Hegel in the 1843–44 writings and Marx's subsequent critique of political economy begin to seem very powerful. Under these conditions, rationality is subjected to a process of rationalisation and reduced to an instrumental mode of behaviour linked with strategy rather than epistemological issues. The legitimacy of the state is no longer subject to the ethical and cognitive force of communication on the part of an economically independent community of bourgeois citizens. Legitimacy increasingly becomes a matter of satisfying the material demands of the now enfranchised, economically dependent citizen-clients of the new electorate. These are demands which might best be satisfied through sheer technical methods which can, as the Weimar example clearly shows, place tremendous pressure of a distinctly non-ethical kind on state institutions. Thus in liberal democratic régimes, from the Weimar Republic to the present, legitimacy becomes to a great extent a matter of economic growth and technical efficiency, and politics is reduced to the best strategic devices for working out compromises between struggling classes and other conflicting interest groups. With the erosion of the cognitive dimension of law, law increasingly reflects the balance of forces in society rather than offering a non-ideological account of how, in terms of Kant's critique of Hobbes, truth rather than merely authority is the source of law. Thus the decisive question posed by Marx about the democratic organisation and control of external nature seems at first glance to loom as the great question of modern politics and the reconstitution of legal epistemology on a truly democratic basis. For Marx it is clear that the democratic organisation of the labour process and its products is the key to a materialist critique of Kant that retains all of what must be retained in Hegel's dialectics while dropping the Hegelian defence of the state – for Marx a critique of liberalism must also be a critique of the parliamentary state and liberal law. That is, *all* forms of alienated power must be appropriated in order for humanity to realise a higher level of theoretical–practical unity liberated from oppressive, illegitimate political form. Consequently, Marx knows that attempts to reconstitute the epistemological bases of law by recreating the highly restrictive social conditions of early bourgeois ascendancy are destined to fail or result in merely ideological forms of legitimacy. His analysis suggests that the epistemological bases of law in early liberalism are inseparable from a class structure which cannot be recreated. For Lenin, Lukács and other militants of the Third International (1919–40) that impossibility signals the inevitability of revolution, first in Russia and then across the globe. Following the Bolshevik Revolution, the introduction of communism thus seemed to be the best way to truthfully re-establish the epistemological dimension of law that guarantees the legitimacy of law beyond mere legal formality. In communism the bases of absolute knowledge are created simultaneously with the bases of absolute legitimacy through the revolutionary praxis of the subject–object of history. For Lukács, for example, this is a subject for whom consciousness is no longer 'blocked off' from praxis, but instead whose very essence is a revolutionary theoretical–practical synthesis.[14]

The analysis in this chapter so far indicates that Marx is the first and most far-reaching critic of liberalism. In a manner analogous to a path-breaking painter who represents a point of no return to past understandings of form and content, Marx shows that any uncritical return to liberal theorising about law and epistemology is bound to result in patent falsehoods. After Marx it becomes extremely difficult to theorise about law, rationality, legitimacy and the state without an accompanying analysis of political economy. Normative theories of law and rationality which do not do so are likely to reconfigure positions already outlined by pre-Marxist thinkers such as Aristotle, Kant and Hegel or some uneasy synthesis of such thinkers.[15] Marx forces his readers to directly confront the reality that the epistemological bases of law cannot be taken as static anthropological qualities of humanity, and that these bases must instead be reconsidered and recreated in conjunction with changing class structure, where the term class structure denotes a sociological analysis of the constantly changing social forms in which humanity secures the material conditions of its existence and possible transcendence of brute necessity. The epistemological bases of law and knowledge are thus socio-political bases rooted in historical experience rather than exclusively *a priori* principles grounded in an abstract concept of reason.

But this raises a potentially difficult objection for Marx. It is not just that there is more to the socio-political bases of law and knowledge than political economy and the democratic control of external nature. If it was, it would simply be a matter of adjusting the relative weight of the base and superstructure in Marx's theory. It is also that legalised control of external nature does not automatically liberate human nature from political repression, entrenched hierarchy and institutionalised fear. For this reason it is of the utmost importance how and through what kinds of socio-economic and political institutions the mediation of humanity and external nature is accomplished. In chapter 4 it will be argued that: (1) the possibility of the realisation of a legitimate form of legality turns on the specific modalities of the mediation of humanity and external nature, and (2) that mediation can be enacted in a way that facilitates a genuinely pluralist alternative to liberal democratic forms of mediation of humanity and human nature. It is in this context that Marx is both indispensable and yet inadequate. On the one hand, Marx's continuing relevance stems from his systematic analysis of the external nature component of questions related to legality, legitimacy and rationality. On the other hand, it seems clear that Marx's exhaustive account of political economy left him with little time for the question of human nature. Following on from Hegel's critique of Kant, Marx devises the first of many subsequent epistemological-political projects to go beyond the limits of liberalism by establishing more thoroughly legitimate forms of politics than those characterised by the liberal dichotomies. Common to most of these projects is an attempted reconciliation between the alienated parties of a divided humanity which is undertaken whilst bypassing the humanity–external nature relation. Thus in one crucial respect, Marx's project is fundamentally different from virtually all of those after Marx: he directly confronts the question of human estrangement from external nature. This makes Marx's project radical in his own literal sense of going to the root of the problem that he urges in the 1843–44 writings. Marx locates the practical–cognitive key to political legitimacy beyond the limits of liberal dichotomies in the transformation of nature through sensuous and intellectual labour. Against a Kantian view in which reason and law are cognitively and temporally prior to practice and experience, and in which an *a priori* conception of reason dictates the terms of practical action, Marx implies that the rational unity of theory and practice is realised in the material transformation of the natural world to satisfy human needs and provide the potential bases of human flourishing. It is the forcible expropriation of the products of that process through bourgeois law that is illegitimate for Marx.[16]

Marx is correct in this assessment, but he does not elaborate all of the consequences implied by his analysis. This raises two related issues (i–ii) to be examined throughout the rest of this book. Firstly, despite his methodological boldness, Marx is not radical enough – not even in his own terms. For in taking substantial steps toward solving the question of the relationship between *humanity and external nature* whilst neglecting the issue of the relation between *humanity and human nature*, Marx's theoretical framework can be seen as radical and yet radically incomplete (i).[17] The converse (ii) is also true: in directly addressing the question of the socio-political repression of human nature, thinkers like Nietzsche, Freud, Foucault, feminists, etc., who are taken up by the new left and new social movements since 1968 are radical in Marx's sense. But insofar as they neglect practical questions concerning the democratic mediation of humanity and external nature, they too are not radical enough.

Post-metaphysical thinkers will object that to speak of humanity and nature in this way is to speak of unmediated essences. But it has been seen that the impossibility of a return to unmediated subjectivity or unmediated objectivity in the relations between humanity and nature is already recognised in different ways in the traditional idealism of Kant and Hegel. The more pertinent problem consists in determining to what extent the Marxist interpretation of Kant and Hegel taken up by Marx's followers is adequate to the epistemological, juridical and political problems raised by the post-metaphysical idealism of Kant and Hegel. Thinkers in the Marxist tradition tend on the whole to remain caught in one of two debates. They are generally concerned with winning the battle of hegemony or mounting a critique of instrumental reason and reified consciousness. Non-Marxists have taken up the critique of instrumental reason in their own way. Without directly addressing the question of legitimacy and external nature, a range of non-Marxist thinkers have sought to locate and define forms of post-metaphysical praxis they see in alternative identities and lifestyles, micro-communities, communicative action, radical alterity, etc. What has been largely ignored in the ostensibly post-metaphysical arguments in social and political thought and philosophy in recent decades by Marxists and non-Marxists alike is the possibility of an investigation of the forms of mediation between humanity and nature in both of the two distinct senses implied by A and B sketched above. The history of state socialism offers a good example of what happens when the attempt to move beyond liberal dichotomies toward more legitimate political form neglects the issue of humanity's relation with human nature.

Beyond the liberal dichotomies to legitimate humanity (II) Legitimising legality in state socialism and new social movements

The attempt to establish direct democratic control of external nature by abolishing private property of land and the means of production has historically been one of the central aims of the diverse attempts to institutionalise Marx's ideas. From the former Soviet Union to social democratic reformism, this project has been undertaken with considerably varying degrees of ideological dogmatism and authoritarianism. The Soviet experience offers two lessons concerning the possible reconciliation between humanity and nature. The first is that it is possible to successfully pursue a strategy aiming at the overthrow of liberal democratic property relations through instrumental means, including force. Moreover, command planning can be effectively used to replace market relations with the bureaucratic decision-making hierarchy of a central planning administration. The second is that in terms of truly revolutionising socio-political relations, the 'success' of this strategy is also closely bound up with the likelihood of its long-term failure. This is because the overthrowing of property relations without a concomitant change in what is referred to in this book as human nature is likely to abolish private property without abolishing conformity, hierarchy and resentment and the key ingredient of political tyranny, fear.[18] In addition to contributing to political tyranny, the persistence of hierarchy and fear after the revolution exerts a deleterious effect upon the project of democratising the economy itself. In *The Civil War in France* (1871), and in other writings, Marx seems confident that the organisation of the economy according to a common plan can be combined with decentralised forms of democratic participatory government. In the *Critique of the Gotha Programme* (1871) he asserts that after a short, possibly authoritarian transition period in which the working class consolidates its control over production, the state is likely to be replaced by a system of democratic administration in which the motto 'each according to his ability, each according to his needs' becomes the reality of legitimate politics. Once the causes of social conflict have been eradicated root and branch, the state can 'wither away'. As far as one can surmise from Marx's cursory remarks in these writings, the abolition of classes is sufficient to inaugurate the non-coerced unification of the distinct theoretical-practical entities that are separated in liberal régimes. In attempting to interpret Marx's ideas in these works, his followers continually return to two essential points: (1) the existing politico-juridical state apparatus cannot be seized and wielded in the interests of the working class. This means that the parliamentary, executive and judiciary institutions of alienated political power have to be reappropriated and democratised on the basis of a network of communes roughly based on the radical democracy of the Paris Commune analysed in *The Civil War in France*; (2) the private appropriation of the collective transformation of external nature under capitalism has to be democratised at the same time that the former state apparatus is dismantled.

A number of questions are raised by framing the question of legitimacy in this way. How can one organise the collective appropriation of external nature in a way that is compatible with the decentralised character of the commune? What might be the role of the communist party in a society characterised by decentralised, spontaneous political participation? The history of the Russian Revolution points to the thesis that a disciplined vanguard following the principles of Lenin's democratic centralism is ideal in terms of organising a centralised and hierarchical appropriation of external nature. In the Bolshevik experiment the price for this particular form of public appropriation of publicly created wealth is the authoritarian unification of state and civil society, with obvious consequences for the repression of nature in both senses used here. A closer look at Soviet history also suggests that the question of the vanguard party is not reducible to a left-wing authoritarian programme of legal reform of property relations. The Bolshevik approach is revealing of a fundamental tendency within state socialism generally: rather than really altering the premises of liberal thought and capitalist economic practices, attempts are undertaken to wield liberal legality in the interest of a collective subject. This strategy is pursued with the aim of widening the bases of legitimacy in a socialist direction. As in liberal practice, a legal form of legitimacy culminating in a version of state sovereignty is still the norm, and as such, law continues to regulate rather than reconcile. In state socialism the law no longer serves the anonymous competitive, autonomous individual of liberal inspiration discussed in chapter 1, but serves forcibly collectivised liberal interests in the name of the régime's openly proclaimed legitimation subject – the working class.[19] The fact that there is no openly proclaimed legitimation subject in liberal democracies in which private ownership systems structure the economy is an important consideration when analysing the differences between liberal and other, more ostensibly democratic, forms of legitimacy. It is also important for understanding how and why attempts to democratise liberal régimes generally fail to re-invest law with the epistemological dimension that law has in liberal idealism. Instead of re-investing law with the epistemological dimension needed to make law legitimate, legitimacy is immediately personified by the struggles of new social actors whose very existence on the social landscape bridges the theory–praxis divide; the legalisation of their legitimate needs thus eliminates one of the central dichotomies of liberalism.

In the previous chapter it is observed that the separation of private, civil law from public, political law undermines the claim of liberal versions of legal universality to be able to dispense with a dogmatic, legitimating 'who' subject. Liberals claim that modern law replaces the rule of tyrants with the rule of law or *Rechtsstaat*. In reality, the dichotomisation of law sanctions the conflation of the pursuit of private interest with liberty. The resulting divisions of state and civil society also help constitute the sphere of competing private interests as supposedly non-political, and thus create an un-named – but decidedly non-universal – legitimation figure in the anonymous subject of private law. The dichotomisation of these spheres introduces an often overlooked functionalist dimension in liberal thought and practice, in the sense that the conflicting standpoints between private individuals and public citizens are assumed to be reconciled by transforming the horizontal contract between private trading partners in economic exchange into a vertical contract between citizens and the state in political elections. Through the bifurcation of law and the deployment of contract as a political as well as an economic institution, liberal régimes are compelled to secure legitimation by staging a functional continuity between the public and the private. This is accomplished by legally uniting all citizens and the state in an ideological form of community at one level, and by legally separating them into privately competing individuals and social classes at another level. This uniting at one level and separating at another transforms all individuals into citizens regardless of their class position, and simultaneously ensures that citizenship can only ever secure minimum access to the humanly transformed natural world, i.e. to the products of the labour process. Hence liberal democratic political practice violates the liberal philosophical injunction not to fuse what cannot be reconciled without coercion. Moreover, instead of making good on its claim to institutionalise legal form rather than legitimate essence, liberalism offers an anonymous and privatised version of human essence. The argument in this chapter is that, far from being conclusive steps beyond metaphysical conceptions of essence, state socialism offers a workerist account of legitimate essence, whilst new social movements offer an expressivist account of legitimate essence. The aim of this discussion is not to whip the dead dog of state socialism, nor to belittle the important enfranchising achievements of new social movements. But there is strong evidence to suggest that to date state socialism and social movements have not effectively challenged the hegemony of liberal democratic governments. Whilst this is obviously true as regards state socialism, it is becoming increasingly clear that the transformative élan of new social movements has slowed to the extent that movement demands have been met. Without ignoring the differences between them, both phenomena assail liberalism from positions that are not fundamentally hostile to it, once, that is, liberalism is not obliged to come up with forms of law that transcend natural necessity by reconciling humanity and nature in both senses used here. Returning just for a moment to an observation made in the introduction concerning Marx's position in *On the Jewish Question*, it is not being argued in this chapter that sexism, racism and gender discrimination are unimportant. The point is rather that if one regards the dichotomies in liberal thought to be symptomatic of epistemological questions with immediate political consequences which are in large measure solved by entitling non-liberal humanity to valorise its experience of marginalisation in liberal terms, liberalism is able to perpetuate its hegemony by re-articulating the conditions of existence of liberal political form on new social bases. In other words, *an epistemologically legitimate form of law based on the reconciliation of humanity and nature in both senses poses a much more destabilising threat to liberalism than the legitimate humanist alternative to liberal man.* This will become clearer as the discussion proceeds.

The conflation of the pursuit of private interests with liberty sanctioned by private law in liberalism is reorganised as a collective enterprise in state socialism. Here the notions of rationality, interest, freedom and autonomy closely associated with legality in liberalism are made legitimate through collectivisation and state ownership. The introduction of Taylorism and other management techniques employed in private ownership systems offers a telling example of the tendency in state socialist ideology to conflate collectivisation with democratisation. Lenin was deeply impressed by what appeared to be capitalism's ability to organise the productive forces according to growth-maximising criteria of rationality and efficiency. He maintained that the Soviet

Union would be able to rationalise capitalism by eliminating the privileges of private ownership and control: communism would combine capitalist principles of organisation and efficiency with socialist principles of planning and distribution. Lenin was in fact convinced that Frederick Taylor's time-and-motion studies of energy expenditure on the shop floor could be implemented in order to secure increased collectively controlled profits, i.e. collectivising the gains which Taylor sought to secure for the owners of capital within market economies. When read out of context, certain passages in Marx's *Capital* could be taken to mean that communist society might be organised in the manner of a large factory of co-ordinated productive operations, which meant that Lenin's ideas on Taylorism and industrial organisation did not seem unduly revisionist. In Soviet practice the legacy of the Paris Commune became increasingly distant, as the one-party state and the essentials of the capitalist factory system were combined with by and large symbolic forms of worker participation. Even these were dismantled when Stalin outmanoeuvred his opponents in the leadership struggle that ensued after Lenin's death in 1924. Announcing a programme of 'Socialism in one Country' to counter Trotsky's internationalism, Stalin called for the extension of Taylorism and other management techniques used in capitalist economies in order to accelerate the industrialisation of the Soviet economy. These measures were accompanied by the forced collectivisation of agriculture.[20]

The First Five Year Plan was announced in 1929. During 1929 to 1930 the number of agricultural workers on collectivised farms rose from 4 per cent to 58 per cent of the agrarian work force. At the same time, the industrial bases of the future Soviet economy were established. Doctrinal rigidity and centralist command planning contributed to large-scale inefficiency and corruption. In fact, rather than producing the bases for the legitimate appropriation and organisation of nature, Soviet society was highly stratified and inegalitarian. This was not immediately reflected in the huge income discrepancies that help contribute to the periodic legitimation crises which characterise capitalist societies. The pyramidal structure of the planning bureaucracy was paralleled by highly unequal access to the best apartments, holiday homes and a range of other consumer privileges reserved for the vanguard and their families. The economic system was based on a combination of coercion and incentives. The latter came in the form of material rewards for the Ministers of the most productive industrial sectors and their plant-level managers and workers. The system – Stakhanovism – complemented the Taylor system of management with comparable notions of performance and reward. Trotsky analysed the resulting inequalities as characteristic of a system marked by the partial socialisation of the means of production combined with an incentive structure borrowed direct from private enterprise. He predicted that this highly authoritarian form of government was permanently destabilised by the strategic concessions made to the emerging industrial elite, on the one hand, and the ideological commitment to democratic legitimacy, on the other.[21]

This is by no means to say that the problems of state socialism can be simply explained as intensified versions of the problems in liberal democracy. But a cursory glance at Soviet history reveals that the functional continuity between legality and legitimacy that is continually staged in liberal régimes is not so much squarely addressed as displaced in Bolshevism and other varieties of state socialism. Private interests dominate in liberal democratic states through the functionalist technique of uniting and simultaneously disaggregating discussed in chapter 1 and mentioned above. In state socialism, the democratic and legitimate appropriation of the means of production and the products of the labour process secured by public ownership is re-appropriated by the party and state bureaucracy. In both instances 'the people' are nominally sovereign. The reconciliation between humanity and external nature which is proclaimed to be an outright impossibility by liberalism in the first instance fails as a result of the Communist Party's usurpation of legality in the name of its supra-legal legitimacy in the second instance. The Bolshevik version of state socialism never seriously considers the possibility that law might attain legitimacy by establishing itself on an epistemological basis. As in liberal régimes, conflict can be regulated or, in the case of Kronstadt, brutally suppressed.[22] Like liberal law, Soviet law is thus ideological and regulatory. This is not altered by the more overtly authoritarian police and propaganda institutions at work in the Soviet case. The project of reforming the juridical-epistemological dimension of early liberalism's public sphere and legal system is not taken up by the Russian revolutionaries, for whom liberal legality is broadly synonymous with bourgeois legality, i.e. a legality that can simply be replaced by the party's legality. From this vanguardist standpoint, legality serves to defend and protect interests directly related to external nature and the scientific organisation of industrial production. Legality has no significant epistemological dimension – the legitimacy of legality stems directly from the fact that it protects vital interests. When the processes generating those interests are legally controlled by the organised majority of producers via the party, instead of by the usurping minority of capitalists, legitimacy automatically ensues. In this way state socialism continues the functional continuity between legality and legitimacy characteristic of liberal regimes by other, more authoritarian, means. Since the party presides over the democratisation of humanity's relations with nature, the party becomes the repository of legitimate science and political knowledge in state socialist society. The dismantling of the liberal form of legality is informed by the supposition that, regardless of the form of regime under consideration, liberal or communist, legality has no significant epistemological dimension. This is because what really matters in politics, hegemonic legitimacy, is always supra-legal. Understood in these terms, legitimacy is the substantive essence or content behind legal form. Legitimacy consists in what the sovereign people think and do rather than in any universal legal principles not directly derived from individual, group or class experience. Once one group or class has become definitively hegemonic, the interests of that group or class, organised in the party, represent the happy union of form and content as well as the realisation of theory in practice. Legality becomes a formality, though not in the liberal sense of post-metaphysical form discussed in chapter 1. Formal liberal legality can be dispensed with, since the union of theory and practice is at the same time the transition from legal quantity to legitimate quality: consciousness is 'unblocked' and reification overcome in the newly created institutions of post-capitalist society. Communist legitimacy liberates the people from the oppressive legality which separated them from the fruits of their labour under capitalism. Like the liberal state, the *workers'* state is a class state. The workers' state is, however, a much more legitimate and democratic class state, since the working class constitutes the vast majority of the population.[23]

The strident anti-liberalism of state socialism reveals itself to be in practice a clumsy attempt to widen and extend the limits of liberal legality, beyond every person's right to be a citizen, to the heart of the class interests protected behind the dichotomies of liberal law. The process of that widening and extending of the law in an effort to transform formal law into legitimate law results in the forcible collectivisation of the very interests which are organised in accordance with a model of law and a model of rationality flaunting the impossibility of a reconciliation between humanity and external nature. The underlying antagonistic rationality itself is not directly addressed, so that the attempt to legitimise through collectivisation results in a distorted, badly conceived collectivised liberalism rather than the creation of a genuinely new political form beyond liberal social and political relations. As one would predict, the politics of expropriation are marked by authoritarian methods and the ideological identification and glorification of a political subject charged with the task of unveiling and expropriating private interests. This unveiling and expropriating in its turn assumes the form of a constant police action against Kulaks in the Russian case and counter-revolutionaries and insidious class enemies of all sorts in the former satellite states. The vigorous policing suggested by the liberal model of law and rationality is expanded into the practice of an outright police state. The end result is the well documented institutionalisation of surveillance and fear in countries ruled in the name of communist legitimacy. The structural implantation of fear in socio-political institutions can be interpreted as one particularly striking aspect of the first major and largely unsuccessful attempt to leap beyond the universal but abstract principles of liberal legality to more directly experiential forms of legitimacy. One could add in this context that fear is not a timeless aspect of 'the human condition' or the manifestation of 'Being' in the midst of human beings. Explanations of this type obscure socio-political reality with flimsy psychological and ontological generalisations. On the contrary, the real is rational, and the rational structures the legal delimitation of the political: a socio-political reality characterised by fear and tyranny can be studied in terms of the institutional unfolding of a particular conception of rationality and a corresponding practice of law which is not timeless but itself capable of being reformed. The citizens of a modern political community are not compelled to live with institutionalised fear any more than they are compelled to live with tyranny, hierarchy, conformity or hunger, as if such phenomena were earthquakes or incurable illnesses. In modern societies with advanced economies, fear and hunger are not primarily natural, psychological or ontological phenomena. Given the right forms of rationality and legality, fear could be minimised, and hunger could certainly be eliminated. In the context of this necessarily brief discussion of the theoretical implications of the failure of state socialism, the Russian experience indicates that a real political-epistemological reform of liberalism cannot take shape as a drastically one-sided attempt to square humanity's legal relations with external nature. The overview of some of the problems raised by new social movements provided below indicates that it also cannot be an equally one-sided project of reconciling humanity and human nature without adequate consideration of the issue of democratically organising humanity's relations with external nature.[24]

A credible political-epistemological move beyond liberal political form is centrally concerned with several questions, one of which can be formulated as follows: is it necessary to push beyond liberal legality into democratic legitimacy by diluting liberal legal form? This seems to be the impasse suggested when the push beyond legal legitimacy to legitimate legality entails the identification of a single social subject (state socialism) or a plurality of social subjects (new social movements/identity politics) entrusted with the task of directly embodying legitimacy. Might there not be instead ways of rethinking legality itself beyond its specifically liberal instantiation, so that legality might begin to approach the boundaries of *legitimate form* (instead of sovereign, democratic-legitimate essence) whilst simultaneously retaining the universal dimensions of modern legal normativity in such a way as to obviate the designation of an identifiable legitimation subject? The identification of such a subject tends to result in more or less openly authoritarian states with varying degrees of surveillance and systems of control. State socialism represents the first of many attempts to create more democratic forms of legitimacy than the legal form of legitimacy offered by liberalism. In general terms, increased legitimacy beyond liberal legal form is pursued by widening the scope of what counts as valid political-epistemological experience in liberalism, in order to reconcile theory and practice beyond the limits of liberal guarantees of non-interference. That is, in liberalism theory and practice are already reconciled to the greatest extent possible within the institutional boundaries constituted by a theory of individual liberty understood as enforced non-interference: reconciliation in positive terms is deemed impossible and undesirable. Positive forms of reconciliation and positive conceptions of liberty in discourses of legitimacy are often articulated in recent theory and political struggle by assigning positive attributes and reconciling power to various instances of collective experience. They include feminism, various civil rights movements for racial equality, non-governmental environmental groups and development projects, and other projects that have attempted to take the baton from the labour movement. In the particular case of the labour movement and the ideology of state socialism, the purview of liberal political-epistemological experience is inflated to include the collective processes through which external nature is transformed for the purposes of survival, research, productivity and innovation, i.e. labour. The Bolsheviks are thus the first in a long line of anti-liberal theorists of legitimacy. Theorists of legitimacy after the Bolsheviks respond to specifically liberal discourses of legality in a great variety of ways. In fact, from the new social movements first appearing on a large scale in 1968 to contemporary debates about recognition, communication, community and identity, discourses of legitimacy attempt to succeed where the Russian revolutionaries have failed: they seek to transform society beyond the contours of liberalism in a non-authoritarian way. However different they may be, there are several key common features which unite the state socialist and the post-1968 attempts to theorise and bring about this transformation. Instead of thinking about enlarging the contours of legality in ways which would no longer imply an exclusively negative conception of liberty rooted in individual consumption, personal security and private property, and instead of thinking about legal rationality in ways which would no longer imply a punitive conception of justice restricted in large measure to disciplinary measures enforcing protection and retribution, theorists of legitimacy tend to assess negatively and at times even dismiss the liberal account of the links between legal-rational epistemology and legitimacy. Rationality is not so much in need of reconceptualisation as it is in need of tempering by the lived content of emotions, identities, the practices of nurturing, the bonds of community, etc. Though pragmatic strategies of legal reform including affirmative action are pursued in an effort to transform liberalism, the juridical-epistemological project of transforming rationality in order to transform relations between humanity and nature in *both* senses used here is in large measure ignored.[25]

Much of post-1968 social and political theory has set itself the task of moving beyond metaphysics and idealism to the real world of subjective experience and agency of actually existing social actors and groups. However, it is argued below that, despite the great differences of method characterising their respective approaches, the various currents of post-state-socialist theories of democratic legitimacy theory do not successfully manage a qualitative theoretical step beyond the state socialist critique of liberalism insofar as they: (1) posit that what really matters in politics, i.e. legitimacy, is always supra-legal rather than legal-epistemological, even if legal reform is at times adopted as part of political strategy; (2) are compelled to humanise the anonymous, *a priori* subject of liberal legality by identifying an equally questionable humanist alternative first embodied in state socialism by workers, and now personified by women, gays, ethnic or religious minorities, etc.; (3) are one-sided in their approach to the question of reconciliation, often stressing direct reconciliation between human-ity and human nature; (4) are just as compelled as liberalism and state socialism to stage an ideological continuum, albeit on the basis of a completely different social structure than that of early liberalism, between legality and legitimacy. In other words, rather than indicating definitive steps beyond liberalism, most theorists of new social movements, identity politics, communicative action, etc., make a fundamental theoretical mistake which is made in a more palpably authoritarian way in state socialism: they attempt to give legitimate expression to collective experience without really questioning models of law and rational-ity which flaunt the impossibility of a reconciliation between humanity and nature in liberalism. This casts doubt on the long-term capacity of these proj-ects to do substantially more than deforming liberalism in a different way than state socialism did. Like the supporters of state socialism before them, they too go against the grain of early liberalism and implicitly accept what looks like the inevitable decoupling of epistemology from legality with the gradual implemen-tation of universal suffrage. Instead of re-articulating the link between political legality and epistemology on the basis of an entirely different social structure than the one which made the legal-epistemological project of early liberalism (at least theoretically) possible, these projects identify direct links between episte-mology and political legitimacy based on various combinations of political identities and new social movements.

Especially with regard to identities, the priority of theory and legality over practice and legitimacy in liberal thought is ostensibly redressed in the episte-mological–practical unity which results from being oppressed in one or more ways by liberal institutions. Taking a step back for just a moment, one can see that the parallel with state socialism is striking in this context as well. Marx's followers in the former Soviet Union and elsewhere assume that when he asserts in *The German Ideology* that social being determines consciousness rather than vice versa, Marx means that a person's position within the relations of produc-tion will automatically endow them with a specific consciousness on the basis of who they are and what they produce. If they are workers they become revolu-tionary because of their exploited social condition. The fact that it is the workers that produce and know what they produce is deemed sufficient to unblock a reified consciousness and directly facilitate a revolutionary overthrow of the relations of production. Understood in one-dimensional terms as the reconcil-iation between humanity and external nature, socialist praxis is realised without

any conditions prior to experience – the experience of being exploited is necessary and sufficient to generate the correct forms of reason and consciousness
required for the rapid transformation of socio-economic relations and a scientific understanding of society. When institutionalised in the form of socialised
property, reason becomes the correct instrument for maintaining a legitimate
form of legality. Yet in the absence of any unmediated relationship between
social being and consciousness, the Communist Party assumes the role of
converting the epistemological claims of Marxism-Leninism into the non-
coerced reconciliation of theory and practice. The revolutionary agency
signified by the theory–praxis nexus is in reality the voluntarist union of theory
and party in which epistemological issues are transformed into ideological
apologies for state power: whatever the proletariat does is beyond epistemological or normative contention, and the party is the articulate voice of the
proletariat. The state socialist reconciliation between humanity and external
nature is not a reconciliation at all, but rather the mastery and control of nature
by a party in the name of the collective natural rights of a socialist humanity now
freed from capitalist legal form. Legitimacy beyond the limits of non-interference is pursued by widening the sphere of direct political regulation in order to
include economic transactions which had been designated as the domain of
contractual relations of natural rights-endowed, private individuals. Hence the
revolutionary transition to a supposedly more legitimate form of legality is
conceived as an automatic by-product of pushing forward on a continuum from
exclusive private rights to increasingly inclusive public rights.

Like workers forced to sell their labour power in order to secure a stable
material existence, members of disadvantaged groups with particular identities
rooted in race, ethnicity, gender, sexual orientation, etc., can claim to have
immediate access to a successful union of theory and practice. This union is
forged as a direct consequence of being excluded from a material as well as a
stable emotional existence by the institutionalisation of the dichotomies at the
centre of liberal thought. Systematic material precariousness ensured by private
ownership of property and the means and products of production is exacer-
bated by institutionalised forms of recognition which are in fact simultaneously
institutions of coerced integration. By making the provision of child care a
private matter with the argument that the 'natural' place for women is in the
home, for example, it has been possible to exclude women from the labour
market for centuries and to perpetuate dependence on their partners' incomes.
In liberal democratic régimes, lack of recognition is systematically reproduced
through ideologies of nature and natural rights, merit and success, normality
and deviation, etc. Such discourses articulate and are the material reality of a
very particular set of values, whilst other values are assigned an inferior status.
This does not occur in a blatant manner in which particular groups are assigned
a fixed place in a feudal-style hierarchy. The ideological construction of the

'normal', 'natural', 'marginal' and 'deviant' unfolds in processes which, like class structure, are in dynamic flux and subject to political contestation. Feminism is just one example of a many-sided and continually evolving identity which combines socio-economic demands with wider political demands for recognition. It is also a good example of a movement which has been successful in articulating grounds for including womanhood in its diverse facets within the parameters of legitimate political subjectivity once monopolised by the anonymous subject of private law in liberal democratic states. Hence the legitimate study of humanity now includes previously excluded experiences of being human such as womanhood and motherhood. Feminist and other New Left movements have been determined to prevent the usurpation of their political agency in the way that the communist party manages to usurp the representation of the experience of wage labour in one-party state socialist régimes. These activists are also keen to maintain the spontaneous union of theory and praxis in social movements by channelling their efforts outside of the bureaucratic and hierarchical structures of political parties operating in multi-party parliamentary systems. This wariness of parties is not so much a rejection of Marx as it is a well-founded reservation about the social democratic and Leninist appropriation of Marx's work in multi-party and one-party political systems. In fact, whether explicitly conscious of it or not, new social movements broadly follow Marx in rejecting the liberal account of the relation between epistemology, legality and legitimacy. This comparison between Marx and movement politics carries important implications for the project of reconciliation and needs some further explaining.

Like Marx, movement theorists and activists do not accept the idea that reason and law are cognitively and temporally prior to experience and legitimacy, nor do they accept the principle that an *a priori* conception of reason should dictate the terms of political action or the contours of political institutions. For Marx and social movements, the distinctions between legality and legitimacy, reason and experience, etc., are symptomatic of precisely what is problematic with liberalism. In his 1843–44 writings Marx develops his analysis of these dichotomies by way of a thoroughgoing critique of liberalism, Hegel's *Philosophy of Right* and the modern state. He criticises the liberal distinction between state and civil society which Hegel employs in his own way in order to critique a contractual understanding of the state. He remarks further that Hegel is correct to note that politics in modern societies is fundamentally shaped by this dichotomy but untrue to his own dialectical method insofar he does not see an eventual overcoming of the rift between state and civil society in a higher epistemological-political synthesis which Marx calls communism. After convincingly refuting liberalism, Hegel gets caught up in the inextricable problems involved in a non-liberal defence of the state. Although radical in comparison with liberalism, Hegel's philosophy is not radical enough insofar as it cannot manage to turn the critique of contract into a full-blown critique of property and bureaucratic power. Hegel wants to persuade his reader that the utilitarian, contractual relations in civil society do not undermine the more consensual, non-contractual bases of political legitimacy in the state. Hence, for Marx, Hegel is a kind of functionalist *avant la lettre* who theorises the harmonious integration of conflictual and consensual modes of action. Hegel attempts to do this by arguing that spirit knows itself fully only insofar that it passes through its conflictual and consensual moments, both of which are necessary for a higher form of uncoerced reconciliation which preserves the epistemological element of truth contained in differences of opinion and struggles for recognition. For Marx, the kind of harmonious reconciliation of competing private individuals in civil society with public citizens that Hegel claims is achieved in the modern state can occur only in the idea of the state – hence the famous eleventh thesis on Feuerbach calling for the translation of philosophy into revolutionary praxis. Marx suggests that Hegelian philosophy must be 'stood on its head', so that what is valid in Hegel's idealism can be converted into materialism. That is, Marx suggests that there is a continuum between idealism and materialism which is also a continuum between theory and praxis. Marx is largely in agreement with Hegel's account of thought as a movement assuming concrete form in consciousness and in institutions as contradiction, negation and mediation. But mediation remains ideological as long as Hegel is content with the idea of the mediation of conflict and contradiction, which for Marx is tantamount to arguing that existing institutions embody a mediating rationality that is strong enough to bear the strain of conflict. Hegel carries the critique of Kant, liberalism and reified consciousness to its furthest limit whilst still remaining within the idiom of idealism, thus preparing the ground for the transition from idealist apology to materialist revolution. But the Marxist and new social movement revolt against idealism creates problems for both which will become more apparent presently.

The liberation of living labour from the command of capitalist direction marks the transition from idealism to materialism, legality to legitimacy and theory to praxis. In communism, freely organised, collective labour recognises its own freedom in the liberation from the commodified form of labour that is perpetuated in the wage system. Where the wage system transforms each individual's creative labour into a commodity in return for the homogeneous medium of money, liberated labour is a non-commodified expression of subjectivity. What liberalism promises in theoretical, private, abstract, consumerist – in short, legalistic terms – authentic individual expression – is made practical and real with the liberation of labour from capitalist legal form. Liberated labour experiences freedom in its own self-creating and world-creating movement instead of being confronted by the alienated, commodified form that labour assumes as dead labour under the direction of capital. The epistemological dimension of legality which is articulated on a highly restricted basis in the bourgeois public sphere in early liberalism is apparently redeemed in this collective reappropriation of control over the processes through which humanity creates itself and comes to know and transform itself and the natural environment. Under the direction of capital, commodified labour is forced into co-operation with capital's power to create consumer demand, shape needs and determine the course of the labour process and its products. Capital's command of labour casts a spell on the consciousness of the working class that is broken in the revolution. The richness of experience that Hegel charts in the movement of consciousness to self-consciousness in the *Phenomenology* finally becomes material and real in communism. The link between epistemology and legality becomes redundant in a superior form of social organisation in which epistemology and legitimacy become the basis of spontaneous order. Order is no longer based on an abstract and oppressive form of rational-legal domination, since the structures of order are no longer linked with an abstract conception of rationality and a negative conception of freedom. Humanity's productive essence has been harmonised with the legitimate political authority of the organised producers for the first time in human history. In a related vein, new social movements seek to move beyond the boundaries of negative freedom and formal equality which have excluded women, ethnic minorities and other groups from socio-economic equality and effective political participation. Social movements seek to give the richness of experience a far more faithful political translation than is possible within the limits of liberal legal form. In a manner analogous to the wage system criticised by Marx, which channels the processes of creative labour into the repetitive cycles of commodity production and systematically distorts humanity's productive essence, the liberal democratic political system criticised by new social movement theorists denies people the chance to give political expression to their essence as women, blacks, ecological militants, peace activists, gay rights advocates, indigenous people, etc. This picture is considerably complicated by the possibility of a myriad of plural identities and allegiances which emerge in the democratic struggles of black feminists, gay peace activists, etc., which makes it difficult to theorise in general terms about new social movements.[26]

Nonetheless, a number of striking parallels between Marxist and movement concerns emerge. The wage system and the political system serve to establish logics of identity and equivalence for things that are non-identical and unique. In the first instance, this is accomplished by subordinating creative individual expression in work to generic criteria of potential profitability whilst keeping wages as low as possible at all times. In the second instance, it is accomplished by reducing the political subjectivity of a plurality of struggling social actors to the aggregation of homogeneous vote totals. What Marx refers to in his early writings as political, as opposed to human emancipation, characterises an institutional structure which keeps levels of participation low enough so as not to destabilise oligarchic decision-making institutions. Combining Marxist and movement critiques of liberalism, one might say that the wage system and the political system work in tandem to blunt the potentially transformative edge of praxis in work (external nature) and in politics (human nature). The possibility of political change in both spheres is forestalled by functional mechanisms which steer socio-political relations toward the predictable modalities of contractual exchange. In the first instance, it is the horizontal contract between those who buy and those who sell labour power that homogenises non-identical forms of work. The horizontal contract transforms labour power into the commodity of wage labour which is exchanged for its equivalent value in wages, thus reducing various forms of work to the common denominator of money. In the second instance, it is the vertical contract through which citizens with radically different perspectives are forced to passively exchange equal votes. The equality of the votes ostensibly guarantees non-preferential treatment for everybody involved. But it is precisely this equality which effaces the history and experience of the distinct individuals who delegate their authority to people that they conceivably have never heard or seen. The worker's labour power is cut to measure for the designs of capital's need for expansion, whilst in a series of parallel processes the words and voice of the citizen are reduced to saying 'yes' or 'no' to the elected representatives of the parties in government or opposition. The transition from the horizontal to the vertical contract is grasped as a continuum between legality and legitimacy in liberal thinking flaunting an antagonistic relation between humanity and external nature as well as an antagonistic relation between humanity and human nature. The antagonism, which is anchored in a very specific account of rationality, negative freedom and private law, regards private property and competition to be the best answer to the economic problem of *natural scarcity*, and regards the sovereign state with a monopoly on the legitimate use of force within a given territory to be the best answer to the political problem of *natural aggression*. On this account, reason is rooted in a fear of natural scarcity in the first instance and fear of the potentially violent nature of one's fellow citizen in the second. The analysis in this chapter aims to demonstrate that the strategy of addressing the systematic modes of exclusion practised in liberal régimes by collectivising property or extending the legal criteria determining who can be politically enfranchised within liberalism is likely to yield authoritarian liberalism rather than a new political form. Since a key dimension of liberalism – a concept of reason rooted in fear of natural scarcity and fear of fellow citizens – has not been surpassed with a different concept of reason and law, anti-liberalism in practice tends to yield a poor version of the liberal original. It is an authoritarian version of liberalism in the case of state socialist societies, and a politically correct and pastoral version of liberalism in the case of post-1968 Western European and North American societies. The key point is that, by not aligning the critique of ideologies of natural scarcity with a critique of ideologies of natural aggression, the revolt against traditional idealism remains one-sided and largely ineffective. This is in some ways a real step backward in relation to the consistently two-sided negativity of liberal idealism.

Marx and new social movements seem to be addressing related problems with liberalism in different but complementary ways. Marx focuses on the question of the relation between humanity and external nature. He succeeds to a large extent in showing that liberation from fear of natural scarcity is directly related to the project of potentially liberating creative labour from the oppressive and homogenising structures of wage labour. In very different ways, new social movements question the logic of legally mediated political fear. They do this by making a good case for the argument that fear of the other is not natural at all, but is actually institutionalised when there is an underlying misconception of what is natural which is implicitly upheld as a universal standard of normality. For social movements, what is natural must be expanded well beyond the boundaries drawn by the white male protagonists of natural rights in the English, American and French Revolutions. That is, fear and aggression are likely to flourish where rationality means renunciation of sensuous impulses, sexual orientation, one's ethnicity, etc., in short, in the continual neglect of the need for recognition, and the simultaneously imposed self-renunciation of who a person actually is and where they come from. In its inception, liberal humanity is rational, white, property-owning or professional, heterosexual, in most instances Christian, and endowed with legally protected natural rights. To meet the criteria of liberal humanity and enter the bourgeois public sphere, a person must first be a professional and, in addition, must renounce the legitimate impulses, emotions and particular experiences that would destabilise the unity of the liberal legal subject. That legal-rational unity is forged in antagonism to nature in both senses used here. From a new social movement perspective, classical liberalism punishes all of those social subjects who do not fulfil the operative criteria of liberal rationality and normality. Such people are in fact irrational and potentially criminal, i.e. they are people who must fear the law in liberal régimes. In very different ways, new social movements insist that, in order to squarely address and solve the institutionalisation of fear, liberal humanity must extend its boundaries to welcome non-liberal humanity within its fold. In this way liberal humanity becomes liberal democratic, legitimate humanity. It redeems liberal ideas of freedom, equality, justice and impartiality. To abolish fear and aggression, liberalism has to become feminist, colour-blind and indifferent to homosexuality, religion and ethnicity. Once this is achieved by making all of humanity liberal instead of just white professional, non-interference need no longer be institutionalised in a negative spirit of exclusion. On the contrary, it becomes positive and all-inclusive as social movements force citizenship to become more than merely formal. Like their state socialist predecessors, social movements have not effectively compelled liberalism to re-articulate the relation between the juridical and epistemological pillars of the liberal cosmos. Instead, liberal interests have been forced to meet the various movements half-way in a gradual twofold process of redefining what is natural and entitled to natural rights, on the one hand, and of collectivising politically legitimate humanity, on the other. This is a process in which the liberal precedence of legality before legitimacy has been challenged and in large measure inverted in the name of democracy. The dethroning of theory, reason, law and the universal maxims of individual conscience by the ostensibly more democratic imperatives of legitimacy, collective identity and collective agency marks a break with the traces of a distinctly legal form of liberal idealism. It has already been seen that, as a paradigmatic thinker of early liberalism, Kant suggests that the conditions of the possibility of humanity are prior to individual experience (*a priori*), formal, rational and legal. Kant's idealism strives to break with dogmatic versions of speculative metaphysics concerned with pure reason, unmediated essence and absolute origins. Yet Kant's break with dogmatic metaphysics is not a break with idealism. Contrary to the Aristotelian notion of *phronesis* taken up in different form by state socialists, pragmatists, social movements and theorists of communicative action, Kant's idealism offers an account of experience which locates reason and law as prior to and constitutive of agency. Hegel correctly perceives that Kant cannot make this argument without conceding the synthetic and dialectical relation between subjectivity and objectivity, and it is precisely these aspects of Kantian philosophy that are radicalised by Hegel. With Marx's materialist critique of Hegel, philosophy, law and politics seem to be racing away from idealism in a terrestrial direction that culminates with Nietzsche, and it is clearly a very short step from Nietzsche to Heidegger, post-structuralism and postmodernism.[27] In the process of gradually emancipating subjectivity from all external and objective constraints, humanity liberates itself from the yoke of metaphysical estrangement from the world and finds itself at the centre of all things. In Soviet Marxism, humanity establishes its dignity against metaphysical abstraction and bourgeois law by way of the world-transformative praxis of labour. In a post-1968 context, the human is now immediately legitimate in all of its diverse feminist, gay, black and indigenous facets in the agency of social movements. Thus, for the advocates of humanism, the death of idealism is also the birth of praxis and agency – praxis and agency dissolve the liberal-metaphysical concepts of law and rationality in the concrete life forms of struggling communities. Where the legal-metaphysical is something other than and hostile to human agency, praxis is emancipation *vis-à-vis* that otherness. Postmetaphysical legitimacy is thus a state in which humanity finally recognises the rationality of the human world in the things that humans make, do and are. Inverting the Kantian ban on experiential particularity – expressed in more contemporary terms in Rawls's veil of ignorance – social movements champion the epistemological validity of the struggles of marginalised non-liberal humanity in opposition to liberal humanity. These are democratic struggles for inclusion and recognition: it is widely held that to oppose them is to engage in a reactionary form of liberal élitism.

It might be objected that it is misleading to distinguish the Marxist critique of the wage system from the new social movement critique of the political system, since Marx's critique of capitalism is also a critique of liberalism and parliamentary democracy.[28] This raises a question: how are the social movement critiques of liberalism different from the Marxist critique of liberalism, which at least in principle inspires state socialism, and which one might call a first-order discourse of legitimacy? Marx focuses on the reconciliation of a liberal and non-liberal humanity by way of ending the antagonistic relations between humanity as a whole and the external natural world; the possibility of a reconciliation between a divided humanity is mediated by the relation between that divided humanity and external nature. Hegel argues that the philosophical mediation between humanity and nature constitutes a totality, and that this totality is the real basis of epistemology and freedom. Marx follows Hegel in regarding the forms of mediation between humanity and nature as the basis of objectivity. But Marx regards the totality of the humanity–nature relation to be mediated by socio-economic forms of law and ownership rather than philosophical forms of consciousness. The relation between liberal and non-liberal humanity is mediated by law, or, more specifically, by private ownership of the means of production and exchange. Without ever stating the matter explicitly in these terms, Marx specifies the first condition of legitimate law: reconciliation between humanity and external nature in a form of libertarian socialism.[29] It is now possible to resume where Marx left off by identifying the second condition of legitimate law as the reconciliation between humanity and human nature. For thinkers and activists working outside of the Marxist tradition in a post-1968 context and seeking to succeed where state socialism has failed, i.e. in bringing about a non-authoritarian transformation of liberal democracy, legal relations of production may at times inform the critique of liberalism, but such relations of production are rarely a central part of their projects. These projects are characterised by the widespread assumption that movements such as Bolshevism articulating first-order discourses of legitimacy which directly address questions of humanity and external nature have failed, and should now be surpassed. How should they be surpassed? They should be surpassed by second-order discourses of legitimacy which aspire to a direct reconciliation between liberal and non-liberal humanity. But, as the preceding discussion shows, first and second-order discourses of legitimacy start by criticising the continuum thinking which in liberalism is rooted in the model of contract, and end up by adopting a modified continuum argument in their turn. The collectivisation of the production process results in an overtly authoritarian form of undemocratic liberalism (sometimes referred to as state capitalism) in state socialism. Private property is substituted with collective property and markets are replaced by planning, whilst individual natural rights are jettisoned in favour of humanity's collective natural rights. The boundaries of liberalism's vocabulary of freedom, justice and autonomy are continually pushed forward from liberal form through to socialist content. The boundaries of liberal legal form are expanded to legitimate content in a different way by social movements. They have taken liberalism's vocabulary of tolerance, neutrality and non-discrimination between different conceptions of the good, and have compelled liberalism to live by its word. This work is by no means complete, since there are still entrenched forms of race and gender discrimination as well as arbitrary pay differentials, obstacles to promotion, etc. But liberal democrats today can argue that these problems are now the subject of parliamentary inquiries, newspaper reports and government reform, i.e. that the problem is in hand.

In this section of the chapter it is shown that first-order discourses of legitimacy have not been able to furnish a non-authoritarian alternative to the liberal democratic understanding of the humanity/external nature question. This section also indicates that the issue of the reconciliation of humanity and human nature has not so much been addressed as displaced by second-order discourses of legitimacy. Liberal humanity has been compelled to welcome non-liberal humanity (barring people labelled as extremists) into its fold, though not by effectively challenging the dichotomies inherent in liberalism. In conclusion one could say that in first-order discourses of legitimacy exclusively concerned with humanity and external nature, *legality is legitimised* in various forms of state socialism. In second-order discourses of legitimacy primarily concerned with humanity and human nature, non-liberal *legitimate needs are legalised*. Albeit in very different ways, both of these discourses of legitimacy imply coerced forms of reconciliation which in practice do not seriously challenge the economic and social foundations of liberal democracy. Chapter 3 attempts to challenge these foundations by showing why freedom from legal oppression is to be sought in a legitimate form of legality, not by tempering liberal democratic legality with humanist conceptions of legitimacy or abandoning law altogether. Chapter 4 develops the broad outlines of a theory of critical idealism capable of elaborating the implications of the argument that the first condition of legitimate law is reconciliation between humanity and external nature. It will be seen that reconciliation between humanity and external nature, as the first condition of legitimate law, requires a form of libertarian socialism. The contours of such a form of socialism are briefly sketched at the end of the chapter. Chapter 5 completes that discussion by demonstrating in detail why the second condition of legitimate law is the reconciliation between humanity and human nature, and by explaining what this means in juridical and epistemological terms.

Notes

1 See Henry E. Allison, *Kant's Transcendental Idealism: An Interpretation and Defence*, New Haven CT, Yale University Press, 1983, chapters 5–6, and Hermann Cohen, *Kants Theorie der Erfahrung* (*Kant's Theory of Experience*, 1871), Berlin, Cassirer, 1919, p. 637. Cohen convincingly argues that there are distinct kinds of idealism with different political consequences. For example, one can distinguish between Kant's critical, *formal* idealism, on the one hand, and Fichte's *metaphysical* idealism. Cohen suggests that the latter has authoritarian implications (p. 739). For a detailed exposition of Fichte's relation with Kantian philosophy, see Klaus Christian Köhnke, *Entstehung und Aufstieg des Neukantianismus* (available in translation as *The Origins and Rise of Neo-Kantianism*), Frankfurt, Suhrkamp, 1993, especially pp. 88–105. Karl Jaspers (1883–1969) signals that, for Kant, we become certain of several *a priori* dimensions of experience by way of experience, but that the forms of experience and experience itself are always – unfortunately – separate (*pace* Hegel). Jaspers adds that what Kant fails to see is that future experience may well make us aware of as yet undiscovered *a priori* forms, with all that such a discovery entails in terms of law and politics. See Karl Jaspers, *Die grossen Philosophen* (*The Great Philosophers*), Munich and Zurich, Piper, sixth edition, 1988, pp. 595–6. In a related vein, one might argue that Kant's critical philosophy points out that reality is neither one-sidedly subjective nor objective. Reality is rather the mediation of the subjective and objective through concepts. But in contrast to what Kant suggests, the concepts that mediate subject and object are not given to us in some timeless and unchangeable fashion. Contemporary critical philosophy holds out the possibility of the creation of new mediating concepts and, as a consequence, of new realities. For this line of Kant interpretation, see Gilles Deleuze and Félix Guattari, *Qu'est-ce que la philosophie?* (*What is Philosophy?*), Paris, Minuit, 1991, pp. 10–12.

2 Not all critiques of metaphysics are necessarily humanist in focus and approach. There are also forms of anti-humanist critiques of metaphysics, such as those found in the works of Martin Heidegger and Niklas Luhmann. For a comparison of their respective projects, see Chris Thornhill, 'Systems Theory and Legal Theory: Luhmann, Heidegger and the False Ends of Metaphysics', in *Radical Philosophy*, 116 (2002), pp. 7–20. It is interesting to note that attempts to move beyond metaphysics are often cast in terms of a projection beyond idealist (often in the works of Kant and Hegel) and/or materialist (usually Marx) accounts of subject–object dialectics. To break with dialectics without embracing some kind of humanism is almost certainly going to mean brushing shoulders with some version of the theories of Luhmann and Heidegger. At their very core, these theories offer apologies for violence in the name of either indomitable biological complexity and flux or the limitless possibility of new forms of historical being.

3 Jürgen Habermas, *Theorie und Praxis. Soziologische Studien* (*Theory and Praxis*, 1963), Frankfurt, Suhrkamp, 1978, pp. 51–5. For a clear account of the Aristotelian notion of *phronesis* and its various applications in the work of Arendt, Gadamer, Habermas and Rorty, see Richard J. Bernstein, *Beyond Objectivism and Relativism: Science, Hermeneutics and Praxis*, Philadelphia, University of Philadelphia Press, 1983, pp. 160–1, 219–23.

4 It is safe to say that these implications have not yet been fully explored. Hegel stands at a junction between the insensitivity to historical dynamics that marks the residual *a priori* rationalism in Kantian idealism, on the one hand, and the various attempts

after Hegel to give the concept of experience a post-metaphysical framework by abandoning idealism altogether in the name of a materialist, pragmatic, phenomenological, interactive or communicative orientation to politics and philosophy, on the other. There are puzzling aspects of Hegel's conception of experience that remain unclear in the terms in which he formulates them. Yet Hegel's theory of experience is framed within a 'philosophy of *right*', that is, of law. It is a theory which attempts to discern the underlying structures of human thought and experience in relation to observable tendencies at work in socio-political institutions with the ultimate aim of reconciling citizens and the law rather than merely regulating citizens through state institutions. An analysis of the particular failings of Hegel's attempt is more elucidating than unqualified assertions of the impossibility of charting any such mediated unity between thought and institutions. For a corroborating view, see the essays collected in Jean François Kervégan and Gilles Marmasse (eds), *Hegel: penseur du droit*, Paris, Éditions CNRS, 2004.

5 Schlomo Avinieri, *Hegel's Theory of the Modern State*, Cambridge, Cambridge University Press, 1972, chapter 9, and Herbert Schnädelbach, *Hegel's praktische Philosophie. Ein Kommentar der Texte in der Reihenfolge ihrer Entstehung*, Frankfurt, Suhrkamp, 2000, chapter 4.

6 Hegel, *Grundlinien der Philosophie des Rechts* (*The Philosophy of Right*, 1821), Frankfurt, Suhrkamp, 1986, paragraphs 257–8, pp. 398–404.

7 Marx, *Grundrisse der Kritik der politischen Ökonomie* (*The Grundrisse*, 1857–58), Frankfurt and Vienna, Europäische Verlagsanstalt, 1972. Characteristically, Marx breaks into another language – this time into English – to explain what he calls 'the great civilising influence of capital' (p. 313). Marx comments further that capitalist relations of production render the great service of completely stripping nature of its externality *vis-à-vis* humanity, that is, that the capitalist mode of production releases humanity from the need to recognise nature in its otherness – it becomes for the first time an exploitable reservoir whose 'natural laws' are not laws at all but a form of cunning that has finally been unmasked ('Die Natur wird *erst* rein Gegenstand für den Menschen, rein Sache der Nützlichkeit; *hört auf als Macht für sich anerkannt zu werden*; und die theoretische Erkenntnis ihrer selbstständigen Gesetze erscheint selbst nur als *List*, um sie den menschlichen Bedürfnissen, sei es als Gegenstand des Konsums, sei es als Mittel der Produktion zu *unterwerfen*', p. 313, my emphases). Marx explains that the demystifying of nature by modern industry is accompanied by a remystification under capitalism. The processes of circulation and exchange assume an external, law-like quality of their own which reduce productive individuals to passive observers forced to conform to the laws of a reinstated heteronomy in the form of oppressive relations of production and an irrevocably entrenched division of labour (p. 111). Thus it is these relations of production that must be revolutionised in order to fully redeem the promise of unbridled technical mastery of nature. See also footnote 89 of chapter 13 of the first volume of *Das Kapital* (*Capital* I, 1867), Berlin, Dietz Verlag, thirty-fifth edition, 1998, pp. 392–3, where in a reference to Giambattista Vico (1668–1744, author of the *New Science*, 1744), Marx seems to suggest that technology helps us penetrate the secrets of the natural world, which, unlike the historical world, is not made by us. Once this technological penetration is accomplished to a sufficient degree, humanity can make history in a fully conscious manner because it simultaneously regulates nature scientifically. This means that human interaction with the natural world is no longer left to the irrational vagaries of overproduction and underemployment that distort the labour process in antagonistic modes of production based on private appropriation. The scientific regulation of

nature in communism is synonymous with the fully rational organisation of society for the satisfaction of human needs and the complete development of human creativity.

8 Without dwelling at length on the differences of emphasis and approach in the respective works of Marx, Nietzsche, Foucault and Freud, the above-mentioned point about inner and external nature has important implications for the present study. For the time being one could say that Marx's neglect of questions of inner nature is paralleled by the lack of consideration of questions relating to the organisation of humanity's interaction with external nature – in short, the economy – in Nietzsche, Freud, Foucault *et al.* For a reading of Marx which attempts to show that a definite sensitivity to questions of inner nature can in fact be found in Marx, see Alfred Schmidt, *Der Begriff der Natur.*

9 Marx, *Grundrisse,* pp. 28–31. From a Hegelian standpoint, the supposed epistemological superiority of materialist objectivity over objective spirit could be considered to be a somewhat hasty victory of materialism over dialectics. It might be claimed that in Marx's hands the Hegelian dialectic of expression–negation–expression charting the movement of the spirit is resolved into the battle for the appropriation of the products of the labour process. Whilst Marx handles this issue with great care, as the works of Alfred Schmidt and Michel Henry indicate, it is not difficult to see that Marx could be interpreted in a reductionist manner, which is what Lenin (1870–1924) and to a much lesser extent Lukács (1885–1971) tend to do.

10 This somewhat formulaic statement of the central thesis of the *Dialectic of Enlightenment* supports the idea that legitimate politics in the sense used here transcend traditional notions of left and right, which is also an idea that has been championed by Anthony Giddens. Horkheimer and Adorno do this in terms which are quite obviously very distant from the reformist social democratic intentions of the author of *Beyond Left and Right.* See Anthony Giddens, *Beyond Left and Right,* London, Verso, 1990.

11 Many structuralists, functionalists and systems theorists attempt to detach thought from the workings of institutions and questions of legitimacy. The result is a metaphysics of one-sided objectivity which does not address issues related to consciousness, knowledge and praxis. It implies that since one can only speculate about the socio-political conditions that might allow praxis to be informed by knowledge, social science and philosophy should dispense with musings about subjectivity and agency altogether and concentrate on explaining what exists. These views became fashionable with the rise of different kinds of structuralism and the notion of the 'death of man'. Theorising of this kind is usually symptomatic of reified thought that forgets that all social objectivity in the form of structure, function and system is mediated by subjectivity.

12 Pierre Manent, *Les Libéraux* (*The Liberals*), Paris, Gallimard, 2001, pp. 19–20. Manent's book is a highly instructive account of what is actually quite compelling in the liberal political argument about the priority of legality over legitimacy. In addition to examining the ideas of classic liberals such as Locke, Constant and Mill, he provides an illuminating analysis of the political ideas of Milton, Spinoza and Bertrand de Jouvenel (1903–87). On the relation between liberalism, epistemology and capital-driven market economics, see Andreas Jäger, *Was ist Ökonomie? Zur Formulierung eines wissenschaftlichen Problems im 19. Jahrhundert* (*What is Economics?*), Marburg, Metropolis, 1999. Jäger remarks (p. 10) that for all of its vaunted value neutrality and impartiality with regard to different conceptions of the good, classical economics weaves together ideas on ethics, economics and politics in

an overarching world-view. This is true of the early liberals as well as more recent thinkers like Kenneth Arrow.

13 Habermas, *Strukturwandel der Öffentlichkeit* (*The Structural Transformation of the Public Sphere*, 1962), Frankfurt, Suhrkamp, 1990, and *Legitimationsprobleme im Spätkapitalismus* (*Legitimation Crisis*), Frankfurt, 1973. Kant's political writings are collected in Hans Reiss (ed.), *Kant: Political Writings*, Cambridge, Cambridge University Press, 1970.

14 See Lukács, *Geschichte und Klassenbewusstsein. Studien über marxistische Dialektik* (*History and Class Consciousness*, 1923), Amsterdam, De Munter, 1967, especially the chapter on reification and the proletariat. It is important to keep in mind the differences between Marx, on the one hand, and the ideas of the various theorists of the Third International, on the other. This is not easy, given the different stages in the evolution of Marx's work and the various lines of interpretation of Marx by Leninists and other state socialists determined to interpret Marx as a political centralist.

15 Very telling examples of this tendency include Arendt (Aristotle), Rawls (Kant), Habermas (Kant, Hegel, Aristotle in conjunction with post-Marxist pragmatism) and communitarianism. (Hegel is often invoked by communitarians to endorse positions which are actually much closer to Herder.)

16 In the *1844 Manuscripts*, Marx credits the Hegel of the *Phenomenology* with the discovery of labour as the key to the unity of theory and practice. In so far as he makes this discovery, Marx says, Hegel is the philosopher of political economy *par excellence*. Hegel's crucial shortcoming is that he reduces labour to its abstract and intellectual dimension ('Die Arbeit, welche Hegel allein kennt und anerkennt ist die *abstrakt geistige*', p. 191, his emphasis). See Marx, *Ökonomisch-philosophische Manuskripte vom Jahre 1844* (*The 1844 Manuscripts*), Leipzig, Reclam, 1988, pp. 190–1.

17 Not only does Marx not address the question of humanity's nature with enough detail, he also does not adequately address the role of consumers in communist society. This deficiency has historically led to a number of urgent practical problems wherever socialism has been attempted or implemented. Without a non-capitalist account of how to democratically aggregate individual and collective preferences in representative institutions such as consumer councils, Marxism tends to gravitate toward authoritarian command planning (Leninism) or different models of worker control (anarcho-syndicalism and anarchism). It is true that anarchists do address this question, but they generally assume that consumers will simply take what they need from a warehouse of goods and services that spontaneously arises from co-operative production. This is unlikely to happen except in the most unusual circumstances, such as the Spanish Civil War. Production and consumption need to be co-ordinated without central planning or faith in spontaneous co-operation. The best model for organising producer control in co-ordination with consumer need is to be found in the writings of G. D. H. Cole. Cole's proposals are outlined in *Radical Theories* and in chapter 4 below. Interested readers should see Chris Wyatt, 'G. D. H. Cole: Politics and Organisational Democracy', DPhil, University of Sussex, 2004.

18 The former USSR offers a paradigm example of a society with public ownership though without the overcoming of fear. Whilst it is true that there is more to state socialism than the USSR, and that the examples of China, Vietnam and Cuba should be considered separately, it is true that the military presence of the Red Army made the satellite states in Eastern Europe viable political entities until 1989–90. In the *Spirit of the Laws* (*L'Esprit des lois*, 1748) Montesquieu (1689–1755) makes a good case for identifying fear as the defining characteristic of political tyrannies, and he would no doubt have seen his views confirmed in the Soviet case by the extensive

system of surveillance, informants and KGB control of Soviet society. See Montesquieu, *L'Esprit des lois*, Paris: Gallimard, 1982. The pervasive fear in formally democratic systems in which legitimacy is restricted by private ownership analysed by thinkers like Foucault and more recently by Beck clearly indicates that the question of ownership is just one aspect of the legitimacy question as soon as one analyses legality and legitimacy in conjunction with questions of epistemology. See Ulrich Beck, *Risikogesellschaft. Auf dem Weg in eine andere Moderne (The Risk Society)*, Frankfurt, Suhrkamp, 1986.

19 The question of the relation between the working class and peasantry is a complex issue which varies a great deal depending on the historical context. For revolutionaries like Bakunin, Lenin, Gramsci, Mao and Che, the peasantry is a key legitimation subject, whereas academic Marxists like Althusser and Jameson rarely mention it at all.

20 Lenin, *Collected Works*, XXVII, Moscow, Progress Publishers, 1975, p. 259. On Soviet experiments with Taylorism and attempts at important capitalist forms of factory management, see Geoffrey Hosking, *The First Socialist Society: A History of the Soviet Union from Within*, second edition, Cambridge MA, Harvard University Press, 1992, chapter 5, and Mary McCauley, *Bread and Justice: State and Society in Petrograd, 1917–1922*, Oxford, Clarendon Press, 1991, Part IV.

21 David McClellan, *Marxism after Marx*, Boston MA, Houghton Mifflin, 1979, pp. 131–9, Chris Ward, *Stalin's Russia*, London, Arnold, 1995, chapters 2–3, and Vladimir Andrle, *A Social History of Twentieth-Century Russia*, London, Arnold, 1994, chapters 5–7.

22 The history of the Kronstadt revolt and its bloody suppression is chronicled by Paul Avrich, *Kronstadt, 1921*, New York, Columbia University Press, 1970.

23 Sheila Fitzpatrick, *The Russian Revolution*, second edition, Oxford, Oxford University Press, 1994, chapters 4–6, and Robert Service, *A History of Twentieth-Century Russia*, London, Penguin, 1997, Parts I and II.

24 Geoffrey Hosking, *A History of the Soviet Union, 1917–1991*, London Fontana, 1992, pp. 159–63, Service, *A History of Twentieth-Century Russia*, pp. 178–81, Vladimir Andrle, *A Social History of Twentieth-Century Russia*, pp. 80–4, 148–51.

25 This is certainly less true of some of the left-wing currents within the green and feminist movements. Yet it has proved extremely difficult for these currents to resist marginalisation at the hands of their more mainstream comrades. For an overview, see Robyn Eckersley, *Environmentalism and Political Theory: An Ecocentric Approach*, London, UCL Press, 1992, Boris Frankel, *The Post-industrial Utopians*, Cambridge, Polity Press, 1987, and the essays collected in Martin Shaw (ed.), *Understanding Politics in Globalisation: Knowledge, Ethics and Agency*, London, Routledge, 1999.

26 This complicated issue is analysed by Alan Scott, *Ideology and New Social Movements*, London, Routledge, 1990, and Sidney Tarrow, *Power in Movement: Social Movements, Collective Action and Politics*, Cambridge, Cambridge University Press, 1994.

27 See Steven Best and Douglas Kellner, *Postmodern Theory: Critical Interrogations*, London, Macmillan, 1991.

28 This is particularly clear in the 1843–44 writings. Yet the distinction between political emancipation and human emancipation which informs the young Marx's critique of parliamentary democracy never really converges with the critique of capital in the *Grundrisse* and *Capital*. Moreover, it is by no means clear what human as opposed to merely political emancipation might actually mean in institutional terms. Marx talks about the reappropriation of humanity's *forces propres* without specifying how the critique of political economy and the critique of political oligarchy might be co-ordi-

nated. Moreover, his writings on the Paris Commune and Russian communal traditions do not give any clear indications of Marx's ideas on the political form of communism. Marx famously predicts that the state will eventually wither away. Considered in the light of the history of state socialism, these theoretical and practical questions suggest that, although related, the critique of political economy related to external nature is not tantamount to the critique of political oligarchy relevant to human nature. Crucial for the argument developed in the next two chapters is that this need not mean a retreat to Hegel's traditional idealism or submission to the creeping functionalism of the mature Habermas.

29 A first-order discourse of legitimacy is transcendental in the legal sense that it posits the democratic reconciliation of humanity and nature as a prior condition to human transcendence of natural necessity in non-mechanical and non-biological-predatory terms. Here one can truly speak of spectres of Marx: without this form of transcendence there are only very limited forms of freedom that are in reality subordinated to the logic of capital accumulation and the private appropriation of publicly created wealth. Thus whilst it is still a discourse of legitimacy, it nonetheless preserves a legal dimension that is largely absent in second-order discourses of legitimacy which hold out the possibility of direct reconciliation between humanity and human nature. One of the lessons of the authoritarian turn of the Russian Revolution is that reconciliation in the second sense is crucial, since it is possible to abolish private property and commodities without abolishing hierarchy, conformity, bureaucratic domination and fear. One of the lessons of the current crisis of movement politics is that second-order discourses considered by themselves will not have a decisive impact on property relations and commodity production, i.e. they will not even be able to redeem the prior condition to human transcendence of natural necessity articulated by Kant as practical reason and Marx as communism.

Chapter 3

Inside the liberal machine

ALTHOUGH it is true that liberal democracy in practice has been hegemonic without ever being legitimate in the epistemological sense used here, liberalism is rarely perceived to be authoritarian by a large majority of citizens in liberal democracies. Moreover, the fact that it has proven to be almost impossible to enact non-authoritarian alternatives to liberal democracy contributes to the continuing hegemony of global neo-liberalism and ideological myths about the end of history.[1] Why has it proven to be so difficult to create more legitimate political institutions than liberal institutions which are not authoritarian in practice? One hypothesis raised in the previous chapter of this book is that, however strange it might sound, it is possible that genuinely non-authoritarian alternatives to liberal democracy have yet to be tested on a large scale since the establishment of liberal democratic hegemony.[2] The discussion of legitimacy in chapter 2 suggests that intransigently anti-liberal movements such as Bolshevism are not really anti-liberal in so far as they do not question the basic premises of liberal thinking about humanity and nature. The argument shows that this inconclusive break with liberalism is also a feature of many new social movements. Albeit in different ways Bolshevism and movement politics are inconclusive in their ambiguous responses to the liberal dilemma. Chapter 2 demonstrates that first-order discourses of legitimacy like Bolshevism as well as second-order discourses of legitimacy such as those articulated by many social movements undertake one-sided critiques of the liberal understanding between humanity and nature, and that this one-sidedness is a key factor in explaining why opposition to liberalism is usually either authoritarian, or is integrated or marginalised by liberal political systems. Because the alternatives to liberalism all too often turn out to be authoritarian, incoherent or simply banal, the critics of liberalism usually end up making the alternatives seem inferior to the original liberal model. The alternatives fail because they are not decisive breaks with a machine which they aspire to steer for their own purposes, and since they did not design the machine themselves, they tend, on the whole, to steer it badly. A viable alternative to liberalism has to begin by venturing to the centre and periphery of the liberal machine, though without immediate political aspirations to take it over and operate it for ostensibly non-liberal aims. This investigation is undertaken in this chapter.[3]

The attempt to manoeuvre liberal institutions toward non-liberal destinations has been undertaken in the belief that the liberal dichotomies analysed in chapter 1 can be overcome by 'de-reifying' liberal epistemology with post-metaphysical theory which is immediately practical. Theorists who support this claim maintain that whereas liberal epistemology is mired in a system of dichotomies symptomatic of an anti-humanist metaphysics inherited from theological systems of belief, post-liberal thought transcends those dichotomies in various forms of post-metaphysical humanism at work in already existing institutions, movements and political identities. As such, its proponents hold, post-metaphysical thinking takes place beyond liberal reification, and is suggestive of potential forms of political authority beyond the legality and legitimacy as well as the theory and practice divides. The argument in chapter 2 suggests that, in practice, post-metaphysical humanism does not conclusively point toward post-liberal politics. This becomes clear when observing instances of supposedly post-metaphysical practice such as state socialism, new social movements and varieties of communicative action. Whilst state socialism is in the process of disintegration in the few places where it is still in power, most social movements and institutionally recognised structures of communicative action operate firmly within the contours of the liberal democratic system. The argument in the previous chapter also observes that post-metaphysical humanism does not even really point toward post-metaphysics in either theory or practice. This becomes clear when one considers that the cornerstone of metaphysical thinking is the belief that humanity has access to and can know supra-sensible essences unmediated by conceptual form. In fact, liberalism remains hegemonic among other reasons because it actually comes closer to a credible account of post-metaphysical form than its humanist rivals in search of post-liberal legitimacy. It is observed in chapter 1 that whereas one might contrast essence with form as the content contained or framed by form, Kant's legal idealism achieves the paradoxical result of arriving at a formal formulation of human essence. By refraining from a positive definition of freedom, and simultaneously insisting on the primacy of legality over legitimacy, Kant defends a formal conception of human essence that never definitively discloses what that essence consists of. Liberals from Kant to Rawls are convinced that once in power, a positively determined conception of freedom based on a revealed conception of human essence will result in the enforcement of an arbitrary vision of the good life bound up with that particular conception of positive freedom. It is argued that, if this occurs, spontaneity and pluralism will necessarily be abandoned, since politics will be directed in advance toward constructing social and political institutions that are designed to match a single conception of human essence by the institutions of political authority, i.e. such as the notion of man as worker in state socialism. In such cases, the alienation between the individual and authority is overcome at the prohibitively expensive cost of coerced reconciliation. That is to say that the strength of liberal theory consists amongst other things in the identification of a direct correlation between theories of *revealed human essence*, on the one hand, and practices of *coerced reconciliation* on the other. Liberal theorists are correct to suppose that the least coerced political moment short of fully uncoerced reconciliation is a liberal democratic moment because of the formal as opposed to revealed concept of essence that liberalism manages to articulate with the help of legal theory.[4] State socialism is probably the most obvious instance of a largely unsuccessful effort to address legitimation deficits in liberal democracies by championing a concept of revealed essence, though one could cite fascism and other examples as well. The history of these movements in practice indicates that liberals are correct to insist that attempts to widen the bases of political legitimacy beyond liberal formalism often end up diluting legality through extra-parliamentary discretionary measures. Rather than redeeming the Enlightenment promise of rational mediation of disagreement and the possibility of legislation based on knowledge, conflict is managed from above and legislation is reduced to executive fiat. The theorists of new social movements, communicative action and other second-order discourses of legitimacy claim to represent more pluralist attempts to formulate a democratic concept of legitimate human essence than those found in state socialism, fascism, etc. They argue that these 'friendlier' versions can be variously grounded in broad anthropological categories like speech, interaction, love and identity. But there are two reasons why these practical and theoretical innovations of the new left do not represent the last word on political legitimacy. First, these activities are to a large extent integrated or marginalised by liberal democratic systems of government. Second, whether conceived of in revealed or formal terms, the institutionalisation of such activities does not compel liberal democracies to reform themselves in a direction that would mark a conclusive step beyond essentialism altogether. Social movements, plural political identities and communicative life-worlds do not manage the step beyond the formal conception of essence enforced by liberal democracy, short of which reconciliation remains coerced and legitimacy remains hegemonic, albeit to a comparatively lesser extent than in other régimes. Thinkers like Habermas with a critical allegiance to liberalism and law clearly recognise this problem. Habermas advocates an epistemologically grounded praxis of legitimacy, but he undermines his own project by limiting the epistemological dimension of legitimacy to the cognitive content of the speech acts of life-world participants in functionalist isolation from the economic subsystem of money and bureaucratic administrative subsystems of power. Despite his claims to the contrary, Habermas is deeply indebted to a functionalist account of legitimacy. His post-

Legitimacy Crisis (1973) writings clearly suggest that social differentiation and the systemic autonomy of the economy are distinctive features of modern democratic polities, such that democratic political systems in effect cannot challenge the systemic logic of economic processes without ceasing to be democratic. He takes the view that although economic processes unfold according to the logic of instrumental reason, there are structures of communicative action in civil society sustained by cognitive rationality aiming at substantive agreement.[5] Against the view propounded by Arato and Cohen and other creative elaborations and departures from Habermas that remain committed to the main features of the functionalist model, it is argued in *Beyond Hegemony* that a much more consistent and extensive praxis of epistemological legitimacy than that suggested by the communicative action approach is possible. It will be seen that epistemological legitimacy based on a theory of legitimate law can redeem the early liberal and Enlightenment project to ground the law in knowledge rather than the effective exercise of power.[6] In the previous chapter it is argued that the supposedly post-metaphysical search for this-worldly humanist legitimacy turns out to be a project to realise legitimate human essence against abstract legal form as the key to the theory–praxis nexus. As suggested at the start of this chapter, if one considers one of the decisive hallmarks of metaphysical thinking to be a belief in the possible knowledge of the noumenal essences beyond sensory appearances, then the political struggle to realise legitimate human essence remains in large measure fought on a decidedly pre-Kantian metaphysical battlefield. This is still a long way from either post-liberalism or post-metaphysics, and, crucially, a long way from post-authoritarian political form.[7]

On the basis of the preceding discussion, one can distinguish between (1) a legal conception of formal essence that never discloses its essential core in liberalism, (2) a first-order conception of legitimate essence which is embodied by the socialist workers of the traditional left, (3) a second-order conception of legitimate essence embodied by the new social movements and the various communicative action theorists of the new left, and (4) an anti-essentialist postmodern position which has largely given up on legality, legitimacy and politics, and which is undoubtedly a pyrrhic victory over the problems of legitimate essentialism. The various projects to realise legitimate human essence against abstract legal form can be seen as attempts to undermine liberalism's undisclosed legal essence by confronting liberal democratic régimes with dimensions of legitimate human need that are not satisfied by liberal political institutions. The question of need and its possible transformation into legitimate knowledge will be briefly discussed toward the end of this chapter and then at length in chapters 4 and 5. For now it can be noted that until now the various modes of articulating the politics of legitimate, humanist need have generally tended to illustrate the strengths of liberalism rather than its weaknesses. Here liberalism seems to win a decisive epistemological-political victory: if one is intent on securing Enlightenment forms of post-metaphysical epistemology and the triumph of reason over dogma, a legal conception of undisclosed essence is clearly preferable to a legitimate conception of revealed essence. This would point to the definitive triumph of liberalism if need did not have a rational and epistemological dimension, and if the claims of Enlightenment were satisfied by forms of law that regulate without reconciling. To very briefly foreshadow the argument in chapters 4–5, it will be argued that there is a rational as well as an epistemological dimension to need. This implies that, like legality, legitimacy has a transcendental (not *a priori*) and idealist dimension that resists immediate disclosure (humanism) and infinite deferral (liberalism, negative theology). Humanist versions of disclosure attempt to fuse legality and legitimacy in more (state socialism) and less (movements and communicative action) authoritarian alternatives to liberal deferral. In these forays into legitimacy, the anonymous functionalist dimension in liberalism is attacked by confronting it with a concrete human face in the person of a specific legitimation subject, or a 'legitimation who'. The attempt to de-transcendentalise the transcendental subject of liberal idealism by giving it flesh and bones in this particular way leads to a humanist trap and a functionalist impasse that have been of great service to the social interests driving liberalism. This claim must be briefly explained below.

Since the publication of Kant's *Critique of Practical Reason* (1787), defenders of the promise of the Enlightenment version of modern law affirm that it is in reason, and by extension law, that humans transcend the mechanical and biological-predatory instances of freedom operative in the domains of matter, plants and animals, etc., in order to create the institutional bases of a distinctly human form of political freedom. The obvious question is: what kind of reason and what kind of law will best secure the transcendence of the necessity operative in nature? According to Kant's liberal idealism, a government is not legitimate unless its laws conform to the dictates of reason institutionalised in collective self-legislation. In practice, an absolutely decisive break with this rational and juridical account of experience, knowledge, political legitimacy and human freedom in the quest for a thoroughly terrestrial, consistently post-metaphysical epistemology and politics in opposition to idealism would probably imply one or a combination of the following alternatives: (1) an espousal of Nietzsche's or another account of vitalism, an espousal of Heidegger's or another account of fundamental ontology, aesthetic-ironic protest, structuralism or structural functionalism with a minimal role for individual subjects. It could also mean (2) a thoroughly voluntarist/decisionist account of extra-legal legitimacy based on political-sociological notions of the primacy of party, class, race, gender, etc. This confronts most of the contemporary advocates of post-metaphysics and humanism with a dilemma: they do not want legitimacy to be tied to consciousness, because this commits them to some form of idealism, nor do they wish to embrace the alternatives suggested by 1–2, since these offer no discernible normative grounds for political obligation. That is, post-metaphysical forms of legitimate humanism seem to want to sever the idealist link between legitimacy on the one hand and mind and reason on the other, though without embracing the conclusive break with legality that a consistent decoupling of mind and legitimacy would imply. Humanised post-metaphysics offers itself as a form of post-idealism, though without knowing how to be post-legal. It has been argued at various points in this book that liberal régimes survive by staging a functional continuity from the horizontal contract between anonymous buyers and sellers of labour power, on the one hand, to the vertical contract between citizens and the state, on the other, thus mediating the public and private in an ideological community of citizens. Liberal hegemony is perpetuated by legally uniting all citizens and the state in a compulsory community of citizens at one level, and by legally separating them into privately competing individuals and social classes at another level. This legal tactic of uniting at the level of state and separating at the level of civil society transforms all individuals into legitimate citizens regardless of their position within the division of labour, whilst simultaneously ensuring that citizenship cannot guarantee anyone a secure material or emotional existence. Liberalism's critics are correct to draw attention to the ideological sleight of hand implied by this coerced form of mediation between public and private and state and civil society. But the problem is not solved by calling for the replacement of the traders' model with an ostensibly more communicative or expressivist model at the level of civil society, whilst leaving the model of citizenship linked to the traders' model pretty much in its place at the level of state. This is not a decisive break with idealism, and indeed there are no decisive breaks with idealism that are not also decisive breaks with legality. Legality entails some form of idealism suggestive of a corresponding theory of transcendence. The question is: is it an idealism that is also critical, mimetic and materialist enough in order to transcend forms of economy and bureaucratic domination which continue to perpetuate necessity for many in the form of wage labour and fear for all in the form of non-transparent institutionalised hierarchies? Or is it a traditional form of idealism justifying wage labour and hierarchy as the only way to get the better of natural scarcity as best one can within what is officially declared to be the limits of what is possible and knowable?[8]

As a hegemonic movement capable of changing tactics and engineering passive revolutions, liberalism has been more politically astute on this fundamental point than any of its rivals. Idealism makes an epistemological discovery that is crudely inverted in Soviet Marxism-Leninism and effectively hi-jacked in different ways by liberalism in its various classical, humanist and functionalist guises. It is the discovery that in the medium of thought humanity comes into contact with forms of reason and law that make freedom and a substantial transcendence of natural necessity for humanity a real possibility, though only on condition that reason and law are apprehended as mediating instances and not as anthropological properties of humanity. Reason and law mediate between humanity and nature in a series of processes structured by the labour process and the creation of values in the widest sense. This is a philosophical, aesthetic and juridical discovery pursued in critical theory beyond the terms of traditional idealism. When reason and law are subjugated to the social interests driving liberalism and liberal humanity's fear of external nature as well as nature in humanity, reason and law are reduced to a series of techniques designed to subjugate nature in order to stave off liberal humanity's fear of the rest of humanity, hunger, illness and death. When liberal versions of reason and law assume coercive political form in the institutions of liberal democracy, the possibility of freedom is forfeited to the grinding quest for survival. The forms of economy and politics that sustain that quest produce wealth for some and prolong survival for many, though at the great cost of creating an accompanying climate of fear, conformity, hierarchy and domination. Here it is important to stress that this loss of freedom is a question of consciousness, reason, law and transcendence, and not a question of destiny, efficiency, ontology, the human condition or survival of the fittest. This means that freedom is still possible if the trajectory of reason and law can be inflected. Selected texts in critical theory and specific works of art indicate that the subjugation of nature for fear of humanity, hunger, illness and death is likely to engender relations of hierarchy and conformity amongst humans at the same time that it produces seemingly impressive monuments to (post-) industrial capitalism. This is because humanity is part of nature but not reducible to the natural world thanks to humanity's relation to reason and the possibility of transcendence. Conversely, humanity maintains contact with materialist and mimetic reason in the medium of thought, though humanity is not reducible to thought since humanity is also a part of nature. The reconciliation (not fusion or separation) of humanity and nature signals the possibility of a politics of epistemological legitimacy.

The natural dimension of humanity which is not reducible to reason and which is repressed by institutionalised forms of instrumental reason continually revolts against its subjugation. The forms in which that revolt takes place are at the centre of the critical reflections on legitimacy which run through this book. A central claim of this chapter to be explored throughout the rest of this book is that the revolt in question is a revolt of individual values against instrumental manipulation, and that these irreducibly individual values could acquire an epistemological relevance for a post-hegemonic theory of political legitimacy if the struggle for survival can be legally transformed into a struggle to create the socio-political conditions of non-instrumental objectivity. If Kant convincingly establishes the reality of form beyond metaphysical essence, and if preceding chapters demonstrate that only a legitimate form of legality can ground political authority in knowledge rather than hegemony, then the project to create legitimate forms of legality assumes key importance in the struggle to make law a barometer of knowledge rather than of force or opportunistic compromise. The discussion in this chapter and the chapters to come attempts to show that there is a potential epistemological revolt by critical reason against instrumental reason, and that this revolt is capable of outlining possible forms of economy and politics allowing for the transcendence of natural necessity without disciplining nature in either humanity or the environment. It will be seen that the union of critical theory and legal theory is necessary for the elaboration of the political contours of those forms. Against liberal deferral and humanist fusion, critical theory holds out the possibility of an uncoerced reconciliation of humanity and nature, but critical theory needs legal theory and relevant aspects of libertarian socialism taken up by theorists like Cole in order to make the idea of reconciliation politically relevant. The possibility of making reconciliation politically relevant turns on the possibility of there being forms of law that do not isolate the instrumental, aesthetic and cognitive moments of reason with the aim of reharmonising them in functionalist fashion to solve liberal democratic legitimation deficits. The matter is complicated by the fact that the concept of reconciliation has certain elective affinities with the liberal idea of deferral that it does not share with the humanist notions of fusion. That is, liberalism thinks in harmony with critical forms of idealism in resisting the coerced reconciliation of humanity and nature and in opposing the institutionalisation of revealed forms of human essence. From the moment of the birth of practical reason onwards, distinct strands of liberalism share the idealist position that humanity is part of nature but not reducible to the natural world, and that there is a constellation of related concepts constituted by the ideas of freedom, law, reason and the transcendence of necessity. But liberalism undermines the utopian moment in idealism by 'naturalising' the separation between ethics and politics, private and public, state and civil society, theory and praxis, as well as legality and legitimacy. This makes the liberal dichotomies seem inevitable and eternal, and helps propagate the view that there are only authoritarian and populist alternatives to liberal régimes.[9] Theorists of communicative action such as Habermas do liberalism a great service by giving it an ostensibly post-metaphysical vocabulary in an era in which almost everyone tends to equate metaphysics, idealism and authoritarianism. Framed in these terms, the metaphysics of liberal legality and the fusion of humanist legitimacy are both highly problematic, but the former can at least be reformed. Hence an effective way to shore up liberalism whilst denying that one is a liberal is to argue for the functionally effective mediation of the spheres separated by liberalism whilst denying that one is a functionalist. The point, however, is not to consolidate liberalism from within or assail it from without. What might happen if one tried to simultaneously dismantle and radicalise it from within?

One would begin to sever the link between a concept of transcendence rooted in a fear of nature and a concept of freedom and autonomy grounded in non-interference, though without embracing statist collectivism or pastoral notions of inclusion. The project to surpass statist collectivism and pastoral control is a project to dismantle institutionalised human fear of nature, bearing in mind that fear itself is not natural or ontological, but rather mobilised through various modes of instrumental reason. The mobilisation of technique and strategy sustains systems of hierarchical surveillance and regulation which make reason irrational by attempting to make it sovereign *vis-à-vis* nature. The alternative can be conceived in epistemological terms as freedom to know instead of conceiving and enacting freedom as freedom of the will. In other words, liberalism may be able to dispense with a revealed concept of essence in the guise of a legitimating class, race, party or identity, but it reintroduces an essentialist metaphysics of the will in the guise of the liberal understanding of negative freedom.[10] Freedom to know would not be an example of positive freedom in the sense used by Isaiah Berlin in his famous essay *The Two Concepts of Liberty* (1959), in which, as he points out, positive liberty usually means coerced reconciliation. One could think about freedom to know as a praxis of justice, enacted as an instance of affirmation and discovery of the epistemological moments of rationality in nature and humanity, and how these moments might relate to one another in new constellations in the future. In other words, reason can mediate between humanity and nature in a variety of different ways. That mediation depends on the political conceptions of freedom, justice and law that underpin reason, and the particular forms of reason which in turn guide the institutionalisation of different conceptions of freedom, justice and law. The regulatory theory and practice of reason invoked in punishment, discipline or retribution imposed to adjudicate between conflicting wills in pursuit of their divergent notions of negative liberty will be different from the reconciliatory theory and praxis of reason. The latter would constitute a decisive break with the liberal idea of freedom of the will which a whole range of parties and movements invoking discourses of legitimacy against liberalism have sought to collectively appropriate or democratise rather than challenge in terms of its very premises and assumptions. It is suggested above that, against revealed notions of legitimacy, liberalism appears to be virtually unassailable because it can defer the disclosure of its formal essence. Yet matters change from the moment one considers that it is impossible to really know what justice is unless one has an idea of what freedom is. Liberalism parades its defence of negative liberty as the basis of its capacity to resist coerced forms of reconciliation by enforcing the priority of the right before the good. Yet liberal democracies nonetheless make extensive use of systems of justice in order to discipline and regulate their populations. Liberals must concede this point: if they want to remain steadfast in their defence of the idea that freedom cannot be determined in positive terms, and they remain committed at the same time to a conception of freedom as freedom of the will, then they are compelled to admit that justice in liberal régimes is basically punitive justice. According to the codes of punitive justice, a judicial sentence demanding either payment, a prison term, military service or execution is the closest thing one gets to the impartial mediation of conflict in politics. That is a lie that has been exposed by political theorists, activists and artists like Kafka, and which must be fully explored in order to avoid the pitfalls of discourses of legitimacy. [11]

Unwritten laws (I) On legality and the commodification of labour

Liberalism articulates a set of connections between highly disparate elements of a complex world view comprised of different levels which may at times seem unrelated. These elements include freedom, equality, rights, autonomy, justice, punishment, guilt, political obligation, rationality, contract, culture, privacy, pluralism, utility, society, needs, values, merit and democracy. The liberal understanding of these individual subjects attains systematic coherence within the wider framework formed by the ideological commitment to the political and epistemological priority of legality over legitimacy in liberal theory. It is argued in this book that the legality–legitimacy framework offers the most appropriate starting point for an analysis of liberal social and political institutions as a preliminary step toward the construction of theories of mimetic materialism, epistemological legitimacy and a political understanding of freedom as freedom to know. These three theories are formulated in an attempt to offer a theory of legitimacy as reconciliation as an alternative to the specifically liberal defence of legality as regulation. This is a complicated undertaking which lends itself to added confusion due to the centrality of law in liberalism as well as its central-ity in the alternative to liberalism proposed here. Moreover, the complexities are heightened when one bears in mind that the theory of a legitimate form of legal-ity outlined in *Beyond Hegemony* is neither a variant of legal forms of legitimacy common to liberalism and most of its supposed opponents, nor an anti-legal approach to direct legitimacy found in the writings of postmodernists and post-structuralists, who in a variety of ways imply that direct legitimacy is to be found in the face of the other, friendship, the care of the self, i.e. in forms of action which attempt to stake out positions outside of or on the margins of the liberal democratic legal system. It has been demonstrated that liberals employ a variety of strategic arguments to defend the view that the mediation of humanity and nature must assume regulatory forms with regard to the reciprocal relations between humanity and nature, and that several distinct modes of instrumental reason are required to organise the regulation processes to secure desired outcomes that satisfy regulatory criteria in the economy, state and society. The smooth operation of these processes is dependent upon a series of premises and results which liberals are either not consciously aware of or not explicit about, and which opponents of liberalism largely ignore in their projects to reform or overthrow liberal political institutions. These premises about the relationship between humanity and nature are the necessary conditions for the particular forms of rationality operative in liberal democratic states. In a manner analogous to the two forms of sensible intuition and the twelve categories in Kant's philosophy, the conditions of liberal reason lay the groundwork for the structure of individual experience inside the liberal machine. This chapter lays bare the conditions of one particular form of rationality that one can call liberal. The project to create new, post-liberal political forms cannot dispense with such an analysis. This section will analyse the epistemological relation between humanity and external nature mediated through the labour process. The next section explores the epistemological relation between humanity and human nature mediated through the expression of values. The discussions in these sections lay the groundwork for the arguments to be developed in chapters 4–5.

Like many modern states, liberal democratic states are rational in a specifically legal sense analysed by Max Weber.[12] Weber analyses the rationalisation processes through which the areas of social life once structured by myth and tradition are steadily transformed into domains subject to legal scrutiny and codification. Weber's analysis prefigures Luhmann's thesis that in modern societies the law is increasingly likely to embrace virtually every dimension of existence. That is, whether one is referring to the codes of scientific research, the ownership of land and the products of the labour process, the statutes governing the practice of medicine, the control of biological reproduction and the provision of child care, etc., one is referring to the reciprocal relations between humanity and nature and their mediation through law, and legality, it will be remembered, exists prior to legitimacy for liberals. However, these examples illustrate the point that there is much more to law than ownership of entities external to human consciousness such as property. Indeed, a central claim of this book is that law can either reconcile or regulate in a much wider sense than that implied by ownership of goods such as labour power and land; this wider sense is captured by the term human (inner) nature.[13] Human nature cannot be owned in the strict sense applicable to external goods and services, but it can certainly be regulated, controlled and disciplined. Hence the most effective forms of regulation are those which purport to restrict the spheres of their jurisdiction to matters concerning external nature, but which in reality legislate on matters of internal nature as well. This is the point where the tenability of the liberal dichotomies is undermined, since the control and discipline of human nature are a condition for the steady functioning of many different modes of production. Depending on the mode of production in question, such discipline is very likely to make people neurotic, submissive or potentially violent to varying degrees at the same time that it makes them 'productive'. Different historical epochs characterised by different modes of production tend to engender quite distinct modes of pathology and escapism. What does the historical evolution of liberalism suggest in this context? The private appropriation of the fruits of collective human labour upon external nature, combined with wide-reaching innovations in technology, finance, and increased political enfranchisement, resulted in unprecedented levels of wealth and urban development during the industrial revolution. The accelerated transformation of external nature through the rise of manufacture and heavy industry was accompanied by new forms of surveillance and control of human nature that have been documented by Foucault, Braudel, Hobsbawm and many other social historians and social philosophers.[14] These forms of control do not merely accidentally accompany the industrial revolution and its continuing aftermath in such phenomena as Fordism, post-Fordism and globalisation, but are rather an integral component of its history: the trauma of human nature in modern industrial societies theoretically analysed by Nietzsche and clinically examined by Freud is unthinkable without the mastery of external nature brought about by liberalism, capitalism and the rise of what Weber calls legal-rational domination. This raises immediate questions about the validity of establishing a credible separation of a legal level of politics governed by rational rules which apply to external nature and which are valid in equal measure for all, on the one hand, and a legitimate level of politics restricted to private considerations of happiness varying from person to person, on the other. It also raises questions about the coherence of conceiving of justice as the rational mediation between legality and legitimacy by taking into account the claims of universality and the reality of particular cases and needs.

At first glance, liberalism appears to limit the claims of civil law to (1) ownership of property and commodities and (2) the right to command labour power to objectify itself in the commodity form (a form of command secured through the wage contract). The commodity form is an important phenomenon to analyse carefully, since it represents a relation between humanity, nature and need in which the direct satisfaction of need is deferred by the production of a good or service which must find a buyer before it can be enjoyed. Under these terms liberalism allows people to freely enter and annul contracts in accordance with their will, and at the same time, liberal law claims that it does not attempt to secure coerced forms of reconciliation between citizens by legislating on matters of individual ethical conduct and personal need or happiness. The function of the liberal democratic state is to secure the legal conditions which ensure that the processes of exchange of land, commodities and labour power proceed rationally and predictably. Minimal degrees of state authority are required to enforce the sale of exchangeable goods and services. Liberals claim that the liberal democratic system is a libertarian system based on consent, since there is no force – there is only enforcement. Although contracts are enforced, nobody is forced into contractual relations; although allowed, nobody is compelled to take part in communities or other instances of collective solidarity. This is said to be one of the bases of liberal freedom, since the creation of a public space governed by minimal levels of force simultaneously creates a private space of non-infringement in which autonomous citizens are free to think and say whatever they like and go about their private business in freely chosen contractual arrangements and emotional commitments with other autonomous citizens. It is in these private, freely chosen activities that citizens can pursue their own visions of happiness and spontaneously unite in any number of communities without state interference.[15] From the liberal perspective, if individual initiative in these matters is stifled by state planning or corporatist steering, an arbitrary conception of the good is imposed in an authoritarian spirit of contrived community. Thus for liberals the state must be there to enforce contract, but political considerations about possible forms of positive freedom or the good life or the collective satisfaction of human need – considerations about legitimacy – cannot be allowed to interfere with the freely chosen designs of the privately oriented citizenry that bestows on the state the legitimate authority (the right) to enforce contract and protect individual liberty. Yet if specific modes of scientific research, the buying and selling of labour power, the rules for deciding issues related to custody, etc., are barometers of the reciprocal relations between humanity and external nature, it is also evident that these processes do not unfold in abstraction from needs, values and desires for happiness linked with legitimacy and human nature. Here one would be right to ask liberals the following question: if it is reasonable to proceed on the basis that there is a consensus for the necessity to enforce contract (established in a transcendental original contract with no basis in empirical historical reality or experience), why is it not equally reasonable to proceed on the basis that there is a transcendental consensus for the satisfaction of legitimate needs? This is an important juncture in the overall argument: demanding a radical overhaul of liberal legal form whilst at the same time retaining the centrality of legality for the mediation of humanity and nature is now able to become the starting point in the theoretical endeavour to deconstruct liberalism from within instead of trying to patch it up or assailing it from without. From the moment that the indissolubility of legality and legitimacy is firmly established, the liberal dichotomies can be called into question without recourse to extra-legal notions of legitimacy. Social and political thought is thereby released from an oppressive straitjacket juxtaposing *liberal argument* for the epistemological dimension of legality, on the one hand, with *non-liberal appeals* to extra-epistemological bases of legitimacy, on the other.

Within the framework constituted by (1) the liberal dichotomies and the priority of legality over legitimacy, (2) the instantiation and protection of negative liberty, and (3) the practice of punitive forms of justice correlative to the insistence on negative liberty as the only possible non-authoritarian liberty, liberal states are able to legislate invisibly on matters of human nature (level 2) at the same time that they publicly legislate on the control and exchange of external entities (level 1), and nonetheless maintain that the law is impartial with regard to level 2 considerations. This is the real, legal basis of liberal demo-cratic hegemony. The two–tier architectural structure of liberal law introduces a barely discernible and highly arbitrary dimension of power into the liberal democratic legal system. In this process, very particular and decidedly non-universal fears about the limits of reconciliation and human nature infiltrate legislation that is supposed to enforce the neutrality of the state between differ-ent conceptions of the good. The arbitrariness of what appears to be a neutral system can be examined by tracing liberal humanity's unspoken desire to prohibit a public and political discussion of the legitimate and rational dimen-sion of need. By the time creative and potentially system-transformative needs are allowed to find expression through systemic channels they are stripped of their rational and legitimate dimension and treated as preferences, so that it is they that seem arbitrary. Concessions made to preferences give state neutrality a generously pluralist appearance, thus inviting people to ask, what can be so amiss with a system of legality and legitimacy in which there is enough social space for business interests, the interests of labour, artists, athletes, gamblers, layabouts and even vociferous critics? At the same time, the liberal democratic legal system privileges certain energies linked with very definite ambitions and misgivings which do indeed pertain to values and conceptions of the good. The class relations implied by (1) to (3) are perpetuated or challenged via legal rela-tions that in formal terms pertain exclusively to relations between humanity and external nature. As a corollary, matters of human nature are held to be a matter of private individual and ethical choice. Yet it was just established that the specific modes of health care, scientific research, etc., are barometers of the reciprocal relations between humanity and nature in both senses, since it is clearly demonstrable that these processes do not unfold in abstraction from considerations of legitimacy and human nature. Legislation which in theory is legal in form because it abstains from arbitrary judgements about the good of humankind and positive liberty, and which bans issues connected with human nature to a supposedly non-political private sphere in the name of the priority of the right before the good, legislates on issues of human nature while it is legis-lating on matters concerning external nature. To put the matter very crassly for the moment, one can argue that if someone has legal control over someone else's access to external nature through the labour–capital relation codified in the wage contract, they also have a significant degree of control over that person's imagination and their legitimate needs and desires as well. That person is then invited to buy back their own needs and desires in the form of goods and services promising security, happiness, adventure, fantasy and fulfilment. They are free to buy back what is theirs in a commodified form; their choice in making those purchases constitutes the basis of their formal freedom. Just as they are not made to work for any particular firm, they are not legally compelled to buy any particular car, house or holiday package. They can choose the one they want, provided they can afford it.[16] The implication is that law is the form in which the humanity–nature relation in all of its diverse aspects is mediated, and, as such, there is no form of law that does not structure that relation in both senses used here. To argue that there are rational rules to mediate humanity and external nature which are operative in civil and public law, on the one hand, and simultaneously maintain that the humanity–human nature relation is a non-rational, non-political and private affair not subject to legislation, on the other, is to create a bureaucratic power structure based on the combined force of rules and lies. The problem for reform-minded liberal democrats and social democrats is that more rules or even better rules cannot solve this problem as long as they are brought to bear on lies. The lie is the official dichotomy between legality and legitimacy which in reality turns out to be a legally legitimated form of hegemony based on the socio-political relations implied by commodity production and a deeply ambiguous conception of freedom of the will as freedom of choice. The rule is that, in any clash of wills, one prevails over another on the model of a contractually mediated zero-sum exchange.

Once they have been exposed in these terms, it becomes clear that liberal forms of legality are not plural in any meaningful sense. Legality is rather the expression of a form of regulated conflict in which plurality is negated by the organisational pressures imposed by a reality principle structured by the need to compete against rival organised wills for the right to survive. This point is of considerable epistemological-political importance for evaluating different liberal visions of practical reason from Kant to Rawls and Habermas: legally regulated conflict does not constitute the transcendence of necessity through reason, and, as such, liberal law is not legitimate law. This is a form of legality that guarantees the legal appropriation of control of the labour processes in which humanity interacts with external nature, and establishes mechanisms of hegemonic manipulation of creativity and need. The labour process and the various articulations of need are in constant flux and as such constantly change the very terms in which transcendence beyond mere survival can be imagined. Private control of the labour process contrives to create a political climate of despotic fear so that even in wealthy liberal democratic societies the struggle for survival contrives to reduce reason to strategy. Regulation of this kind serves one particular reality principle whilst shutting out alternative reality principles that may in fact be more real precisely because domination and fear are liable to distort human experience of reality. An immediately evident consequence is an insight developed by critical theory that informs the approach to legitimacy taken here: practical applications of reason that confront the issue of natural scarcity by perpetuating unfreedom in socio-political form are indeed rational but only instrumentally so. This holds if one wishes to adhere to the Enlightenment project of enlisting the mediation of reason in the search for political liberty. Otherwise one would have to conclude that there is no contradiction between rational praxis and the perpetuation of bureaucratic domination and fear. In this case there would be no grounds to want rational politics more than non-rational politics. It is in this context that liberalism is a complicated political phenomenon. Whilst in theory liberalism seems to be based on reason and law, and as such appears to champion rationality and freedom, in practice it pursues and generally achieves very different ends. Even if these ends are collectively controlled through forms of state ownership, they remain liberal ends, however idiosyncratic this understanding of liberalism might seem to be. This means that the only way to dismantle liberalism from within is to definitively break with the particular form of traditional idealism that underpins liberal conceptions of autonomy, reason, legality and legitimacy, though without renouncing all forms of idealism *per se*. The reasons why will become clearer in the next chapter. In any case it is evident that opposition to liberalism which attempts to redistribute the products of the liberal machine in more equitable terms or reduce restrictions on the conditions of entry therein does not effectively challenge the workings of that machine.

To summarise the argument in this section, one could say that the decoupling of legal rules from legitimate values depoliticises and commodifies needs at the same time that it systematically reduces legality to regulation. In accordance with these systemic premises and the production of predictable outcomes following from them, one can see that conflict in liberal democratic societies is bureaucratic and ideological rather than political and transparent. This is because legality and legitimacy are formally separated and informally re-articulated in the cycles of commodity production and commodity consumption in what one can truly designate as a *system* which shapes the contours of the human experience of reality and the rational understanding of what might be possible individually and collectively. This is a system with totalitarian implications: whilst the mode of production transforms labour power into a commodity which is bought and sold on the labour market through the wage contract, the mode of consumption in its turn effectively transforms the needs and the creations of the imagination into commodities that have to be bought and sold for the smooth functioning of the mode of production.[17] Within the terms dictated by this system theory and praxis cannot be reconciled in any significant sense: praxis is reduced to a passive model of consumption rather than expanded into an active model of cognition based on knowledge of humanity's real relationship with nature in a given historical moment. The analysis so far suggests that in order to move toward an active model of cognition in opposition to a passive model of commodified re-appropriation, the articulation of individual values has to be released from the struggle for survival which chains the expression of value to largely negative statements about the unnecessary perpetuation of need. The systematic disarticulation and re-articulation of legality and legitimacy take place in a series of parallel processes which secure the prevalence of a practice of freedom based on the notion of free exchange enforced in civil law. Exchange-based freedom blunts the plural dimension of political struggles between different standpoints. Conflict can be efficiently managed when the incommensurability of different energies is suppressed and marginalised by the energies needed to compete successfully in the disputes over control of the fruits of the labour process and external nature. Instrumental efficiency, dogged determination, hierarchy, calculation and strategy are able to flourish at the expense of the imagination and Eros in the widest sense of creativity, investigation and play. Under these terms conflict is almost always a conflict about (1) 'how much?' and rarely a question of (2) 'what kind?' and bureaucracy provides the best institutional matrix for mastering type (1) questions through predictable rules, statutes and techniques. To argue that this is a political system that is neutral with regard to different visions of the good life is to be silent about the values that are privileged by a form of legality that claims to exclude normative considerations of legitimacy from the law, but which nonetheless legislates about the good of humankind as if the latter was monolithic instead of radically plural.

Unwritten laws (II) On legitimacy and the commodification of the political imagination and individual values

It is suggested in the last section that the commodity is far more than a neutral object. The commodity is a phenomenon that embodies a relation between humanity, nature and the possibility of need satisfaction. To this extent it is the visible, objective form of a particular mode of thinking about law and a conjecture about possible forms of legitimacy. Commodity production – production for exchange and the generation of money and capital rather than direct use – legislates that the satisfaction of need is to be deferred until a good or service finds an individual buyer. Instead of organising the labour process as a dialogue between producers and consumers in which consumers have a direct say in what is produced and are able to learn about the individual stages of its manufacture, commodities are produced in private and subsequently thrown into circulation. Since its value is not determined in advance as a function of use but is instead revealed in the decisive moment of exchange, the commodity must attract an interested party to deliver it from the shop shelf. Until this moment of exchange it must sit and wait in a limbo state. The unsold commodity continues to wait until it is either finally sold at a discount or shamefully taken out of circulation and destroyed or discarded. The idea of a libertarian socialist economy based on a producer–consumer dialogue as an alternative to commodity production is a horrifying thought for the liberal imagination, since it would mean that the power of the will to choose as a free, autonomous individual before God would be undermined by collectivist provision of the good life imposed by the state. In other words, God gives the liberal freedom of the will, which is a price worth paying in the face of the possibility of evil, whilst the liberal state gives official sanction to all exchanges completed by freely contracting individuals. God and the state are the rarely acknowledged transcendental conditions for the existence of liberal humanity and law; they precede real humanity in space and time insofar as they are grounded in a transhistorical and mythical origin rather than experience or history. They are both moments of faith which are framed in legal-rational terms: faith in the divine origins of humanity despite the threat of evil, and faith in the existence of a fictitious collective decision to leave the state of nature in a mythical first contract to give validity to all subsequent real contracts. Whilst the threat of evil can be effectively met with the right forms of deterrence and punishment, breaches of contract can be prevented to the greatest extent possible by efficient methods of enforcement. Hence it is intrinsic to the liberal political imagination that the conditions of humanity are transcendental and not located in various instances of terrestrial historical experience or individual/group identity of the kind analysed in chapter 2. What is at issue in the critique of liberalism in this chapter is not the transcendental argument about the possibility of knowledge being contingent upon knowledge itself - it is argued that this is liberalism's great strength *vis-à-vis* the various discourses of democracy and populist legitimacy. It is instead the particular way that transcendence is understood in relation to legitimacy in the liberal tradition that is contested. On the basis of what has been demonstrated so far, the question of transcendence can now be rethought in critical distance from liberalism as well as the discourses of legitimate humanity. One can take the premise that the possibility of knowledge is contingent upon knowledge itself and radicalise it in socio-political terms with materialist arguments and explanations rather than in *a priori* terms with state-of-nature arguments and explanations.

It is seen in the previous section that the liberal democratic state must enforce contract, but political considerations about possible forms of positive freedom or the collective satisfaction of human need must not be allowed to interfere with the freely-chosen designs of the privately oriented citizenry that bestows on the state the legitimate authority to enforce contract and protect individual liberty and conscience. The commodity form is a particular manifestation of the awkward mixture of liberal as well as idealist reflections found at the centre and periphery of the liberal democratic system. It does not tell outright lies as such, but lies indirectly in two ways. The commodity form lies obliquely by diffusing a variety of mendacious accounts about the rationality and desirability of deferral of the satisfaction of need through production for exchange, and it is coquettish about the desirability of not revealing the essence of freedom. In contrast to the example of state socialism analysed in chapter 2, these stories are not diffused from a centre of ritually legitimised power. An intrinsic dimension of power relations in liberal democratic societies is the manifest absence of a centre of power and the dispensability of outright lies in the typical form of authoritarian propaganda. This follows from the fact that there is enforcement of contract rather than the direct use of force in such societies, as well as freedom of speech rather than the official promulgation of the truth. No one has to work for someone else, as in slavery, feudalism or state socialism, and indeed it is true that citizens of the liberal democratic *Rechtsstaat* do not have to work at all or do anything against their will except pay taxes. From this standpoint, to make people work for a particular firm or the state would be tantamount to resurrecting feudal social and political relations. According to liberal history, these paternalist relations thankfully perished in the modern bourgeois revolutions of the seventeenth and eighteenth centuries. Instead of openly declaring that it is bad or wrong to want to act collectively in order to bring about the greatest possible transcendence of natural necessity, the ideologies in circulation in the commodity régime imply as much by suggesting that freedom is a matter of duty, and duty is a matter of individual conscience, not a matter of collective provision. To want such provision is silly, childlike, unrealistic – in short, irresponsible in view of the necessity to choose as an individual if one wants to be a free adult capable of earning one's own livelihood and taking control of one's individual destiny. Once one accepts the fallacious claim that this value-laden construction of rationality is really a value-free account of how liberal law enables everyone to pursue their liberty without infringing the liberty of another, one is also ready to accept the specious idea that one's dependence on commodity production is actually the basis of one's freedom and autonomy. The key to understanding this subtle conflation of dependence with autonomy is to be sought in the gradual evolution of liberal theory and praxis. It is a shift marked by a slow but persistent transition from the theories of freedom of conscience and ethics in early liberal thinkers like Kant and J. S. Mill, on the one hand, to the understanding of freedom as consumer choice, on the other. The latter has dominated daily life in liberal democracies at least since the transition to post-war capitalism in the 1950s. Important in this context are the very different models of legitimacy that these conceptions of freedom imply.[18]

The transition just alluded to is closely related to the demise of the early liberal project aimed at securing an epistemological basis for the law through the discursively grounded ethical truths arrived at by the economically independent participants of the bourgeois public sphere. At various points in the evolution of liberalism toward liberal democracy and subsequently toward nationally specific models of social democracy, it became clear that the project of formulating a concept of legitimacy based on knowledge would have to be either abandoned or renewed on the basis of an entirely different legal mediation between humanity and external nature. This implied the necessity of a number of far-reaching institutional transformations, and a completely new economy in particular. The Kantian model of the public sphere is contingent upon quite specific economic relations and a specific moment in the development of the changing interaction between humanity and external nature in Western Europe. It is seen toward the end of chapter 1 that the Kantian formulation of a possible epistemological grounding of law through free discussion on the part of university professors, government administrators and other economically independent élites is predicated on factors which were operative in Kant's day but soon to be swept away, as Hegel clearly foresees even before Marx's critique of political economy. These factors included highly restricted suffrage and low levels of literacy amongst broad social strata, incipient forms of industrialisation, limited forms of transport and urban growth, etc. Thinkers in the liberal tradition like Tocqueville and Mill intuited that liberalism was going to have to transform its socio-political institutional profile in order to cope with the inexorable demands for the end of restrictions on suffrage and for more democracy generally. Tocqueville poses the most pressing theoretical and practical question of his day. He predicts that, as a form of government, democracy is firmly inscribed in the historical process and will eventually come to all societies around the world. His question is: will democracy be liberal or despotic?[19] In order for democracy to be liberal by remaining committed to the project of instituting forms of epistemologically based legal practice, the property relations underpinning that project and making it possible in its original form would have to be extensively democratised. This would then allow a much broader, and one day fully representative, segment of the population to participate in the discursive processes which in the Kantian model guarantee for a small minority that law is legitimate rather than just formally legal. That is to say that the possibility of liberal rather than despotic democracy turned decisively on fulfilling the political condition of reorganising the relationship between humanity and external nature in such a way as to legislate the transcendence of natural necessity for the entire adult population of liberal democracies, rather than protecting the economic independence of the administrative élite and other figures of the bourgeois public sphere. The legitimation of legal norms through rational discussion freed from the battle for survival could then be practised on a society-wide scale, and liberalism could assume a democratic form.

The choice, in effect, was twofold. Liberals could have attempted to preserve the epistemological integrity of law under the new social conditions emerging with the democratisation of society, or liberal élites in the economy and polity could begin searching for political compromises with anti-democratic forces in the army, church, state executive, remnants of landed power, etc., which is in fact what happened. The search for alliances with other socio-political interests of course varied tremendously from country to country. But in any case, this historical development constituted the demise of the classical version of liberalism based on clear demarcations between public and private, state and civil society, etc. It marks the initial appearance of a social ensemble without clear boundaries in these matters, i.e. the beginning of the total state in liberal democratic form which does not fully emerge until after the turbulent authoritarian transitions of the 1920s and 1930s and the establishment of the post-war capitalist order.[20] Apart from rare exceptions, liberals generally refused to accept the loss of socio-economic power which the end of private property would have entailed had they chosen the first option. In so doing, they embraced the far more strategic view that the gradual enfranchisement of the masses spelled the end of classical liberalism as well as the end of the feasibility of any real transparency between social relations and the legal system. In terms of Tocqueville's question, acceptance of the latter was open acceptance of the likelihood of despotic rather than liberal democracy. As a consequence, the utopian moment in early liberalism was lost to the necessity of mobilising popular support in favour of government policy; the claims of knowledge ceded to the claims of power organised as competing collective wills. The legitimation processes involving a potentially independent and democratically enlightened citizenry would have to be – and in fact were – usurped by parties claiming to represent the wishes of the sovereign people. In a series of socio-economic processes charted by Weber, Michels and other political sociologists, political parties from right to left began articulating populist and strategically reformed neo-liberal visions of legitimate authority, thus helping to reduce participation in the newly emerging post-classical liberal public sphere to a small number of avant-garde artists, that is, to an even smaller minority than the liberal élites of the former bourgeois public sphere. Contrary to the claims of theorists of communicative action, the remaining socio-political public space has subsequently been thoroughly colonised, with the exception of the avant-garde and underground, by commercial enterprises and in particular by the commercial media.[21]

The commercialisation and medialisation of the public sphere in conjunction with the virtual monopoly of legitimate political opinion usurped by political parties vying for control of state power has resulted in a chronic reduction of the epistemological questions of legitimacy to tactical questions concerned with hegemony. Whilst hegemony is by no means reducible to the legal mediation of humanity's relations with external nature in the concrete terms posed by class structure and class struggle, the question of who owns and controls the means of production is the key to understanding its exercise. The first question for any government regardless of the party or parties comprising it is economic growth and its distribution. Under conditions that have been operative in Western Europe and North America for quite some time now, it is clear that no government will be perceived as legitimate unless it can guarantee an acceptable balance of economic growth and social welfare, though the provision of the latter is becoming increasingly precarious.[22] The analysis points to the thoroughly commercialised nature of the relation between the citizen and state in liberal democracies. But there is really no point in bemoaning clientelism, corruption, consumerism and voter apathy in view of the reality that the citizen is in fact to all intents and purposes a depoliticised client and a passive consumer of goods and advertising. The parties make promises to the electorate they usually cannot keep, and the electorate rewards them with votes on the day of the election: clientelism is in no way an aberration, it is rather the foundation of this system. After the elections the voters return to a passive existence taken up by work, leisure and private concerns in which they can exercise their negative freedom.[23] To assail this phenomenon with moralising sermons or by exhorting a return to republican virtue is to lose sight of the fact that the liberal democratic system is now based on a private and commercial-contractual conception of freedom and a legal form of legitimacy in which legislation that purports to legislate about control of external nature (legal issues) actually legislates on matters of external as well as matters of human nature (issues concerning legitimacy about which liberal law claims to be neutral). Contemporary apologies for liberal democracy which enlist the old arguments whilst refusing to acknowledge new realities are either hopelessly naïve or extremely cynical; they are in any case pathetic in comparison with the lucidity of Tocqueville. Such apologies ignore the point that the systematic functioning of the liberal democracy and the control of political experience in liberal democratic régimes is marked by (1) the deferral of matters of need and creativity through commodity production, and (2) legislation that is legal in form but which is also empowered to dictate the terms of legitimate needs and wants due to non-transparent legal structures which regulate humanity's relation to nature in both senses. The system secures the transformation of labour power into a commodity which is bought and sold through the institution of wage labour codified in contract. At the same time it transforms needs and aspirations into commodities that are bought and sold according to the principle of deferral. It is this latter transformation that is central to this section of this chapter, since it is this which effectively blocks consciousness by prohibiting the transformation of needs into individual expressions of value. This point will be examined in detail in chapter 5.

Because needs and wants are commodified according to the terms established by liberal democratic property relations, individual citizens must either renounce those needs or attempt to partially satisfy them by buying them back. If they are renounced, the citizen is confronted with the trauma and fear that long-term renunciation will probably engender. Likely responses to structurally induced renunciation include depression, violence and/or passive conformity.[24] If they are bought back, the likely result is the renewal of the spiral of dissatis-faction. This is because the commodity offers the buyer an experience in the form of a thing that fits into a package; it promises an experience limited in scope and duration to the dimensions of the package itself. Since the terms of the sales contract specify that the internal contents of the package must conform to what the package promises in terms of its external form – violation thereof constitutes fraud – the experience itself is predictable and devoid of any active role for the imagination. The completion of the exchange satisfies the need the consumer has deferred until the moment of purchase and use, whilst starving their imagination in the very same process. At one level they have gained posses-sion of what their will has aimed for. At another level they have been cheated, since they are only buying back in a commodified form available to any buyer what was already theirs alone in a non-commodified form. What was theirs in a non-commodified form and what is absolutely unique to each individual citizen is the rational desire – what is discussed in this book as a legitimate value with an epistemological dimension – to imagine the terms of transcendence of natural scarcity in a way that does not reproduce need in socio-political form due to the institutionalisation of exclusively instrumental forms of rationality regulating human nature. This reference to the rational and desiring political imagination may seem to constitute a leap in the argument, but it is in fact the liberal imagination that first posits the liberating moment of Enlightenment in the transcendence of mechanical causality and natural necessity through reason. Liberalism raises the possibility of transcendence of necessity through the medi-ation instances of law and reason and then abandons it, whilst most movements and parties in opposition to liberalism simply ignore it. That is why this chapter attempts to critique liberalism in terms of its own premises and suppositions, so that the project of enacting a legitimate form of law can be considered, bearing in mind the critical and radical implications of the Enlightenment view that reason and law are incompatible with ideology and political domination. An economy which paradoxically perpetuates need as it satisfies it through struc-tural deferral legislates this possibility of rational transcendence out of existence. That economy and the legality that underpins it are thus unsuccessful in guaranteeing the transcendence of need. This means that the attempt to collectivise such a form of economy or redistribute its fruits more equitably does not go to the centre of the machinery that drives it. As seen in chapter 1, the legitimacy of liberal law is claimed to derive precisely from the rational and cognitive dimensions of liberal legality through which the mechanical causality operative in the world of minerals, plants and animals is practically transcended in a way that enables humans to enjoy a particular form of political freedom not found in nature. The analysis in this chapter shows that liberalism undertakes the project of liberating humanity from nature through reason in hostile antagonism toward nature in the two senses used here. The twofold result is that reason is reduced to its instrumental dimension both in the economy and in the polity, and law becomes a tool of oppression. People are oppressed by people, though rarely directly: they are oppressed by a particular form of rationality, commodities, money, contracts, justice as punishment, deferral of need satisfaction and bureaucratic rules. The truth is not dogmatically imposed through discourses of legitimacy or the official celebration of humanist essence supposedly embodied in specific actions such as love, work, communication or recognition. Instead, there is an ongoing lie about the absence of truth, and that lie is told in the form of the alleged necessity of deferral and the characterisation of a situation of dependence as one of autonomy. Liberals like to claim that liberal legality is legitimate in an historically distinct sense signalled by the rationality of law championed by Enlightenment intellectuals and their followers. In contrast to previous forms of political authority codified in authoritarian forms of law and arbitrary customs, the legitimacy of liberal law is constituted by its rational basis. It is this rational basis which also secures political freedom against tyrannies of the past and potential tyrannies of the future. But it has just been demonstrated why and how liberal democratic legality legislates illegitimately without pronouncing directly on legitimacy. This is because the types of transcendence that this form of rationality promulgates actually create relations of hierarchy between citizens, to say nothing of the neurosis perpetuated within citizens. This is symptomatic of a political condition of widespread dependence rather than the greatest possible transcendence. The legal *authority* to enforce rather than impose force thus finds its complement in various forms of diffused social *power* that do not need to ban or censure the imagination in an obviously tyrannical or authoritarian manner. The imagination is regulated by the structural constraints of a mode of production which can exist only on condition that commodities are sold to consumers who are not defrauded; this extends from money privately spent on advertising in one domain to votes publicly cast in another.[25] But advertising is not real information or communication, any more than deferral is real satisfaction or a credible basis for the transcendence of necessity. A further point can be deduced which is part of the critique of liberalism offered in this chapter: if (1) deferral does not allow for the transcendence of need, and (2) by definition there is not sufficient freedom without the greatest possible transcendence of need, and (3) liberalism understands the transcendence of natural necessity to be accomplished in reason and law, then (4) liberal legality which systematically perpetuates need as socio-political need (no longer natural need in the form of scarcity) is only instrumentally rational. In terms of their own argumentation, law which is not rational is not legitimate for liberals.

Two preliminary conclusions follow from the foregoing analysis. The first conclusion is that only forms of law which meet the conditions required by the greatest possible transcendence will be more than merely instrumentally rational and strategically legitimate. This chapter has shown that such law is incompatible with private property and commodity production. The second conclusion is that if natural necessity and its transcendence through philosophy and science can be conceived of as a political-epistemological project with an Enlightenment lineage, and if *the legitimacy of legality*, i.e. the quality of legality, is intrinsic to the successful realisation of that transcendence, then there is a transcendental and rational dimension to legitimacy, not just to legality. This means that there is very significant epistemological dimension to legitimacy that is suppressed by the liberal democratic practice of legality. To speak about the legitimacy of legality is to speak about reason, provided that one wishes to base legality and freedom on philosophical and scientific grounds rather than on force, tradition, ruse, strategy or regulation. When one speaks about reason one is talking about possible forms of mediation between humanity (subject) and nature (object), bearing in mind that subject and object are not unmediated essences. The argument initiated in the first chapter thus comes full circle at this point, since this study began with the thesis that rational mediation is made possible by thought in the widest sense which is given institutional expression as praxis in law. To show that rational mediation is made possible by thought is not the same as saying that thought is inherently rational or that humanity is born rational and in possession of reason as if it were property or a natural right. It is to demonstrate something different, to wit, that in thought humanity makes contact with reason, and that reason is the key instance mediating subjectivity and objectivity. Assessing the quality of that contact and reflecting on the kinds of political institutions that structure it become an issue of major importance in any non-ideological discussion of freedom. In order to dismantle liberalism without quickly articulating yet another discourse of legitimacy incapable of challenging the real economic and social foundations of liberal democracy, this chapter seeks to give the critique of liberalism the space it requires so that the next two chapters can draw out and evaluate the theoretical and practical implications of the two preliminary conclusions that have just been reached.

Notes

1 One might ask, what is social democracy, if not a non-authoritarian alternative to liberalism? The years following the implementation of the Marshall Plan and the oil crises of the 1970s may well enter history as the time in which steady growth, nearly full employment and extensive welfare provision seemed like inviolable gains of the social democratic post-war era. That period came to an abrupt end in two waves which perhaps signify a terminal crisis of social democracy – at least in its post-war form. The first wave follows the arrival of Thatcher and Reagan in power in 1979 and 1980, soon followed by the right-wing turn of the first Mitterand government not long after the French elections of May 1981. This first wave might be called the neo-liberal moment in the battle against social democracy. The second wave unfurls in the

wake of the end of the Cold War with the fall of the Berlin Wall in 1989. Instead of signalling the onset of a new era of political possibility with the removal of the threat of nuclear annihilation, this second wave is marked by the union of neo-liberalism and globalisation in a continued assault on social democratic gains. The austerity programme adopted by Schröder and Blair's neo-liberalism indicate that social democratic parties in the new millennium find themselves compelled to continue the neo-liberal war on the welfare state instead of returning to the commitment to work and social security once associated with social democracy. The thirty years of welfare state capitalism and Keynesian economic management following the Second World War were characterised by steady growth, corporate agreements between strong labour unions, government and business, and Fordism in the workplace. These have been succeeded by faltering growth, high unemployment (especially in Germany), substantially weakened labour unions and post-Fordist flexible specialisation at work. In view of this, it might be the case that social democracy is not an alternative to liberalism, but rather a luxury of growth years that is rescinded when growth stagnates.

2 Thus for the purposes of this discussion, I will leave aside smaller-scale examples such as the anarchist co-operatives in the Spanish Civil War, Mondragon, etc.

3 It will be objected: does not Marx say as much when he declares in *The Civil War in France* that the history of the Paris Commune indicates that the working class cannot lay hold of the ready-made state machinery and wield it for its own purposes? This is certainly true. Yet Marx's argument remains incomplete to the extent that Marx integrates this insight about political form within the framework of a first-order discourse of legitimacy without directly addressing the relation between humanity and human nature in the sense used here. For the young Marx, humanity is directly reconciled with external nature (legality) and human nature (legitimacy) in work freed from commodity production and private property. The continuing relevance of Marx stems from the legal dimension of his project concerning humanity and external nature. But it was seen in chapter 2 of this book that his implicit assumption that legality and legitimacy can be grasped as points on a continuum mediated by the humanisation and democratisation of work opens the door to a Leninist interpretation of Marx and the practice of authoritarian state socialism. Chapter 2 also explains why it is equally mistaken to opt for the social movement approach to legitimacy, and suggests why a communicative action approach is also inadequate.

4 The currently dominant liberal democratic union of liberalism and legal theory is challenged in this book by the epistemological union of legal theory and critical theory informed by Cole and Marx on libertarian socialism as well as Kant and Hegel on idealism. Union in the first case is forged on the basis of essentialist notions of human nature which culminate in theories of human autonomy based on the circular idea that humanity is *naturally* autonomous from *nature* with the help of practical reason. Union in the second case is conceived not as unmediated union with nature, but rather as reconciliation based on the idea that mediated non-identity between humanity and nature is possible given the fulfilment of specific socio-economic conditions. Those conditions and their implication will receive further elucidation as the argument unfolds in this chapter and the rest of the book.

5 This is particularly true of the line of argument pursued in *Faktizität und Geltung. Beiträge zur Diskurstheorie des Rechts und des demokratischen Rechtsstaats* (*Between the Facts and the Norms*), Frankfurt, Suhrkamp, 1992, pp. 17–19, 108, 215–16, 359, 363, 429, 435, 443, 462, 465, 553.

6 Foucault distinguishes between the *knowledge* that each person gains in the course of their personal investigations and struggles, on the one hand, and the ideology that

there is a *truth* that exists independently of individual experience before which everyone must bow, on the other. Foucault develops this distinction in the course of five
lectures he gave on the juridical forms of truth in Rio de Janeiro in 1973. The themes
in these lectures are published in *Dits et écrits, 1954–1975*, Paris, Gallimard, 2001, pp.
1406–513, as part of the entries for Foucault's conferences, articles, etc., for the year
1974. The lectures are also published in as book as *La Vérité et les formes juridiques
(Truth and Juridical Forms)*, Paris, Gallimard, 1994.

7 The notion of legitimate human essence is closely associated with Marx's concepts of
human emancipation beyond political emancipation, creative labour and species-
being, though Marx is by no means the only one to approach the issue of legitimacy
in this way. Theorists of communicative action, existentialists and even ontologists
usually deploy some notion of anti-liberal post-metaphysical praxis which stems the
divide between the ideal/material and thought/being. Whilst the existentialist attempt
at post-metaphysics is famously summed up in the idea that existence in its plurality,
openness and unpredictability precedes all forms of essence, ontologists argue that
being precedes essence in the form of ontic entities (things). For the existentialists,
freedom is an act rather than a thing, whereas for ontologists being is a horizon rather
than a thing. The existentialist cult of the act nonetheless posits that the essence of
humanity is its ability to choose to be free. The ontological cult of being offers a
phenomenological account of an historicised version of essence: being reveals itself
and withdraws again behind the ontic clouds, waiting for its human shepherds to
prepare being's next dramatic act of self-disclosure. The problems with existential,
ontological and existential ontological views have been amply documented elsewhere
and are not central to the argument in this book.

8 The idea of mimesis offers a fertile way in which one might begin to think about legitimate need in epistemological, i.e. in transcendental, terms which interrogate the
changing socio-historical conditions stipulating that one must already have knowledge of some sort before one can know at all – otherwise one would not know that
new knowledge is knowledge. Mimesis in the sense sketched by the negative dialectics
of critical theory and aesthetics suggests the somewhat paradoxical idea that it is
possible to imitate what does not have an original, i.e. what does not yet exist. To
imitate what does not yet exist in mimetic anticipation of harmony with nature means
to sublimate historically mediated drives seeking uncoerced reconciliation with social
order in an aesthetic form of human communication, i.e. in art. What is communi-
cated does not reproduce the instrumental rationality expressed in most
manifestations of existing forms of reason. On the contrary, it shows why existing
forms of reason are not rational enough. Aesthetic praxis of this kind contains a
rational moment capable of evoking forms of social organisation which attest to the
rationality deficit of a régime of social norms that enforces the sublimation of needs
as the price for individual expression, and imposes commodity production as the
price for survival. Hence the transcendentally legitimate – what is theorised in this
book as epistemological legitimacy as opposed to hegemonic legitimacy – can be
conceived of as that which is not identical to what already exists in institutional terms,
but which exists as knowledge in the form of a possible future norm reconciling
humanity and nature. Without this transcendental dimension, demands for legitimacy can be neutralised as affirmations of already existing individual, group or class
identity. As seen in chapter 2, *such affirmation is the starting point of liberalism, not its
eclipse.* It will be objected: is it really possible to invoke this aesthetic-juridical-
rational idea of legitimacy? The short answer is yes. One can begin by returning the
objection: liberals, liberal democrats and liberal democratic republicans celebrate the

notion of the virtuous citizen-soldier, with all of the bellicose implications that this notion entails. Why might one want to continue to reform this outdated and in any case imperialist notion in an ostensibly humanist and democratic direction? As an alternative, critical theory in conjunction with legal theory offers the possibility of a coming citizen-artist. Gramsci makes a convincing case for the idea that everyone, not just academics and party leaders, is an intellectual, whilst Benjamin shows that modern industrial societies offer everyone, not just students and professional artists, the possibility of an aesthetic education.

9 The attempt to 'naturalise' the dichotomies can be seen as a political concession to the reality that the only way to hold on to the liberal rejection of coerced reconciliation whilst maintaining liberal political institutions is by clinging on to the *a priori* argument in its various guises as the state of nature, veil of ignorance, etc. The radical idealism defended in this book thus distinguishes between the liberal *a priori* argument based on the speculative requirement to think 'as if' one did not know anything about oneself and the world, on the one hand, and a materialist argument about the transcendental bases of knowledge, on the other. Both liberals as well as 'idealist materialists' (or, if one prefers, radical idealists) accept the hermeneutic paradox that knowledge must already exist in order for there to be knowledge, i.e. that knowledge is the condition of knowledge. Radicalising the premises of the paradox points beyond liberalism whilst retaining what liberalisms promises in terms of uncoerced reconciliation but cannot redeem.

10 Heidegger observes that the crisis of liberal humanist civilisation is signalled among other things by Nietzsche's identification of the essence of truth with the will to power. In terms of this particular reading, Nietzsche is not a post-metaphysical ontologist as much as he is the last metaphysician – he carries the implications of a conception of human freedom based on the will to their furthest and most consistent conclusions. See Martin Heidegger, *Nietzsche* I, sixth edition, Stuttgart, Neske, 1961, Part III.

11 To be more precise, this is a lie to the extent that it is only true within the totality of socio-political relations between humanity and nature constituted by legal forms of legitimacy in conjunction with the enforcement of negative forms of liberty. For a political reading of Kafka that deftly manages to avoid the usual truisms of most of the existential readings, see Gilles Deleuze and Félix Guattari, *Kafka : pour une littérature mineure*, Paris, Minuit, 1975, pp. 81–2. Kafka is not primarily saying that the world is absurd or meaningless or hostile to human purpose. He suggests among other things that the *Rechtsstaat* as it currently exists is oppressive in a murderous way which weaves together rules and lies. This dimension of Kafka's work attains a moment of particular brilliance in the penultimate chapter of *The Trial* in K.'s discussion with the pastor in the cathedral about the nature of legality.

12 In the posthumously published *Economy and Society*, and in other writings on political sociology, Weber contrasts legal-rational forms of authority associated with the modern state with traditional and charismatic examples of legitimation of authority characteristic of earlier state forms. Weber admits that legal-rational, traditional and charismatic forms of authority are ideal types which in reality manifest themselves in hybrids such as the volatile legal-rational/charismatic combination characteristic of authoritarian forms of modern populism. See Weber, *Wirtschaft und Gesellschaft* (*Economy and Society*, 1920), Tübingen, Mohr, 1983. For an exposition of Weber which enlists his ideas for the purpose of a critique of state sovereignty, see Schecter, *Sovereign States or Political Communities?*, chapter 2. The argument in that book on the metaphysical bases of sovereignty is developed further in the present book.

13 Niklas Luhmann, *Rechtssoziologie*, Opladen, Westdeutscher Verlag, 1980, and *Das Recht der Gesellschaft*, Frankfurt, Suhrkamp, 1993. The point that there is much more to law than ownership of entities external to human consciousness will be taken up in more detail in the next chapter as part of the project of reformulating philosophical idealism 'in non-idealist terms'. The legal theory informed by a critical idealist account of legitimacy sketched in this book attempts to project beyond the primacy of mind or matter debates in political theory which reach an impasse with Hegel and Marx's critique of Hegelian idealism.

14 See Fernand Braudel, *Civilisation matérielle, économie et capitalisme* (*The Wheels of Commerce*), three volumes, Paris, Colin, 1979, Michel Foucault, *Surveiller et punir* (*Discipline and Punish*), Paris, Gallimard, 1975, E. J. Hobsbawm, *Industry and Empire*, London, Penguin, 1968, and Charles Tilly, *Coercion, Capital and European States, AD 990–1992*, Oxford, Blackwell, 1992.

15 Hence virtually all political parties and movements in opposition to liberalism have demanded more extensive state intervention in the economy, family, education, etc., if only as the precondition of the state being able to 'wither away', as it is sometimes phrased. Yet because there is no legality–legitimacy continuum, attempts to implement those demands often confirm the liberal claim that to reverse the individual terms of the liberal dichotomies is in practice likely to create a paternal society managed by the state.

16 A number of surrealists and situationists argue that the commodification of work on external nature finds its complement in the commodification of key dimensions of human nature such as desire and the political imagination. The situationist critique of the authoritarian turn of the Russian Revolution is broadly consonant with the argument developed here, i.e. that the decommodification of work without the decommodification of human nature is bound to result in a form of bureaucratic tyranny more oppressive than liberal democracy. Hence the project of establishing a legitimate form of law entails disentangling the liberal subterfuge involved in merging issues of legality and legitimacy, in order to re-articulate their relation as one of pluralism, difference and incommensurability of values.

17 Some readers accustomed to Cold War terminology will be surprised to see the term totalitarian applied to liberal democracy and will perhaps ask: was it not rather fascist Italy and Germany and the former USSR and its satellites that offered paradigm examples of the total state? Several factors point to the conclusion that the term itself is a misnomer when applied to those historical examples. With regard to former Eastern Bloc countries such as Poland, one might ask: if the system was so total, why was Solidarity so prominent, i.e. a form of articulate if disparate opposition which is conspicuously absent in Western Europe and North America? How can a system be total and yet suddenly crumble? Did not the use of force in 1956, 1968, 1981 and the extensive deployment of ridiculous propaganda indicate weakness rather than total control? There is much evidence to suggest that these were authoritarian polities marked by the absence of hegemony rather than totalitarian polities in which the totality constituted by external nature and internal nature is regulated by legal-rational forms of domination. The argument in this chapter suggests that liberal democracies are totalitarian to the extent that, in claiming to separate issues of legality and legitimacy in theory whilst quietly merging them in practice, liberal democratic legislation is more effective in stifling dissent and curtailing pluralism than more overtly authoritarian political forms in which a revealed conception of political essence is openly declared to be the source of régime legitimacy. Liberal democracy ushers in more insidious institutions of regulation by legislating into exis-

tence formal and deferred forms of essence that acknowledge only revealed (overtly authoritarian) and informal (marginalised or insignificant) forms of opposition.

18 Consumer choice is and will remain in large measure ideology until humanity's relation with external nature is guided by a transparent dialogue between knowledgeable producers and informed consumers in which both sides decide what is to be produced and how. Such an economy is a prerequisite for an updated public sphere which carries forward the project abandoned by liberalism and ignored by most of its opponents.

19 This is the big question that runs throughout both volumes of the seminal *Democracy in America*, which in many respects remains a theoretical work of genius that has lost none of its relevance for contemporary politics. Yet in his sanguine estimation that the social bases of liberal power could be offset or countered by republican virtue, it is also clear that Tocqueville clearly underestimated the extent to which the evolving power of political parties, monopolistic economic interests and bureaucratic state power challenged liberal assumptions about the bases of political authority.

20 Students of political history with an interest in theory will still find Marx and Gramsci particularly relevant for this topic. See Marx, *The Eighteenth Brumaire of Louis Bonaparte*, in Iring Fetscher (ed.), *Karl Marx und Friedrich Engels. Studienausgabe IV*, Frankfurt, Fischer, 1990 and Gramsci's *Prison Notebook* dedicated to the Italian Risorgimento (Rome, Riuniti, 1979). For the case of England see George Dangerfield, *The Strange Death of Liberal England* (London, Constable, 1936). For an analysis of the different ideas and strategies employed by liberal interests in different national contexts, see Richard Bellamy, *Liberalism and Modern Society*, Cambridge, Polity Press, 1992.

21 On the specific national modalities of this process of colonisation, see Habermas, *The Structural Transformation of the Public Sphere*, and Norbert Elias, *Über den Prozess der Zivilisation. Soziogenetische und psychogenetische Untersuchungen*, II (*The Civilising Process*), Frankfurt, Suhrkamp, 1997. The phenomena analysed by Habermas and Elias take up issues examined by Weber in *Politics as a Vocation*. With the notable exception of Piero Gobetti and Carlo Rosselli in Italy, L. T. Hobhouse in England and other mavericks elsewhere, liberals were unable or unwilling to think seriously about Tocqueville's prescient diagnosis of the likely despotic evolution of democracy in the event of liberal silence on what Arendt refers to as the social question, i.e. on the question of the legal mediation between humanity and external nature and resulting forms of social inequality.

22 See note 1 above.

23 It will be objected by many observers that New Social Movements (NSMs) and communicative action and life-world structures neutralise or offset these tendencies. A critical response to these claims is formulated in *Sovereign States or Political Communities?* and at various points in the present book.

24 Elias, *The Civilising Process*, pp. 457–65. Elias makes this argument with convincing clarity in the closing pages of the last section of that book, entitled 'Outline of a Theory of Civilisation'. For a series of theoretical essays that also support the hypothesis that there is a close relation between forced renunciation on the one hand and aggression and conformity on the other, see Herbert Marcuse and Mihailo Markovic (eds), *Aggression und Anpassung in der Industriegesellschaft* (*Aggressiveness and Conformity in Industrial Society*), Frankfurt, Suhrkamp, 1972. Marcuse's essay in that collection, 'Aggressiveness in Contemporary Industrial Society', is available in English in *Negations*, London, Penguin, 1968. *Negations* also contains his 'Philosophy and Critical Theory' (1937), which anticipates some of the arguments in the present book.

25 One might ask: would one would be happier if the mode of production were to sanction the filling of wine bottles with grape juice in order to baffle the consumer rather
than regulate them?! This is not the real question. The real question is: is it possible
to reconcile the ideology of consumer power with the real implications of private
ownership and control over the means of production, i.e. with the power of capital to
structure the production process and decide what is to be made available for
consumption according to the need for capital to expand?

Chapter 4

Idealism, legality
and reconciliation with external nature

THERE are two threads uniting the various arguments in this book. The first is the thesis that, since the Enlightenment and the discovery of modern forms of rationality, only law that reconciles is legitimate law. Law that does not reconcile regulates, albeit on the basis of a wide variety of disciplinary techniques and subtle epistemological hierarchies that tend to be as different from régime to régime as the ones found in liberal democracy compared to those used by state socialism. The second thesis is that the possibility of legitimate law in this specifically reconciliatory sense is closely bound up with the possibility of non-instrumental and non-reified knowledge. In terms of ideal types, such knowledge results from the mediation of humanity and nature when undertaken according to two identifiable conditions that are specified toward the end of chapter 2. Liberal legal doctrine and traditional idealism unwittingly make these seemingly extreme theses plausible by effectively illustrating two points. They show why every theory of law is also a theory of knowledge and a theory of political agency about the appropriate modes of its implementation, and they demonstrate why the only kinds of modern law that are legitimate are based on knowledge in the form of reason.[1] The problem that liberals and traditional idealists rarely address is that the forms of reason and knowledge they generally subscribe to can only be characterised as instrumental because they are rooted in social conflict, the struggle for survival and the attempt to master nature. They are thus neither legitimate in the sense used here nor are they the only possible forms of knowledge.[2] This appears to be an anti-juridical argument. It is initially made with great clarity and far-reaching implications by Marx and Nietzsche, and is subsequently taken up in detail by Weber, Freud, critical theory, Foucault and many other thinkers and activists. Hence one can compare legitimate law that reconciles humanity and nature on the basis of non-instrumental knowledge, on the one hand, with illegitimate law that regulates humanity and nature on the basis of strategic knowledge stemming from systematic social exploitation, coerced integration and socially mediated fear of nature, on the other. It is certain that there is nothing inevitable about exploitation, coerced integration and institutionalised fear. Each of these three phenomena can be explained in terms of the mediation of humanity and nature, of which there are an unlimited number of possible social forms. It is also certain that variously defined conceptions of knowledge, law and reason are created through human transformation of nature in the labour process and through scientific investigation. The question is not whether knowledge, law and reason exist; it is whether they are practised in a non-instrumental or in a strategic way in any given socio-historical context. The answer depends on how the concept of legitimacy is understood and translated into objective social form by thinking and acting humanity which is in turn acted upon by social form. [3] Although it is demonstrated in the first two chapters that strategic knowledge stems from hierarchy and power and is explainable in terms of diverse regulatory modes of mediation, it has yet to be shown that there can be non-instrumental knowledge within social ensembles that are divided on numerous lines and governed for the most part by strategic and instrumental considerations. Without a convincing account of the existence of such non-instrumental knowledge and how it could become the basis of a new praxis of political legitimacy, there is no real alternative to liberal democracy, save in purely aesthetic and theological terms which are not very credible as alternatives. This chapter attempts to show how a materialist reformulation of idealist philosophy provides the broad outlines of a theory of critical idealism that bears directly upon the organisation of the labour process and the first condition of legitimate law concerning humanity and external nature. Toward the end it will be seen that in the first instance legitimate law requires reconciliation between humanity and external nature, and that this, in turn, requires a form of libertarian socialism whose basic contours can be discerned in G. D. H. Cole's writings on guild socialism.

In an attempt to decipher the functioning of the hegemonic form of governance in the world today and outline an alternative, this book focuses on the legal form of legitimacy underpinning liberal democracies. It is suggested at various junctures in the previous three chapters that the insoluble contradiction at the core of liberal democratic legitimacy is the uneasy fusion of traditional idealist and liberal components in a single account of legitimacy. The idealist component stipulates that the epistemological content of experience and knowledge, as well as the political content of freedom, is conditioned by factors that are internal to and external to the knowing and acting individual subject. These internal and external factors account for the synthetic dimension of knowledge and the objective dimension of law and reason. In idealist philosophy, law and reason are not exclusive anthropological properties of humanity. Instead, their existence is evidence that relations between humanity and nature are mediated by factors that are both subjective and objective. Liberals defend the validity of their version of law as an instance of objective knowledge and authority commanding the obedience of all citizens in terms of the idealist discovery that the external factors of the epistemological synthesis condition experience and knowledge. They are the same for all people rather than merely arbitrary inventions based on subjective fantasy and irrational or private conceptions of need. Since liberals and traditional idealists contrast need with freedom, and the terms of freedom have to be the same for all if citizens are to be governed by law rather than tradition, whim or fiat, the legitimacy of modern secular law is based on the premise that the private sphere of needs and inequality is transcended in the political sphere of freedom and universality. Philosophical idealism underscores the bridges between the capacity of consciousness to synthesise, and the very possibility of there being rational and transcendent as opposed to irrational and despotic legal form. Liberalism accepts this argument about the legal bases of transcendence but twists it slightly. Instead of arguing that transcendence of need and particularity is achieved in the synthetic dialectic of consciousness which for a thinker like Hegel achieves material form in objective institutions and particularly in law, liberals argue in different ways that the private sphere of needs and inequality is transcended in the political sphere of freedom and universality through contract. By enabling competing trading partners involved in horizontal exchange to become citizens in a vertical contract with the state, the institution of the contract is in principle empowered to transform a highly divided society of competing private individuals into a community of equal public citizens. Both traditional idealists and liberals regard modern law to be the key to a form of legitimacy that entails the transcendence of necessity. The matter is complicated by the fact that a traditional idealist such as Kant adopts liberal political positions on property and natural rights which do not easily square with key aspects of his idealism. But this should not distract from the fact that the liberal stress on contract and exchange offers a functionalist, pragmatic and consumerist theory of epistemology and legitimacy, whereas the idealist emphasis on synthetic knowledge offers a far more dialectical and, if substantially reformed, materialist theory of epistemology and legitimacy. Although traditional idealism and liberalism converge to some degree on the question of modern law, one has to be careful not to formulate a materialist critique of both as if they are making identical arguments. If one criticises a particular form of law without distinguishing which aspects of the critique are directed against liberalism and which are directed against idealism, one ends up by schematically linking thinkers such as Kant and Hegel with a defence of private property and liberal democracy, whilst linking thinkers like Marx and Nietzsche with political alternatives to law and the state. This erroneously suggests that there is an easy line of interpretation from traditional idealism to historical materialism, and from bourgeois individualism to radical individualism. This undermines critique at the same time that it enables apology to mix and match idealist and liberal arguments for strategic and ideological purposes.[4] Might one think instead about possible moments of transition from traditional idealism to critical idealism, and from a legal theory of legitimacy (sovereignty) to a theory of legitimate law (reconciliation) that draws on all four of the philosophers just cited as well as other relevant contributions to such a project? What this implies will be explained below before moving on to the main sections of this chapter.

In relation to possible moments of transition, one can distinguish between two closely related and yet distinct constellations of ideas and institutional practices suggested by them. In the liberal democratic constellation sketched in chapters 1 and 3, the condition of legitimate law (I) is reason, whilst the condition of reason is humanity. The condition of humanity is explained in terms of an absolute origin such as God, or by way of a naturalistic explanation of unitary origin such as evolution. Within this first constellation the key question is: how does one prove that reason is one of the essential traits of humanity, i.e. that in some fundamental sense the relation between humanity and reason can be characterised as one of identity? This question leads to a series of reflections on the anthropological characteristics of humankind and the political freedom of citizens in liberal democratic polities. In the second constellation sketched in this and the next chapter of this book, the condition of legitimate law (II) is reconciliation between humanity and nature, whilst the condition of reconciliation here is non-instrumental knowledge and non-instrumental reason. The condition of the latter is explained in terms of alternatives to reified essences and linear conceptions of time positing a single origin and an inexorable trajectory toward a single end. The key question here is: how might it be possible to think in non-speculative and non-escapist terms beyond strategy and reification in a society in which thought is still not free from the necessity of strategic thinking and action? This question leads to a series of parallel reflections. The main tenets of traditional idealism would seem to place its protagonists within the first constellation. Yet the critical idealist theory of reconciliation elaborated in this chapter, like the traditional idealist theory of reason, locates the possibility of knowledge in the mediation of humanity and nature; neither of these makes the liberal move of identifying that possibility as part of the definition of humanity or the natural rights of man. If it is the case that there is no substantive knowledge without mediation in this sense, it is also apparent that all processes of mediation which rely on epistemologies of identity are likely to create institutions of technical coercion mediating between humanity and external nature as well as institutions of hierarchy and control (regulation) adjudicating between humanity and other humanity in zero-sum fashion. A momentary leap ahead explains why this is so, and sets out the major lines of argument in the rest of this chapter.

According to the logic and premises framing action in the first constellation, the question about the relations between humanity, nature and reason is solved by positing an immediate identity between the natural creature humanity and the epistemological tool of reason. In an idealist vein, non-rational nature becomes the means to secure the end of human transcendence of natural necessity without which humanity cannot be free. By aligning itself with law and knowledge against brute mechanical causality and sheer natural indifference to human pain and suffering, humanity is able to create the bases of a free community of equal citizens who are governed by reason rather than fate, destiny or unjustifiable tradition and privilege. In a more markedly liberal vein, however, it is simultaneously alleged that whilst all of humanity is born rational, there are clearly big differences within humanity itself in terms of inclinations and abilities. Some are much more adept in using the natural gift of reason to their advantage, and it is generally asserted that they should be free to do so. They should be allowed to develop their talents, become knowledgeable and productive, and rightfully aspire to positions where they can exercise their abilities in everybody's interest by creating wealth for themselves and job opportunities for others. This understanding legitimises hierarchical forms of social organisation which appear to be most conducive to eliminating necessity and creating abundance, thus offering maximum choice to everyone in a way which rewards talent and capacity for future-oriented innovation. Hierarchical forms of social organisation create conflicts and tensions which need to be policed and monitored, but this is the inevitable and legitimate price to be paid for the enforcement of negative freedom. In contrast to revealed conceptions of essence specifying a 'legitimation who' discussed in chapter 2, formal essence allows the results to speak for themselves without compelling people to speak in the language of an overarching ideology specifying the substantive contents of the good life. The inescapable conclusion is that some of humanity is more rational (and hence more deserving) than the rest. For its advocates, this thesis is borne out by the social reality of economic and personal success, upward mobility and differentiated psychological responses to risk. Too much legal intervention aimed at steering and controlling differential ability to fruitfully employ reason to successful ends trammels individual freedom and chokes the motor of the economy by smothering the incentive to get ahead. In so doing, the excessively interventionist law is said to undermine the bases of its own existence, that is, it forfeits its role as the guarantor of transcendence. The clash between the idealist and liberal democratic components of theory and practice in the first constellation thus comes to a head in a way which points to a moment of possible transition to the second constellation via the radicalisation of idealism. Idealists show that humanity must legislate on the basis of reason and knowledge in order to transcend necessity. But, in practice, liberal democracy ensures that, under the heteronomous rule of capital, humanity enacts strategic forms of law codifying instrumental knowledge and reason. The latter undermine the possibility of transcendence by creating hierarchies that exclude on class lines and coercively integrate by not giving anyone a choice in the matter of being a citizen. To the extent that it ties freedom directly to income, liberal democratic citizenship is structurally incapable of going to the root of class inequality at the same time that it is philosophically and politically committed to exclusively negative forms of liberty. Moreover, state socialism does not provide a solution, as the discussion in chapter 2 demonstrates, whilst social democracy seems to be in an inexorable process of transformation toward neo-liberalism. Hence the shift from the first constellation to the second that retains the centrality of law as the basis of legitimacy and transcendence, and which manages to side-step the state socialist and social democratic impasse, turns on the possibility of formulating a form of critical idealism. This has to be an idealism that is materialist enough not to legislate social and economic institutions which reproduce brute mechanical causality in socialised form as the laws of the market and accumulation, on the one hand, and critical enough not to reproduce natural indifference as bureaucratic indifference and administrative and executive *raison d'état*, on the other. [5]

Traditional idealism in question: post-metaphysics or critical idealism?

It has been seen that, in political systems as diverse as liberal democracy and state socialism, the exercise of power and the implementation of hierarchy are justified as necessary means for the rational organisation of humanity's relations with external nature. Although they champion very different conceptions of freedom, both régimes proclaim that scarcity is a natural fact. The discussion of the subordination of possible non-instrumental knowledge to very questionable notions of efficiency and freedom opens up the possibility to investigate the concept of knowledge by way of ideal types. This can be pursued by retaining the humanity–nature framework which has guided the argument so far, and by focusing on the two primary manifestations of knowledge in all modern industrial societies. In the first instance these are collective forms of knowledge yielded by the mediated unity of humanity and external nature in the labour process. In the second instance they are unique forms of knowledge yielded by the encounter between each individual living in society and human nature which is expressed in the affirmation of values.[6] The theory of reconciliation which emerges from an analysis of the labour process and the articulation of values refers to the mediated relations between humanity and nature, not to the direct reconciliation between the different parts of an estranged humanity divided on class, race, gender, linguistic, etc., lines. The reasons for this approach are briefly introduced in chapter 3 but must be elaborated in a bit more detail now in order to explain why idealism is defended as well as why it needs modification. To bracket out the question of a direct reconciliation between humanity and other humanity is to run against the grain of a great deal of contemporary social theory, much of which dismisses the kind of approach taken here as idealist and therefore metaphysical. Such theory strives instead for a supposedly post-metaphysical understanding of conflict and freedom rooted in human relations with humanity itself as they unfold according to an institutional dynamic which is social and communicative in contrast to what is often thought to be the abstract or speculative character of idealism. What is missing in the idealist account of reason and society, it is claimed, is an adequate grasp of the social interaction and communication that occurs between individuals. Hence post-metaphysical theorists are in broad agreement that 'the social' has a kind of ontological status which unites individuals beyond the thoughts they carry with them in their isolated minds. From the standpoint defended here, which is informed by selected ideas from legal theory throughout, idealism in this chapter and critical theory in the next, the currently dominant social anthropological approaches raise a number of fundamental questions which remain to a large extent unanswered within the terms offered by their sociological and communicative frameworks. For example, if current modes of social interaction and the category of 'the social' are to be preferred on post-metaphysical grounds to idealism, what, exactly, are those grounds?[7] What confers on society the *a priori* or transcendental status that consciousness enjoys in traditional idealism? Is it not clear that Hegel's account of the dialectic between consciousness and institutions is already considerably more sociological and materialist than the term 'idealism' suggests? Why should the crisis of traditional idealism, and its postulate that law is the hallmark of post-metaphysical social form, mark the abrupt end of all credible juridical accounts of freedom as the politically mediated transcendence of necessity and scarcity? Further: how post-idealist is post-idealism in reality if it rejects the centrality of consciousness in the knowledge process but retains a normative commitment to law? What would be the normative basis of law if not some kind of knowledge that is understood by a conscious, epistemological, i.e. idealist subject? What is the political basis of citizenship if it dispenses with an epistemological grounding of law? These and other questions are inadequately addressed if one just assumes that idealism is necessarily abstract, solipsistic and speculative whilst sociology is empirical, interactive and concrete. The introduction to the previous chapter calls the post-idealist character of supposedly post-metaphysical thought into question. It is remarked that if post-idealist means post-legal, few post-metaphysical theorists would not balk at the political implications of their own premises. This becomes clear once it is established that a post-legal polity implies either (1) universally spontaneous harmony, where law is superfluous and legitimacy is ubiquitous, or (2) the direct legitimacy of a class, race or some other unquestionable legitimation source such as the nation. If law is unnecessary in (1), in (2) formal-rational law can be dispensed with by a leadership clique organised on the basis of the rule of a charismatic leader or vanguard. In chapter 3 it is argued that the political problem for mainstream as well as radical post-idealist social and political theory is that universally spontaneous harmony clearly does not exist, whilst instances of extra-legal legitimacy tend to be either dictatorial in power or hopelessly isolated in opposition. The result is an impasse for the mainstream and margin alike. Mainstream theorists are compelled to take up complacent and largely uncritical positions with regard to liberal democracy, whilst radicals end up having to make gestures to a notion of radical alterity on the part of marginal groups and subject positions that cannot effectively challenge liberal democratic hegemony. The bulk of post-idealist social and political thought decries the solipsistic and authoritarian implications of philosophical idealism and wants to detach the law from idealism. Yet chapter 3 shows that some kind of idealism is necessary for conceptualising a form of law that locates the possibility of freedom and transcendence in knowledge against purely procedural, pragmatic, contractual or functionalist accounts of legality; whilst the latter may regulate humanity and nature, they cannot reconcile humanity and nature to any significant degree.[8]

This is a key part of the overall argument in this book which will be elaborated at various junctures in the next two chapters. This chapter concentrates on the link between idealism, law and external nature, and explores that link in relation to two questions. First, chapter 3 establishes that there is a clear connection between idealism and law. The question is: what kinds of law are implied by different kinds of idealism? Second, it also clear that there is a close connection between idealism and reason. This raises the parallel question: what kinds of reason are implied by different kinds of idealism? If the first question is posed with the aim of transcending regulatory forms of law, the second question is posed with the aim of transcending instrumental forms of reason. That is, if it is possible to found a praxis of law that transcends a purely procedural, pragmatic or functionalist institutionalisation of legality, it is also possible to found a praxis of reason that achieves knowledge by transcending forms of instrumental reason which are in large measure restricted to establishing classifications, hierarchies and dichotomies. A central hypothesis to be tested in the discussions to come can be expressed as follows: the key to the political project of transcending regulatory forms of law is closely bound up with the epistemological project of transcending the predominance of instrumental over other forms of reason. Stated in these terms, the link between reconciliation and knowledge in its turn appears in a clearer light. Regulatory law and instrumental reason attest to antagonistic and deeply flawed forms of mediation. Hence a non-antagonistic and non-instrumental mediation between humanity and nature assumes paramount significance in the project to overcome human dependence on nature in such a way that nature, both in the external natural world (chapter 4) and within humanity (chapter 5), is not subjected to institutionalised forms of discipline and control. Laying the groundwork for the thesis to be developed in chapter 5, it is suggested at the end of this chapter that the possible reconciliation of humanity and human nature depends to a large extent on the institutional forms implemented for structuring the mediation between humanity and external nature. It will be explained why a libertarian socialist mediation of the latter is the key to a non-hierarchical and pluralist mediation of the former. The discussion in chapter 3 shows that the depersonalisation of modern forms of liberal democratic legal mediation cannot be confused with the desubjectivisation of legality. On the contrary, that analysis demonstrates that the depersonalisation of legal-rational domination is a key component in the hegemonic strategy for mastery of nature and people which is pursued in societies characterised by systematic economic exploitation and bureaucratic domination by some subjects over others. In order to desubjectivise the law, legal theory has to help disentangle and then re-articulate the relation between legality and legitimacy beyond the reified and residually metaphysical frameworks provided by the liberal dichotomies (formal essence) and direct appeals to humanist legitimacy (revealed essence). The epistemological and political problems of formal essence associated with liberal legality (chapter 1) are not solved by various accounts of revealed essence associated with democratic legitimacy (chapter 2). It is not difficult to see that there are obvious philosophical and political problems with a third possible position which can be identified in negative theological terms as infinitely deferred essence. Advocates of this third position might say that truly legitimate humanity is conceivable only in terms of the trace of what it is not, i.e. only as the negation of that face which presents itself in its flawed manifestations at a particular historical juncture. What humanity happens to be in those moments is merely an oppressed and subjective incarnation of what it might look like when it achieves objectivity in science, perfection in the arts and freedom in politics. Those moments of objectivity, perfection and freedom can be glimpsed in their absence, but never actually arrive. According to infinitely deferred conceptions of essence, law that is based on knowledge is only possible in a free society without power struggles. In other words, social relations must already be economically and politically free in order for there to be freedom of inquiry and law that reveals instead of codifying and concealing. Since one is palpably never free in this absolute sense, law will always be mired in relations of force; legitimacy will inevitably be fraudulent, i.e. hegemonic. Hence even if one can distinguish between legality, hegemony and legitimacy – and one can convincingly argue that the difference between hegemony and legitimacy is law that is based on knowledge – the political conditions that would enable law to be knowledge-based praxis are not attainable.[9] One alternative is pragmatic and affirms quite simply that whatever works or seems to function reasonably well is knowledge and should be accepted as such.[10] The other alternative position to these conceptions of essence which is worked out in these pages attempts to map out a stringent alternative to all three which enters into a critical dialogue with each. The aim is to show that although objectivity, perfection and freedom are indeed in large measure now absent, one can discern two ideal (not *a priori* or speculative) conditions for their realisation. This claim is first made in chapter 2 and is elaborated in chapters 4–5.

A close inspection of mainstream political and social theory which abjures idealism quickly reveals a marked tendency to steer a path between what it construes to be the solipsistic pitfalls of transcendental philosophy (retaining as much of a juridical dimension as is necessary and compatible with various forms of *phronesis*) and the authoritarian implications of direct legitimacy (an unacceptably populist solution to the problem of imagining law beyond formal procedure). This compromise position usually entails adopting some version of the argument that the rationality limited to formal law by philosophical idealists such as Kant is actually embedded in social action, life-world communication and institutional modes of recognition first discerned by Aristotle. Accordingly, it seems to mainstream theorists that rationality which is dispersed in the interstices of the social matrix is shored up in various kinds of deliberative assemblies and life-worlds, thus conferring a significant degree of legitimacy on official public decisions and legalised political authority.[11] It is widely argued that structures of communication and recognition place a non-formal, experiential pressure on legal formality so that the law becomes receptive to legitimate needs not recognised by formal rationality, though without falling prey to the irrational potential inherent in exclusively needs-based and voluntaristic conceptions of politics characteristic of attempts to establish direct legitimacy. Theorists who put great store by civil society or the 'return of the political' rarely want to argue that communication and recognition might become the basis of law itself, which is why they have to resort to the functionalist fiction that the power of private interests driven by instrumental reason is balanced out by the rational claims of social actors driven by communicative reason and republican activism. According to this line of argument, (post-)modern societies are far too complex for there to be any long-term resolution of the legitimacy problems posed by the antagonisms between the particularity of organised private interests and the universality of the claims of citizenship. Legitimacy in such societies is secured instead by the systemic equilibrium between civil law and public law, and, by extension, by the equilibrium reached between instrumental reason and communicative reason. Yet unless one believes in something like Luhmann's notion of *auto-poesis* – an alleged property of social systems which allows them to generate their own autonomous forms of agency without recourse to the ascription of communicative or political capacity of individual citizens – it remains somewhat unclear how and why systemic equilibrium produces and reproduces itself by adjusting to crises and insufficient information without citizen knowledge or direct participation. Rather more unclear is why such systems are not only legal but legitimate. Instead of ushering in the transcendence of necessity and the realisation of a credible praxis of autonomy, force rules over knowledge through legal-rational domination, economic exploitation and commodification. Systems theory takes the liberal idea that modern legality is the necessary and sufficient condition of legitimacy, and then dispenses with anthropological and epistemological attributes of humanity that underpin the idealist component of the liberal argument.[12] Instead of arguing in the vein of much of contemporary theory that practical reason of idealist lineage is flawed in its very conception and needs to be replaced by a dialogic model of communicative reason and pragmatic exchange in order to stem systemic rationality and colonisation of the life-world, this chapter attempts to rethink the relations between idealism, law and transcendence. It will be argued that the theorisation of a feasible reconciliation between humanity and external nature turns on the possibility of formulating a revised form of idealism – what one might call critical idealism or radical idealism as distinct from the traditional idealism of Kant and Hegel – capable of showing how the legislation of the transcendence of socio-politically created scarcity is possible.[13] Once the links between idealism, legality and the institutional bases of reconciliation between humanity and external nature are established in this chapter, it will be possible to conclude the study with a discussion of the links between materialism, legitimacy and reconciliation between humanity and human nature in the next. It is suggested in chapter 1 that the particular way in which traditional idealism conceives of reason and autonomy is indeed flawed, yet idealism does manage to make an immensely important discovery by explaining the links between reason, law, synthetic knowledge and transcendence. These findings have been obscured to a significant extent by the specifically liberal version of democracy that in moments of transition during the course of the Enlightenment, the industrial revolution and thereafter manages to articulate liberal interests in an idealist vocabulary, and which has become dominant in Europe and North America. Legality, reason and law continue to hold the key to a credible account of transcendence as non-reified knowledge and political freedom. This has to be shown whilst also showing that traditional idealism must be substantially revised to make the argument in favour of a new form of idealism convincing. Otherwise this book will have failed to demonstrate that the crisis of idealism does not signify the inevitable triumph of either various humanist conceptions of law and politics rooted in pragmatism and communication, or of post-humanism in its structuralist, post-structuralist, ontological, postmodern, deconstructionist, system-theoretical and various other guises. Despite what the advocates of these theories may say about the political implications of their theoretical positions, they offer ideas that defend liberal democracy or are merely academically subversive of it.

Citizens need not be confronted with the epistemologically impoverished choice between the dignified escapism of traditional idealism or the positivist/functionalist compulsion to embrace existing institutions because they supposedly have their own inherent systemic or communicative rationality. The emancipatory potential of a renewed form of practical reason and non-instrumental thought need not be jettisoned in favour of the various reality principles underlying the theories of communicative reason, *auto-poesis*, overlapping consensus or 'the political'.[14] It is clear on post-metaphysical grounds already found in Hegel that society as an ensemble of social and political institutions provides the form through which individual knowledge of the external world is mediated. What must be explored further is the evident reality that the power relations and ideologies in society are of central importance for ascertaining what specific kinds of rationality and knowledge prevail at any particular historical juncture. Contrary to what is sometimes suggested by the adherents of liberalism, functionalism, systems theory or positivism, the structure of society and the possibility of its modification delineate a key dimension of the knowledge process; social structure and individual conscious experience are mutually conditioning factors. This holds at the theoretical level unless one views the reality of social form as a static reality that either should not be tampered with in the name of objective inquiry, or need not be changed because it is already inherently rational or in the process of becoming rational. It holds at the practical level unless one wants to argue that élites of various kinds – the wealthy, powerful and 'successful' – are more intelligent and rational than everybody else. Traditional idealism comes close to making this point about the structure of society and epistemological conditions by stressing the synthetic dimension of all knowledge, but it stops decidedly short of consistent critique by limiting synthesis to acts of consciousness in Kant (radicalised in an idealist idiom by Husserl and other phenomenologists that remains traditional) or automatic *Aufhebung* in the theory of objective spirit of the mature Hegel (radicalised by historical materialists attempting to elaborate the work of the mature Marx in a scientific idiom that for the most part remains mechanically materialist and as such traditional).[15] This is a materialist reading of debates in philosophy which suggests that, unless crudely formulated, idealism and materialism can be hermetically separated only by caricaturing them both. But this signals neither a possible return to the idealist tradition nor the systems-theoretical or ontological destruction of tradition which actually shores it up.[16] It signifies its demise and the beginning of critical idealism. The traditional idealist theory of synthetic reason is based on the transcendental subjectivity of the rational will. It implies a practice of political freedom grounded in individual or collective autonomy and the individual or collective reappropriation of alienated essence. The problems with these notions of autonomy and essence in their various guises have been explicitly spelled out and will be further elaborated in the next section in order to show why the theory of idealist reason can now cede place to a critical idealist theory of reconciliation.

Idealism, legality and external nature

Since non-essentialist form is an indispensable dimension of post-metaphysical knowledge, and form in this context is socio-political and in no sense limited to consciousness, one can begin to think about which social forms are likely to produce instrumental and non-instrumental kinds of knowledge. The first step is to deconstruct the idealism/materialism impasse which juxtaposes humanity and nature in a relation of antagonism favouring instrumental over mimetic reason as well as hegemonic over epistemological legitimacy. What is meant by mimetic reason and mimetic materialism will become clearer in the final chapter. For now it might be noted that to reconcile humanity and nature is to transcend instrumental reason in forms of knowledge that are not rooted in an historical experience of nature as a threat which implies socio-economic relations of hierarchy and control. This understanding corresponds to the conception that nature is a danger to humanity that must be dealt with through efficient administrative techniques and ideological incentive systems based on socially constructed ideas of merit, freedom and reward. There is no continuity between legality (idealist universality) and legitimacy (materialist need in its unlimited particularity) or between external nature and human nature. This indicates that non-instrumental and mimetic idealist materialism has to recognise the absence of that continuum without feeling compelled to subordinate the human nature dimension of the knowledge process to the external nature dimension for the purpose of survival. Political utopia is an epistemological utopia of transcendence, but transcendence is not in the first instance an anthropological issue about the best possible form of humanism, or, what amounts to more or less the same thing in different guise, the most fashionable form of anti-humanism embracing structure, function, system, linguistic sign, being, etc. The possibility of transcendence is bound up with the possibility that reason and law, as the chief forms of mediation between nature and humanity, can assume institutional forms which know and legislate in ways that point beyond the idealism/materialism and subject/object schisms. This is the condition for legality to be legitimate rather than a mode of legitimation.

To argue against continuity in the aforementioned sense implies that, although related, the legal modes of exclusion from the fruits of the labour process secured through private property and the division of labour are not the same as the modes of symbolic violence which are invoked in the production of discourses of social unity and legitimacy. Each of these dimensions in the dynamic of forced separation and coerced unity bear upon discrete moments in the relationship between humanity and nature. If it were not so, this would be the final chapter of the book. In other words, it is clear that in comparison with state socialist societies, for example, the fusion of issues concerned with legality and legitimacy is achieved in an almost surreptitious way in liberal democracies which champion the idea of state neutrality and impartiality with regard to competing conceptions of what the good life should be. This surreptitiousness begins as an epistemological problem concerning formal versus substantive knowledge. It is an epistemological problem which quickly turns out to be a juridical problem as well as a political problem: the state of emergency discussed by Schmitt and Benjamin in the 1930s and 1940s, and taken up again by Derrida, Agamben and others in the 1990s and today, is nothing other than a legitimation crisis.[17] The virulent character of the crisis is that it is seems to be permanent and insoluble, since for obvious reasons there is no feasible or desirable political way back to more personal forms of authority typical of traditional and authoritarian forms of rule, just as there is no way back to metaphysical epistemologies which uncover essential knowledge beyond the formal mediations of post-metaphysical reason. What does emerge is that there is a complexly mediated link between the post-metaphysical injunction against more than formal knowledge, on the one hand, and the particular forms of domination in liberal democracies with no essentialist legitimation subjects, on the other. A careful analysis of these implications offers the key to understanding why (1) negative liberty is the only possible liberty in those democracies, (2) liberal democratic justice is redistributive at best and usually punitive, and why (3) the liberal democratic state is for the most part a bureaucratic tax collector for whom the crucial question is income, and is not a site of political community or credible instance of legitimate authority. The legal implications of (3) may be unpalatable to the more naïve liberals, democrats and pragmatists, but the point nonetheless goes to the heart of the matter. Liberal democracies do indeed manage to dispense with personalised forms of domination politically at the same time that they dispense with metaphysical essentialism epistemologically. But there is much evidence to suggest that formalised knowledge in advanced industrial societies is to a significant extent strategic knowledge which is chained to the reified categories produced by thinking that is deeply implicated in and decidedly not above the social conflict and oppression in those societies. As the work of Nietzsche, Weber, Adorno, Bourdieu, Foucault, certain feminists and a wide range of activists amply demonstrates, there is more than a little residual will to and reverence of power in formal knowledge that translates into the exercise of merely ideological forms of legitimacy in regulatory polities with formal structures of law and political representation. A deep fear of nature as well as the will to mastery embedded in formal knowledge is particularly transparent in the reasoning of liberal thinkers broadly affiliated with traditional idealism such as Kant. But it will presently be shown that the radicalisation of traditional idealism offers unique possibilities to move beyond antagonistic knowledge and regulatory politics. This is because idealism is centrally concerned with two mediating phenomena that for centuries have been enmeshed in antagonistic knowledge and regulatory politics but which also point beyond antagonism, regulation and liberalism: law and reason. One must also bear in mind that there are a number of different ways of radicalising idealism. Hence the possibility of redeeming what traditional idealism promises turns decisively on the way in which the project of radicalising idealism is pursued. [18]

The permanent legitimation crisis of liberal democracies compels them to produce ideologies of unity constructed around national heritage or national interest as well as discourses of economic growth and consumer spending power. Whilst the ideologies of unity help marginalise the creation of independent aesthetic-epistemological values, discourses of economic growth and spending power reinforce centripetal social pressures. Although the organised social interests driving liberal democracy were able to win the Cold War by providing Western European and North American citizens with levels of economic growth and consumer choice that the communist countries could not hope to match whilst trying to be competitive in the arms race, neither liberal democratic nor state socialist régimes are legitimate in the epistemological sense elaborated in this book.[19] This confirms the thesis that, short of a reconciled relation in the humanity–nature question, there is no system of legality that is not also a system of legitimacy with very definite legislation on the good life, the best ways to satisfy need in all its diversity and potential creativity, how freedom is to be exercised, etc. These are all issues which are supposedly matters of individual choice in liberal democracies, but which are actually decided upon by a tiny number of professional politicians at the level of state in parliamentary and regional-level legislation. Since the liberal democratic state is first and foremost a tax collector that needs revenue to finance its operations, legislation is drafted under conditions which ensure that little or nothing is passed that will discourage the business interests which will consent to paying only after a certain margin of profit has been gained. Otherwise the tax rate will be rejected as prohibitively high by conservative élites in industry, the media and academia, and decried as inimical to everyone's freedom. This specious claim is then likely to be followed by the predictable chorus of voices from a variety of pro-private industry spokespeople against excessive state intervention in the economy. Scenarios of this kind are increasingly common in the post-Keynesian world of global capitalism. It is now considered a commonplace that (1) over-taxing prevents investment, and that (2) without investment there is no growth in the economy, such that (3) without economic growth there is neither enough job creation nor sufficient consumer power to legitimise governments.[20] It has already been seen that state socialism proposes to overcome the inequalities in liberal democracies by solving the humanity–external nature question with a 'people's democracy' that vaunts its superiority by being legitimate not only in formal–legal but in substantive-popular terms. This turns out to be a Pyrrhic victory over the liberal dichotomies. Little is done for the project of moving beyond liberalism if this means embracing the premature union of theory and practice characteristic of state socialism and other instances of coerced integration.

But under what conditions would unity not be premature? In the case of state socialism unity is coerced unity (to say nothing of other forms of coerced unity such as those found in fascism); far less clear, and far more important for a non-authoritarian alternative to liberal democracy, is ascertaining under what conditions mediated unity and reconciliation would not be coerced. Liberalism wins the day over all brands of revealed essence until this can be done, despite all the problems with it that have been discussed in the preceding chapters. It is asserted above that, short of a reconciled relation in the humanity–nature question, there is no system of legality that is not also a system of legitimacy. This argument can be rephrased as follows: short of a reconciled relation in the humanity–nature question, there is no model of autonomy (legality, theory) that does not also bring in its wake a model of totality (legitimacy, practice).[21] Whilst this was perhaps not necessarily the case prior to the industrial revolution, critical social theory from Weber to Foucault suggests that the complexity of legal systems in industrial societies is symptomatic of the intertwining of issues related to legality and autonomy with issues related to legitimacy and totality. Stating the matter in this way would seem to suggest an almost insurmountable impasse for everyone except perhaps negative theologians and anarchists. Theologians and other theorists of deferred essence can argue that autonomy/legality without totality/legitimacy is possible only if domination and power have *already* been renounced by beings more perfect than humans in a world more perfect than this one. Reconciliation is posited as the indispensable premise of reconciliation itself. Anarchists could argue that since every form of state represents an instance of coerced reconciliation, no forms of state or law will meet anarchist criteria of freedom. Yet theological contemplation (theory) and anarchist direct action (praxis) tend to reproduce the terms of the liberal dichotomies anew in radicalised form. The communicative action approach, which views a possible solution in separating the instrumental moments of domination of external nature from the cognitive moments of agreement, has already been diagnosed as offering only a very compromised form of reconciliation. Communicative action theory accommodates a decidedly unreconciled set of legal relations in economic and epistemological questions concerning humanity and external nature in the name of systemic differentiation and environmental complexity. This concession to instrumental reason casts considerable doubt on the degree of real reconciliation between the different representatives of humanity that is actually achieved in existing forms of political compromise. Moreover, if the theological position is a radicalised version of the liberal separation of theory/practice, and the anarchist position is a radicalised version of Marx's dictum in the *Theses on Feuerbach* (1845) that philosophers have only interpreted the world whereas the point is to change it, new social movements and communicative action perspectives tend to hover inconclusively between reformist participation in existing institutions and refusal to accept the rules of the game as it is now played.[22]

The attempt to theorise the steps in a transition from traditional idealism to a qualified union of critical idealism and legal theory is an attempt to move beyond these impasse positions. However extreme the anarchist and theological positions may sound, there is a core of truth contained in them that is not at all precious, but simply epistemologically rigorous. That is that either power, domination and exploitation are not compatible with knowledge, or knowledge is in large measure a tool in the struggle for power, domination and exploitation. In the last of the aphorisms contained in *Minima Moralia* (1951) Adorno refers to this kind of reflection as thinking from the messianic perspective of redemption.[23] The argument developed here is that rescuing redemptive thought from political oblivion requires an epistemological perspective on legitimacy framed in terms of legal form. It is an attempt to rethink the concepts of (1) legality and autonomy in relation to the concepts of (2) legitimacy and totality in such a way that the forms of transcendence implied by the former are not hopelessly compromised by the totalitarian and authoritarian forms of sociopolitical organisation demanded by the latter in liberal democracy and its largely failed alternatives. The first step in the argument entails asking why the forms of legal transcendence of mechanical causality and natural necessity formulated by most traditional idealists tend to legitimise potentially authoritarian and totalitarian forms of socio-political organisation. Traditional idealism offers a model of autonomy that projects the ideal of transcendence toward the inner reaches of the subject in a kind of self-defence strategy directed against the vagaries of nature. This leads to the implementation of forms of law and a praxis of freedom predicated on the construction of a taboo around issues of need rather than the satisfaction of need, and a rigid dichotomisation between external nature and human nature which tends to subjugate thinking and consciousness to a decidedly instrumental dimension. The institutionalisation of instrumental reason and regulatory law in the economy and polity, in its turn, tends to reach well beyond the domains of property relations and government policy.[24] It is nonetheless traditional idealism that offers the most promising point of departure for a radicalisation of critical thought with epistemological and legal implications which indicate paths beyond instrumental reason, regulation and hegemony. The key issue, then, is to see if juridical transcendence can be thought in harmony with nature, instead of as a bulwark against nature that is constantly at pains to repress and expunge nature from thinking by regulating the nature of thought.

Toward a theory of critical idealism

Within the terms of traditional idealist thought prior to Hegel, the autonomy of reason is unthinkable without the corresponding notion of a unified transcendental subject, which is sometimes referred to as the transcendental ego.[25] In various ways, depending on the position adopted by the idealist thinker in question, it is the unity of the transcendental subject that allows each person to make rational, synthetic judgements that cannot be directly derived from individual experience, but which are prior to experience itself. For Kant, the very possibility of these synthetic judgements suggests that reason mediates between subjective individual experience and the objective world of objects and nature. Reason is the medium through which the subject is both separated from and connected to the world. This simple statement is of the greatest consequence for the preceding discussion as well as what follows, since it is apparent that, once materialised in liberal democratic institutions, separation means exclusion and exploitation through private property and the division of labour, whilst connection is largely synonymous with the political management of coerced integration: there is an idealist way of interpreting the present that is materialist and sociological. It follows that Hegel's dictum that 'the real is rational and the rational is real' need not be interpreted as a hollow defence of socio-political reality as it happens to be structured at any particular stage in world history. It can be interpreted instead as an argument about the knowable contours of a changing reality in which subjectivity and objectivity are mediated through a third term, reason, which in turn assumes objective form in institutions which are codified in law.[26] Hegelian idealism regards that rational mediation to consist in movement, contradiction, negation, i.e. as an unfolding process with an underlying logic and identifiable tendencies in state and civil society. One might accept this notion of developmental tendencies without necessarily embracing a fatalistic or teleological account of history. There is a great deal at stake in ascertaining the particular modalities through which this relation of separation and connection is conceived of and practised: the complete absorption of the object by the subject is as epistemologically and politically problematic as the ascription of absolute otherness by the subject to the object.[27] For Kantians it is the rational mediation of the subjective and objective that allows humans to have scientific knowledge of phenomena as well as freedom of the will. On this account, all objectivity is dialectically mediated by subjectivity: whilst thought without objects of thinking amounts to little more than solipsistic speculation, objects without thinking subjects are only possible in a positivistic dream world of specious objectivity. From Kant's perspective, that dream world came to an end as a consequence of the insoluble dilemmas of rationalism which manifest themselves in the philosophies of Descartes, Spinoza, Leibniz and Wolff. Since no direct knowledge of objects is possible – either through empiricist experience or through rationalist metaphysics – Kant attributes a synthetic function to thinking. Rational individual experience in humanity comes into contact with reason in the external world in a process which is limited by the authority of reason to conceptual knowledge of phenomenal form which never penetrates to the noumenal content of the things in themselves. This synthetic function of reason organises and regulates the interplay between sensible intuition (experience) and the categories humans employ to order the phenomena they observe (understanding). Reason gathers the chaotic and disordered impressions of experience in time and space, and brings them together in the form of an ordered unity. That ordered unity is constructed by a transcendental ego; the ego assures the recipient of sense impressions that those impressions are in fact his or hers. The ego accompanies the subject through all of the mental actions that order experience in accordance with the laws of reason. Knowledge and freedom are achieved by thinking and acting according to those laws. In other words, there is no experience without reason, yet reason (universal) and experience (particular) are nonetheless separate, just as knowing and thinking are separate for a philosopher like Kant.[28] Within this framework, the universality of reason is the basis of its law-giving authority. Freedom and autonomy of individual subjects consists in transcending the particularity of arbitrary individual experience in order to act in accordance with the dictates of internally consistent, non-contradictory principles derived from reason and practised as law.

It has been frequently observed that idealism as originally conceived seems to purchase autonomy from sensory chaos and political disorder at the cost of blocking out particular experience and historically mediated local knowledge. From a Kantian perspective, stubborn refusal to perform this blocking out function in the pursuit of the universal content of particular experience results in the forfeiting of the validity of knowledge. He implies that knowledge is not valid knowledge unless it can be formulated in terms which are accountable to the court of reason itself and nothing outside of it. In order for reason in humanity to be reflexively united with reason in reality, reason must restrict its operations to categorising and organising functions which are identical for all knowing subjects, lest it become irrational by straying into metaphysical or positivist deviations from the non-arbitrary rules of thinking. Those rules stipulate that thinking is performed by a unified subject that is insulated from the threats of the external world and the unstable randomness of particular experience. Insulation is guaranteed by the protective shell of consciousness within which reason is able to stabilise its operations against subjective fantasy, on the one hand, and external chaos, on the other. Subjective fantasy labours under the spell of individual desires and projections which become fixated on the quest for happiness, direct knowledge and other kinds of unobtainable satisfaction and certainty. External chaos presents itself in two guises. In the first instance it presents itself as the uncontrollable flux of senseless impressions that remain senseless until ordered by reason. In the second instance, external chaos appears as mechanical natural causality indifferent to human purpose. Mechanical causality seems to impose a heteronomous order of objective determination which serves to subject humanity to the whims of the elements and other forces outside of the realm of human control. Conventional idealist reason masters these problems by bringing order to the vagaries of sensory apperception, and by defining universally valid rules of conduct that dictate the conditions for overcoming dependence on internal and external factors. As seen in previous chapters, these conditions can be satisfied only by excluding whims and other irrational impulses connected with extra-legal legitimacy, and through individual economic self-sufficiency. Once this occurs, humanity can transcend nature's otherness, obtain valid scientific knowledge of the phenomenal world as well as exercise political freedom over impulse and unpredictability.

The great ambiguity in this way of thinking the humanity–nature relation is that it is potentially emancipatory insofar as it raises the Enlightenment possibility of allowing reason to stand in for fear and faith, and as such to create a world in which humans might progress and flourish beyond dumb dependence. It is thinking that allows individual subjects to explore the reality of separateness and connectedness beyond solipsistic contemplation or the narcissistic retreat inward to individual and group identity. However, in its original formulation in the writings of Kant, Hegel and the other founders of modern idealism, it is thinking that conceives of autonomy as self-defence, mastery and classification. The unity of transcendental subjectivity is constructed as a tactic for grounding the rigid dichotomisation between internal nature (consciousness) and external nature (the world). [29] Hegel manages to overcome the dichotomies of traditional idealist thought, though not by dispensing with the unitary nature of the knowing subject, but rather by identifying the principles of subjectivity with the structure of reality itself. Idealist thought prior to Hegel establishes the epistemological principle that all objectivity is mediated by subjectivity, whilst Hegel demonstrates that the converse is also true: all subjectivity is mediated by objectivity, where the term objectivity refers to the ideas that have assumed objective form in social and political institutions. This is particularly relevant to Hegel's theory of objective spirit and the idea that the reason why social and political change occurs is mind, just as social and political institutions are the key to understanding why mind is in a constant process of change and achieving an increasingly perfect understanding of reality. Hegel takes traditional idealism to a point of no return in that he dispenses with the Kantian distinction between thinking and knowing by uniting these individual terms in an overarching theory of experience which demonstrates the sensuous dimension of thinking and the intellectual dimension of experience. Yet by identifying the principle of subjective experience with reality itself, and positing an inexorable march from sense certainty to absolute knowledge, Hegel abandons his own insight into the reality of contradiction and negation within an antagonistic social world. To this extent he becomes an apologist of thinking as mastery. This is why mimetic materialist thought has to break with the attempt to simply 'stand Hegel on his feet' in the manner undertaken by many of Marx's dogmatically materialist followers. This attempt does not subvert thinking as mastery as much as it re-articulates it in an ostensibly materialist idiom.[30]

The possibility of realising the emancipatory potential of idealist thought – the possibility that humanity might be able to realise a non-antagonistic form of unity with human and external nature mediated by the practical-cognitive exercise of non-instrumental reason whilst shedding the colonising and reifying tendencies inherent in a conception of reason rooted in mastery – turns on the possibility of radicalising a key feature of the idealist project which is at the centre of Kant's philosophy. This is the project of attempting to think independently from any one of many possible first principles such as the cogito or the monad, or hypothetically unconditioned origins. It is to reflect instead on the conditions of possible experience in opposition to the speculative primacy of mind or matter defended by rationalists and empiricists. The point is thus not to abandon idealism for communicative action or some other ostensibly more practical social theory which actually turns out to be a very inconclusive break with idealism, but to radicalise idealism by compelling it to modify its relationship with its own premises. Insofar as idealism poses the question of the conditions of possible experience it is not reducible to traditional rationalism, and, more important, it is subversive of the attempt in Kantian idealism to distinguish rational thinking from non-rational experience. That is because when one reflects on the conditions of experience, rather than the unmediated primacy of mind or matter, it becomes clear that included in the conditions of experience are socio-political factors related to humanity's relation with external nature – what Marx refers to as political economy – as well as somatic and sensuous moments related to human nature signalled by Adorno, i.e. impulses that are not identical to thought, though not necessarily inimical to thinking once thinking has been reconfigured outside of the terms staked out by an autonomous subject. The price to be paid for this kind of individual autonomy is prohibitive: the subject is limited to the exercise of instrumental knowledge and the negative freedom of non-infringement. Idealism prior to Hegel undermines itself to a significant extent by positing analytical distinctions between knowing, thinking and experience. This is one of many distinctions that Kantian philosophy cannot sustain at decisive moments of exposition and which evidently collapse in the process of application.[31] The collapse of these distinctions marks the end of traditional idealism, whilst leaving open the question what knowing, thinking and legitimacy might some day be like under different socio-political conditions in which sensuous and somatic moments of thought are not banned from thinking for the sake of the construction of the self-legislating unitary thinker imagined in isolation from the world and other thinkers in a spirit of antagonistic self-defence.

The end of traditional idealism signifies the end of traditional legal anthropology, thus raising several epistemological-political possibilities. The first is refusal to acknowledge the reasons for the historical demise of the cognitive integrity of the unitary thinker and the demise of traditional idealism, whilst retaining forms of law and political institutions that suggest their continued good health. This is in large measure how things stand at present. This work of denial can be attempted by rejigging anthropological ascriptions in one or more humanistic directions, usually in a communicative-pragmatic one, or by adopting a systems-theoretical approach by saying that one can have perfectly well functioning systems of legal legitimacy without the traditional legal subject or the forms of knowledge corresponding to it. This is fine, it is implied, as long as social relations are relatively stable, since no one really seems to notice the disappearance of that subject anyway apart from a few forlorn republicans. The second possibility is to seek an alternative in 'the multitude' or some other immediately legitimate collective subject armed with various forms of anti-juridical knowledge gathered in the daily experience of being oppressed by the law. A third possible response to the end of traditional idealism, which has been largely overlooked in social and political thought since the arrival of postmodernism and the 'linguistic turn' discussed in the introduction to this book, begins with the formulation of a critical idealism in opposition to traditional idealism and supposedly post-metaphysical communicative reason. The theory of critical idealism incipiently emerging from the discussion in this chapter indicates that reason ceases to be instrumental when it is released from the task of protecting the autonomous subject from other autonomous subjects as well as from nature. In order for reason to be relieved of this role, however, conventional notions of knowledge, autonomy and especially legitimacy have to be legally reformed. In order for reason to be freed from instrumentality, the autonomous subject of cognition has to be freed from the threat of other autonomous subjects in non-subjective guise, i.e. as untamed nature resurrected in the socialised forms of scarcity, aggression and indifference. The way beyond the unitary juridical subject, which is a way beyond thinking in which thought is reduced to mastery and regulation, points to the reconciliation of collective humanity with external nature. To argue in this vein is to argue the Kantian epistemological point that knowledge and experience are conditioned, by way of the political point that those conditions are never simply 'given' by human anthropology or the march of history but must be created and recreated. The bourgeois public sphere is gone and cannot be recreated, but the political project of infusing the law with epistemological content retains its cognitive validity and demands the creation of socio-political institutions that make the transcendence of necessity, which was once possible for the members of the bourgeois public sphere, a reality for the entire electorate. In accordance with the critique of metaphysics set out in the *Critique of Pure Reason* and the *Critique of Practical Reason*, rational thought is thinking that liberates humanity from the dependence on faith and the darkness of superstition, but only on condition that the mind is able to recognise and apprehend the products of thought as its own productions.[32] Hegel takes the argument a step further by demonstrating that, just as thought involves the cerebral as well as the material, production is both intellectual and sensuous. He understands production in terms of a continual process in which the alienated forms of mental work are re-appropriated by a collective thinking subject that is able to reappropriate the various stages of its thinking because all of reality is produced as sensuous and intellectual thought. The way to move beyond Hegel and idealism is not to simply reverse this tendency and argue that all of reality is material that is ripe for collective reappropriation by a collective acting subject, since reappropria-tion is itself an instrumental moment in a mediation process that does not so much mediate as assimilate. The key is to move beyond a mode of subjectivity that reappropriates and assimilates.

The form of critical idealism developed here acknowledges the historical demise of the cognitive integrity of the unitary thinker by showing that an autonomous thinker is not really autonomous in the first place. The cognitive integrity of this version of the unitary thinker is predicated on institutionalised forms of sensuous renunciation as well as a subsequently obsolete bourgeois model of economic independence which in practice, as explained in chapter 3, actually undermine legal autonomy by creating entrenched forms of real dependence on commodity production and market forces. In accordance with the developmental tendencies of market economies, these forces acquire a quasi-law-like autonomy and dynamic of their own which operate indifferently of considerations of human creativity in labour and legitimate human need. Undermining legal autonomy, in its turn, sabotages cognition rooted in experi-ence, i.e. it sabotages thought, since relations of socio-political dependence reduce thinking to strategy and instrumental calculation. Through instrumen-tal thinking of this kind humanity forfeits the chance to transcend need and dependence by shackling thought to the individualistic logic of self-preserva-tion. This may raise the standard of living for some in accordance with the legitimising ideology of consumer power and choice, but it creates a chasm between individual producers and the objects they collectively produce.[33] How might that chasm be closed without resorting to collectivist state socialist reap-propriation or commodified, individualist reappropriation, i.e. without resorting to institutional mechanisms of separation and connection which oppress individuals whilst yielding largely strategic forms of knowledge and reason?[34]

In chapter 2 it is shown that the first condition of legitimate law is reconcili-ation between humanity and external nature, and it is seen in this chapter that reconciliation implies a qualitatively different *legislation of mediation* from the individualist and collectivist *legislations of appropriation* institutionalised to very different degrees in liberal democracy, social democracy and state socialism. Legislations of appropriation are tied to individualist and collectivist notions of autonomy and sovereignty which have their origins in the unstable fusion of liberal and traditional idealist accounts of legitimacy at the core of liberal democracy. The possibility of legislations of mediation opened up by a theory of critical idealism anticipates a reconciliation of humanity and external nature based on a dialogue between producers and consumers roughly along the lines of the libertarian model of socialism proposed by G. D. H. Cole in three very original, and at the time of their writing influential, works published between 1917 and 1920: *Self-government in Industry, Guild Socialism Re-stated* and *Social Theory*.[35] In contrast to the private appropriation of collectively produced wealth characteristic of liberal democratic (and to a lesser extent of social democratic) systems of ownership, and in contrast to the collectivised versions thereof, the guild socialist alternative does not leave the satisfaction of need to the play of calculated risks on the part of entrepreneurs, share-holders or largely unaccountable state planners. Acute problems related to inefficiency and lack of responsiveness to consumer demand in state socialism have led to the collapse of that particular model of humanity and external nature relations, as well as the widespread proclamation of the end of history, not to mention the remarkably unimaginative conclusion that there is only one way to organise a modern economy and aggregate the preferences of sophisticated consumers.[36] In a form of libertarianism based on the guild socialist alternative, the satisfaction of need facilitating the possible transcendence of fabricated necessity is accomplished on the basis of a constant exchange of information between producers working together in non-hierarchically structured guilds, and consumers assembled in consumer councils. It is important to stress the difference between long-standing trade union practice, on the one hand, and what guilds once were in places like England and Germany and what they might become if reformed on the basis of a new philosophy of political legitimacy, on the other. With the exception of some syndicalist and anarcho-syndicalist unions in Spain and other countries, unions have generally defended the interests of workers in specific trades to protect social gains concerning wages, hours, and benefits, whilst accepting the principles of wage labour and private ownership of the means of production. That is, the members of unions have entrusted the union leadership with the task of protecting the interests of workers practising a given trade against attempts on the part of management to lower wages, and against attempts to damage union bargaining power through an excessive influx of more vulnerable (usually female and immigrant) wage earners. Though unions sometimes combine their efforts in federations, union strategy has remained for the most part defensive and sectional. Rather than defending the bargaining power and integrity of individual trades, guilds co-ordinated the efforts of workers in a number of different trades, all of which were involved in the production process. Insofar they resembled the *bourses du travail* (labour exchanges) first organised on a large scale in a modern industrial economy by Fernand Pelloutier (1867–1901) in France at the end of the nineteenth century. Far from protecting the position of workers in a single trade, under Pelloutier's leadership the labour exchange performed an educational and technical training function for workers across trades whose combined efforts were needed for the life of a given branch of industry. In addition, it helped workers from different industries by providing information and advice on educational, health and housing issues. Like the French labour exchange, the guild challenges the division of labour and the fragmentation of the working class into different trades by organising workers on an industry-wide basis. Whilst anarcho-syndicalists agitated for similar organisational structures, Cole also envisages a radically democratic organisational structure for consumers, as well as networks of mediation between production and consumption which call into question the separation of mental and manual work as well as the split between active workers and passive consumers and citizens. Cole reasons that every worker is also a consumer, though working and consuming are discrete activities in the life of each person. This is the reason why production and consumption require their own representational structures with an equal legal status which effectively deconstructs the monolithic state and the notion of all-encompassing citizenship. It is also the reason why there is no immediate identity between producer and citizen in libertarian socialism. It is not that work, consumption and citizenship are to be categorically divided. Libertarian socialism rejects the neat separation of the private producer and public citizen characteristic of liberal legal systems. It also rejects the fusion of those figures in the theory and practice of state socialism. In both of these sovereign systems, one is born into citizenship whether one likes it or not, and then faced with the reality that citizens are subjected to a series of unwritten laws that they have had no hand in drafting. By contrast, pluralist citizenship is an active process of reconciling (not separating or absorbing) production for need with the desideratum of legislating creative modes of production. Cole's ideas on how this can be accomplished are outlined below.[37]

Communes at all levels composed of guild members, consumer council members and non-partisan citizens adjudicate guild–council conflicts in a way that respects the view articulated by each standpoint. Consumer needs are aggregated on personal, household and public levels, taking account of and harmonising individual preferences with efficiency criteria concerning collective provision and economies of scale. This model implies a legislation of mediation between humanity and external nature in which the consumer is truly empowered beyond the ideological glorification of work in the commodity economy and in paternalist state planning systems. Need is neither manipulated nor decided upon from above, bur rather satisfied in accordance with the diversity of need as it is expressed along individual, regional, national and international lines. In contrast to the legal principles governing liberal democratic and socialist versions of state sovereignty, the commune promotes dialogue and compromise between producers and consumers, i.e. between people who would otherwise not meet at all except in highly random and passive instances of shuffling by one another in privately owned shops or waiting together in queues. A couple of brief examples illustrate the central point that communication between the different parts of an estranged humanity is an issue which really concerns the social and political institutions mediating humanity and external nature, rather than any direct rapprochement between citizens pursued through dialogue or some other notion of pragmatic exchange, however broadly conceived. A legal revolution of property relations and the division of labour is thus required in order to introduce forms of mediation that do not destroy the environment whilst setting up mechanisms of exclusion and coerced integration. This revolution is the only rigorous response to the futility of patching up the cognitive integrity of the traditional legal subject with vari-ously conceived attempts to balance Kantian and Aristotelian positions in what is usually construed as a dilemma between liberal legal metaphysics and anti-metaphysical democratic humanism.

Take the example of pollution. If a factory pollutes the air and the quality of life of the local population within the private property régime, the residents are likely to be forced to choose between poisonous air and jobs. The same popula-tion in a state socialist setting has to accept that the general will, established by the party and its planners, has decided that everyone's real interests are best served if production is carried on regardless of the consequences for the human and natural environment. In Cole's libertarian socialism, the interest of the producers to carry on earning a living and the need of the population to breathe clean air are negotiated in a dialogue between guilds and consumer councils mediated by the citizens of the communes, keeping in mind, however, that it is entirely possible for a person to be a producer, consumer, citizen, or all three. The classic problem of who decides when dialogue leads to a legislative impasse takes on a completely different complexion as soon as production is no longer fuelled by calculations of immediate profitability or the long-term interests of the competing factions within the planning bureaucracy. Once workers are producing directly for consumers rather than for private capital or the state, the mad rush to meet artificially imposed deadlines ceases to be the major looming background factor in collective decision-making. The federation of communes is in the position to enact a qualitatively different set of compromises from those ordinarily reached by juxtaposing the power of private and state capital with concern for the local environment. Take the issue of consumer choice: in a system where consumer demand is consciously aggregated in accordance with an ongoing discussion of how to satisfy individual needs (in areas like food, clothing, housing and culture, all of which also have a marked collective dimension) and collective needs (in areas like education, transport, health and sport, all of which also have a salient individual dimension), consumers can actively decide on what they wear, the houses they would like to live in, the kind of education that best suits the talents they would like to pursue and the deficits they hope to change. By discarding the plan versus market straitjacket and providing every consumer with a *political* voice through council representation at the individual and collective levels, control and choice are decoupled from income. Decoupling control and choice from private income as well as from one's political status in the communist party marks the beginning of a transition from *de facto* heteronomy dressed up as autonomy (the problem common to all attempts at mastery which backfire in the end), to a genuine form of pluralism in tastes, abilities, needs and values. Without wishing to push the comparison too far by ignoring the different institutional translations of individualist and collectivist modes of separation and unity, the reality of liberal democratic (individualist) and state socialist (collectivist) autonomy is an economy based on mass-produced goods. Such goods do not really satisfy anyone because they have been thrown on to the market or the shelves of the state shops without having been asked for by anybody. Libertarian socialism raises the possibility of another relation between humanity and external nature and a non-instrumental organisation of the labour process yielding non-instrumental knowledge. Privately owned and state-controlled capital ceases to dictate the terms of production on the basis of immediate term and five-year calculations of profitability. Production is geared to satisfying the creative needs and abilities of skilled workers trained in schools, universities and guilds, as well as the individual and collective preferences of knowledgeable consumers. The consumer is informed about every stage of the production process because their values and imagination are built into the process itself. If someone wants a suit, they have to know something about tailoring and materials when they communicate their ideas to a tailor; if they are thinking about a house to move into, they have to be able to converse with an architect on the various aspects of construction and design.[38] To argue that most people are either too busy or incapable or unwilling to learn such complex but ultimately straightforward things amounts to saying that they are pretty dim and should confine themselves to the things they already know something about. Do dim people know something about budgetary politics and foreign affairs? Why can they vote in elections which have a major impact on how decisions in these fields are made? Should the dim people that comprise the electorate be allowed to decide on tax rates, foreign policy and internal security? The point is that dim or smart, they are not. Coerced integration which simultaneously removes people from effective control of government is the apparent consequence of liberal democratic legislations of appropriation. People are denied control of decision-making at work, where they do have relevant knowledge of the processes involved, and invited to vote on areas of macro-policy, where they do not. Can it really be surprising or shocking that there is acute voter apathy and easy populist mobilisation? For all of its authoritarian and oligarchic tendencies, state socialism at least has the virtue of openly declaring political matters to be the jurisdiction of the party, even if the power of the party and especially its leadership is loathsomely celebrated as the incarnation of the people's democratically sovereign will.

Cole severs the right of consumer control and choice from the privilege of private income, and simultaneously deconstructs the rigid separation of production and consumption through council representation for consumers. The commodity form is abolished, though not by state appropriation or another attempt to counter domination with another kind of domination. The commodity is dismantled by making the transcendence of need the basis of production and the legal framework for organising humanity's relation with external nature. Rather than satisfying need through commodities that re-create the same and new needs, the structure of need itself is transformed along with the structure of law and the experience of objects. From the standpoint of the consumer, law that had previously regulated the relations between humanity and external nature in institutionalised forms of individualism and collectivism begins to cede place to a different form of law in which the act of waiting, once embedded in the fetishistic spiral of deferral–satisfaction–deferral, becomes an instance of observation, experimentation and knowing. This subverts the very subtle liberal democratic fusion of legality and legitimacy discussed in the previous chapter. Instead, each individual is authorised to arrive at their own understanding of the changing relations between legal knowledge and legitimate need, and the possible transformation of the latter into an aesthetic-epistemological value. That is, on the basis of libertarian socialist legality, legitimacy ceases to be centrally concerned with suppressing antagonism and conflict for the purposes of unity and order, and begins to acquire an epistemological dimension that is reserved for legality in liberal democratic thought. This point about legitimate epistemology will be taken up in more detail in the next chapter. For now one might say that there are clearly different political consequences implied by childlike waiting for satisfaction, on the one hand, and learning to know, on the other. Being in a situation of dependence in the first instance is likely to engender an unstable dynamic of passive submission punctuated by interludes of impatient rebellion in which the relation between the individual and authority vacillates between uncritical adulation, hatred and fear. When one learns to know and accepts that knowing is a continual process, one is not undermined by having to know in order to survive. As law becomes legitimate rather than merely formal, knowing becomes aesthetic and pleasurable rather than instrumental and strategic.

There is not enough space to elaborate the details of libertarian socialism as

Cole and others envisage it, or the implications of a theory of political economy based on the epistemological dimension of the labour process underscored by Marx, or the importance of producer–consumer dialogue for the quality of consumer goods and environmental protection found in the writings of William Morris (1834–96) and John Ruskin (1819–1900). Nor is this the appropriate place to examine the merits of the libertarian alternative as a brilliant response to the problems that Cole diagnoses in the alternatives to capitalist legal relations of production offered by syndicalism, state socialism, Fabian socialism and social democracy. This exegetical work has already been done elsewhere. Detailed commentaries stress the originality and feasibility of most of Cole's core proposals.[39] Instead, it is possible to summarise in view of the fact that the first step in the process indicating the possibility of a transition from traditional idealism and autonomy to critical idealism and reconciliation has now been made. The brief excursus on libertarian socialism at the end of this chapter may seem like an abrupt shift from philosophy to politics. It is not a digression but rather a conscious movement from the abstract to the concrete from the perspective of theory and *anticipated praxis*. This perspective theorises the concept of freedom in epistemological terms which offer a significantly different set of legal and political mediations from those demanded and practised by the currently dominant epistemologies of autonomy and reappropriation which are directly implicated in the current crises of the legal subject. Two key points emerge from the discussion in this chapter. First, attempts to ignore or paper over the implications of these crises characteristic of the writings of systems theorists, theorists of communicative action, theorists of the new multitude and new social movements, etc. largely fail to clarify the issues at stake by not addressing concrete issues concerning the political economy of a libertarian form of socialism. Second, there is a way to retain the link between legality and legitimacy by retaining the cognitive dimension of law. But it has been shown that there is no plausible way to salvage the epistemological or juridical integrity of either the individual knowing subject or the collectively self-legislating political subject within the frameworks offered by liberal democratic, social democratic and state socialist institutions. Stated somewhat differently, there is no credible way beyond instrumental reason without a change in the basis of legitimacy. Hence the argument for rational and juridical legitimacy is an argument for libertarian socialism, not for liberal democracy or one of its most famous rivals. The term anticipated praxis refers to the non-speculative, i.e. materialist attempt to think about and know the conditions of freedom in the midst of palpable unfreedom, rather than despairing of the absence of freedom, celebrating the presence of freedom or musing about the infinitely deferred reality of freedom. The theory of critical idealism developed in this chapter anticipates praxis by attempting to liberate knowledge from the paralysing straitjacket of having to be either an instrumental response to the hierarchies and threats of the present or a utopian longing for non-instrumental knowledge in an already emancipated society that does not exist.

Notes

1 There is disagreement about what defines modernity and when it actually begins. Some will say that it begins with the English, American and French Revolutions, whilst others will insist that there is a much older and continuously ongoing modernity in Europe since the first political upheavals connected with the separation of church and state, and later with the Reformation. For an excellent overview of the juridical issues involved, see Harold Berman, *Law and Revolution: The Formation of the Western Legal Tradition*, Cambridge MA, Harvard University Press, 1983. For a similarly brilliant overview of the relevant intellectual and philosophical issues, see Hans Blumenberg, *Die Legitimität der Neuzeit* (*The Legitimacy of Modernity*, 1966), third edition, Frankfurt, Suhrkamp, 1997.

2 In his defence it might be argued that by the time of the third critique of reason (1790) Kant is more resolute in his determination to separate power and interest from disinterested cognition than is the case in the first two critiques. See his *Kritik der Urteilskraft* (*The Critique of Judgement*), Stuttgart, Reclam, 1963.

3 A part of what is undertaken here is the opening up of a dialogue between the Foucauldian critique of power and the Frankfurt School critique of instrumental reason by way of a Marxist reading of Kant and a re-evaluation of idealism. The contrast between strategic versus non-instrumental knowledge and power, as well as some of the other juxtapositions that arise in the exposition of the main arguments, will inevitably seem crude to readers familiar with the complexities involved in the work of Foucault, Adorno, Marx, Kant and Hegel. It is hoped that the reader's patience is not too sorely tried by the abbreviations and short cuts necessary to accomplish the work of synthesis.

4 Hence the striking philosophical and political ambiguity of a great deal of what has been written in the last twenty years against metaphysics and idealism. The argument against traditional idealism which does not also offer a critique of liberalism supports the social interests which defend and militarily export liberal democracy by quietly ignoring the idealist debate about the many different possible forms of mediation and the wide variety of possible forms of conceptualising and legislating transcendence. That is a debate about law which one cannot afford to leave to liberal democratic theorists and interests. An analogous point can be made about critiques of instrumental reason, colonisation of the life-world, the demise of 'the political', etc., that do not also offer a critique of capitalism. The path beyond liberal democracy begins with a radicalisation of the premises of traditional idealism, not with a simultaneous dismissal of liberalism and idealism which effectively shores up liberalism by settling for some version of corporatist or neo-liberal social democracy that its apologists like to call pluralist and defend in the name of civil society. Many observers suppose that the radicalisation of traditional idealism begins with Hegel and ends with the young Marx via Feuerbach (radical humanism with no clear political implications), or begins with the mature Marx and ends with Bolshevism or some other version of state socialism (political authoritarianism). Both interpretations ignore the contribution of critical theory to this problem which informs the present study.

5 Ante Pazanin, 'Die Überwindung des Gegensatzes von Idealismus und Materialismus bei Husserl und Marx' ('The Overcoming of the Antithesis between Idealism and

Materialism in Husserl and Marx'), in Bernhard Waldenfels, Jan Broekman und Ante Pazanin (eds), *Phänomenologie und Marxismus* I: *Konzepte und Methoden* (*Phenomenology and Marxism* I), Frankfurt, Suhrkamp, 1977, pp. 105–27.

6 It will become clear that what is meant by values is aesthetic and rational rather than religious or moral in any sense. In opposition to notions of psychological and biological determinism which reduce the structure of experience to genetic make-up, the concept of aesthetic value as it is used at the end of this chapter and in chapter 5 refers to the search for the creation of cultural forms in which individuals are able to make sense of their experience as individual social actors in history. Artistic production is the paradigm example of the creation of aesthetic-epistemological values. Yet all individuals are intellectuals and artists to the extent that they continually attempt to modify institutions in accordance with the knowledge they acquire (are not born with) in their daily struggles against coerced integration. In contemporary liberal democracies that is a struggle against opposing individual values that have successfully managed to shed their identification as value-laden by assuming an ostensibly neutral form in discourses and traditions specifying what is normal, healthy, acceptable and productive. Many readers will be familiar with the idea that much of avant-garde modern art is a lamentation about fragmentation and the impossibility of integral experience in late modernity. Chapters 4–5 of this book submit that if this is perhaps the case, it is not irreversible. The causes of fragmentation can be analysed in terms of the intensification of instrumental reason and the division of labour rather than questionable theses about the inevitable 'decline of the West' and similar metaphors of decay.

7 Sociological thinkers in the tradition of Durkheim and Parsons are wont to argue that the social bond that 'holds society together' despite increasing social differentiation offers a key starting point for answering this question. Durkheim maintains that society is a 'moral fact' that exists prior to individuals and decisively structures their action. As Raymond Aron puts it in reference to Durkheim, the individual is born of society, society is not born of individuals (*Les Étapes de la pensée sociologique*, Paris, Gallimard, 1967, p. 323). Yet it is not immediately convincing to argue that, because traditional idealism explains social institutions in terms of mind, empirical social science is post-metaphysical because it is able to identify the bases of social action in society itself, for this merely substitutes one transcendental explanation with another.

8 Luhmann intimates that the normative ground of law is indeed nothing more substantive than procedure and systemic adjustment to social and environmental change. The question that Luhmann cannot satisfactorily answer then becomes, what are the normative grounds of procedure? See *Legitimation durch Verfahren* (*Legitimation through Procedure*, 1969), Frankfurt, Suhrkamp, 1983, pp. 141–7.

9 There are times when Adorno's *Negative Dialectics* and Derrida's notions of deconstruction and 'the trace' read like exercises in negative theology. See Derrida, *L'Écriture et la différence* (*Writing and Difference*), Paris, Seuil, 1967. For an elucidation of Adorno's position, see Michael Theunissen, 'Negativität bei Adorno', in Ludwig von Friedeburg and Jürgen Habermas (eds), *Adorno Konferenz 1983*, Frankfurt, Suhrkamp, 1983, pp. 41–66. For a comparison of Adorno and Derrida, see Helga Gripp, *Theodor W. Adorno*, Paderborn, UTB, 1986, pp. 132–44.

10 This view is rejected by the present author but well defended by Hans Joas in *Pragmatismus und Gesellschaftstheorie* (*Pragmatism and Social Theory*, 1992), second edition, Frankfurt, Suhrkamp, 1999. The somewhat uncritical assimilation of the American pragmatists by the early Habermas and then by Joas and Honneth could be viewed among other things as an attempt by these thinkers to make a definitive break

Beyond hegemony

with some of the negative theological aspects of Adorno's work. The question as to
whether the effect of this break is to distance them from critical theory and place them
firmly within the mainstream of liberal democratic discourse is a somewhat separate
issue that cannot be addressed here for reasons of space.

11 This line of argument is put forward by Seyla Benhabib in 'Toward a Deliberative
Model of Democratic Legitimacy', in Seyla Benhabib (ed.), *Democracy and Difference:
Contesting the Boundaries of the Political*, Princeton NJ, Princeton University Press,
1996, pp. 67–94, and by Habermas in 'Three Normative Models of Democracy', pp.
21–30 in the same volume. A similar line is pursued by Axel Honneth in the essay
'Kritische Theorie. Vom Zentrum zur Peripherie einer Denktradition', published
along with a series of other essays in social theory in *Die zerrissene Welt des Sozialen*
(*The Divided World of the Social*), Frankfurt, Suhrkamp, 1990, pp. 25–72.

12 Luhmann, *Legitimation durch Verfahren*, pp. 148, 153, 183. Luhmann defines politics
as the production of power through the recruitment of leaders sustained by legitimating symbols and ideologies (p. 183) that has definitively parted company with
what he calls the classical, 'truth-oriented' conception of legitimacy (p. 148).

13 It is true that Kant called his own philosophy 'critical'. What is meant by this is that
he believed in the possibility of knowledge and freedom without metaphysics. He is
both right and wrong: he is right to think that knowledge and freedom are possible
without metaphysical essences, and wrong to think that post-metaphysics is possible
without a post-traditional concept of the individual knowing subject as well as a revolutionising of the societal conditions constituting the framework of what is known.

14 On Luhmann's theory of auto-poesis, see Chris Thornhill, *Political Theory in Modern
Germany*, chapter 5. Rawls develops the notion of overlapping consensus in his post-
Theory of Justice (1973) writings. See Erin Kelly (ed.), *John Rawls, Justice as Fairness:
A Restatement*, Cambridge MA, Belknap Press, 2001. The invocation of 'the political'
without any particular political implications other than an exhortation for more
republican virtue and pluralism can be found in emblematic form in Chantal Mouffe,
The Return of the Political, London, Verso, 1993.

15 An alternative methodology which is much closer to the approach taken here can be
discerned in the critical realist writings of Roy Bhaskar and William Outhwaite. See
Roy Bhaskar, *Dialectic: The Pulse of Frededom*, London, Verso, 1993, and William
Outhwaite, *Understanding Social Life*, second edition, Lewes, Schroud & Pateman,
1986, and *New Philosophies of Social Science: Realism, Hermeneutics and Critical
Theory*, Basingstoke, Macmillan, 1987.

16 Heidegger's failures to convincingly move beyond Husserl and Kant are revealing of
this tendency to claim victory over tradition whilst settling for its re-articulation.
These failures do not warrant an uncritical return to the latter, however, or a declaration of the arrival of post-traditional times. See Edmund Husserl, *Die Krisis der
europäischen Wissenschaften und die transzendentale Phänomenologie* (*The Crisis of the
European Sciences and Transcendental Phenomenology*, 1936) in *Gesammelte Schriften*
VIII, Hamburg, Meiner, 1992, pp. 165–6, and Adorno, *Zur Metakritik der
Erkenntnistheorie. Studien über Husserl und die phänomenologischen Antinomien*
(bizarrely translated as *Against Epistemology*), Frankfurt, Suhrkamp, 1990, pp. 75–9,
234–5.

17 For the philosophical background to the crisis of political legitimacy that indicates
similarities between the Weimar Republic and National Socialism, on the one hand,
and the post-Cold War period of global capitalism, on the other, see Carl Schmitt,
Legalität und Legitimität (*Legality and Legitimacy*, 1932), Walter Benjamin, *Über den
Begriff der Geschichte* (*Theses on the Philosophy of History*, 1940) in *Illuminationen*,

[*146*]

Frankfurt, Suhrkamp, 1977, Giorgio Agamben, *Homo Sacer: il potere sovrano e la nuda vita* (*Homo Sacer*), Turin, Einaudi, 1995, and *Stato di eccezione: Homo Sacer II* (*The State of Exception: Homo Sacer II*), Turin, Boinghieri, 2003, Jacques Derrida, *Force de loi : le fondement mystique de l'autorité* (*The Force of Law*), Paris, Galilée, 1994. All of these works are available in English translation.

18 The radicalisation of idealism bears within it potentially conservative and even radically conservative implications which have discredited idealism to a large extent. These become especially visible when history is interpreted from a '*völkisch*-populist' standpoint, thus indicating that radicalisation in this context needs to be approached with some care. They are discernible in some of Hegel's mature writings on world history and the state, in which Kant's notions of time and apace are transformed into historical time and national space. The conservative implications become more evident with Dilthey's notion of historical reason, Gadamer's hermeneutics of tradition and Gentile's fascist appropriation of Fichte and Hegel. It could be argued that Heidegger's philosophy is one possible form of Kantianism in which the epistemological problems posed by the noumenal world are re-articulated as ontological problems. As is well known, Heidegger conceives of autonomy in anti-liberal fashion as the lived contingency of an ethnically and linguistically homogeneous national community and its historical 'destiny'. Albeit in highly different ways, these are all flawed right-populist attempts to move beyond what is perceived to be the residual metaphysical dimension in Kant's thought, accompanied by the stubborn refusal to acknowledge the Marxist point first taken up by the Marburg School that there is no credible move beyond Kant, metaphysics and instrumental reason without a change in the socio-economic structure of society. Whilst the main thinkers of the Marburg School have drifted into obscurity, Western Marxism offers various versions of left populism based on notions such as the subject–object of history (Lukács), hegemony (Gramsci), existentialist commitment (Sartre), theoretical practice (Althusser), etc., which share one fundamental common characteristic with right populism: they are attempts to collapse the epistemological and political dichotomies in Kant without showing how this can be done without force or a vague appeal to historical laws or historical communities.

19 If this was not true one would be driven to affirm that the former Federal Republic of West Germany (BRD) was more legitimate than the former German Democratic Republic (DDR), since even though both polities had functioning legal systems, the legitimacy of the East German legal system was undermined by the dominance of a single party (SED) and the state police (STASI). This would imply that the multiparty system and absence of state police are sufficient to qualify a *Rechtsstaat* as legitimate. This is to conflate *legitimate* with politically *stable*, however. At first glance it may seem that common sense requires legitimate to mean hegemonic or stable, but it is really only convenient. With regard to this particular example, legally enacted party pluralism and constitutional protection against surveillance did not stop the reinstatement of myriad ex-National Socialists into prominent positions in West German administration and industry. This 'normalisation' was followed by the *de facto* suppression of the West German communist party by means of the *Berufsverbot* (legalised exclusion from state employment and the civil service) and judicial persecution of its members, etc.

20 This chorus has been most familiar to the citizens of the United States. Yet Blair's neoliberal programme and Schröder's social democratic austerity programme clearly show that people in Great Britain and the Federal Republic of Germany are also being told that the power to make decisions about the extent of welfare provision in those

countries is a prerogative of industry, not a right of the citizen. Contemporary debates about pensions in France and Italy raise the same issue.

21 Emancipation in this context means reconciliation in the sense used here rather than the re-appropriation of an alienated essence of a labouring, loving, communicative, etc., stamp. Iring Fetscher and Alfred Schmidt have edited a collection of excellent essays dedicated to Adorno written in this spirit entitled *Emanzipation als Versöhnung* (*Emancipation as Reconciliation*), Frankfurt, Neue Kritik, 2002. See in particular the contribution by Schmidt on Adorno's understanding of materialism in relation to the concept of non-identity, and the joint contribution by Heinz Brakemeier, Jens Becker and Thomas Zöller on some of the practical details of economic organisation beyond the plan/market straitjacket.

22 This assessment will certainly seem crude to experts on new social movements and proponents of the linguistic turn and communicative action approaches to questions of political legitimacy. But whilst the first wave of social movements following 1968 have been effectively integrated into the liberal democratic mainstream, most instances of life-world communication have been colonised by economic and bureaucratic-administrative systemic imperatives. The current wave of anti-globalisation protest may well mount a more effective challenge to liberal democratic hegemony. It remains to be seen if this is in fact the case.

23 See Adorno, *Minima Moralia*, Frankfurt, Suhrkamp, 1951.

24 The thesis that instrumental reason tends to become all-embracing and cannot be confined within clearly delimited systemic borders in modern industrial societies has been by no means monopolised by Marxists and theorists of deferred essence. For example, Max Weber and Hannah Arendt have illustrated this point with historical argument and rigour. Arendt remarks that the total state is characterised not by the politicisation of all areas of life, but rather by the marginalisation of politics by the insidious combination of the glorification of violence and the exaltation of technology. See Arendt, *The Origins of Totalitarianism*, New York, Faber, 1951.

25 For a summary of the different positions within the idealist tradition, see Frederick Copleston, *A History of Philosophy* VII, *Eighteenth and Nineteenth Century German Philosophy* (1986), third edition, London, Continuum, 2003. Useful information about idealism and other philosophical currents of thought is provided by Bertrand Russell in *The History of Western Philosophy*, London, Allen & Unwin, 1946. The following discussion is based primarily on the ideas of Kant and to a lesser extent Hegel. There is not enough space here to dwell on the specific ideas of other idealists such as Fichte and Schelling or romantic thinkers with distinct affinities to the idealist tradition, such as Hamann, Herder, Schiller and Goethe, or 'renegade' idealists such as Schopenhauer. The ideas of all of these thinkers are relevant to the issues raised by the philosophies of Kant and Hegel, and as such form an important part of the cultural matrix of the idealist tradition. Readers interested in idealism from the point of view of its contemporaries should read Hegel, *Differenz des Fichteschen und Schellingschen Systems der Philosophie* (*The Difference between Fichte's and Schelling's Philosophical Systems*, 1801), Stuttgart, Reclam, 1982, and F. W. J. Schelling, *Zur Geschichte der neueren Philosophie* (*On the History of Modern Philosophy*, 1856), Leipzig, Reclam, 1984. In terms of Kantian philosophy and its immediate impact inside and outside of idealist circles, readers should consult Köhnke's detailed study, *The Origins and Rise of Neo-Kantianism*, which is a great source of background information. A more general view is provided in the brief introduction to Herbert Schnädelbach's *Philosophie in Deutschland 1831–1933*, Frankfurt, Suhrkamp, 1983 (*Philosophy in Germany, 1831–1933*).

26 This may well be another instance where the reader's patience is tried – this time by
repetition rather than by simplification. But it seems necessary to insist on this point
and develop its various ramifications. If a theory of critical idealism can be elaborated
in more detail than is allowed by the space available in this chapter to capture the
rationality of the real through a materialist analysis of ideas and institutions drawing
on philosophy, social theory and empirical social science, it will be possible to
comprehend the dynamics of separation and connection as they unfold institutionally
and historically. Such a theory would enable people to read a thinker like Foucault on
the sociological shifts in the history of power from discipline to control and from
sovereignty to governance, and to understand these movements more systematically,
and in any case beyond the banal assertion often attributed to him that power circulates indifferently to traditional notions of law and human agency. Power circulates
and is not concentrated in a state designated as sovereign, to be sure. But this does not
mean that power is a mystical entity that circulates randomly in the manner of a
hurricane that wreaks havoc and then evaporates. The shift from Fordism to post-
Fordism and from there to flexible specialisation is a similarly under-theorised
dynamic which cannot be explained simply in terms of the collapse of corporate
bargaining structures and the onslaught of globalisation. It fails to see the phenomenon of globalisation itself within a wider set of developments in the social and
political history of humanity–nature mediations. See Foucault, 'Le grand enferme-
ment', pp. 1164–74, and 'Les intellectuals et le pouvoir' (interview with Gilles
Deleuze, pp. 1175–83), in *Dits et écrits I*. In an another article contained in that collection, Foucault explains that his work aims at a history of instrumental and regulatory
knowledge in paradigm instances like sexuality, madness, population shifts and
health. To this end he explores why disciplines such as criminology, psychiatry and
social work arise at a particular historical moment and how, in very different ways,
punitive systems of justice after 1830 increasingly seek to secure two objectives. They
seek to isolate the criminal act of the accused from its social and historical context by
classifying it as a unique 'case' to be filed with broadly similar cases, and they seek to
underwrite judicial sentences with epistemological arguments about the crime
committed. What Marx accomplishes in terms of the critique of humanity and external nature relations with his theory of political economy Foucault achieves in terms
of the critique of humanity and human nature relations by applying Nietzsche's ideas
on power, morality and genealogy to the history of institutionalised values. See 'De
l'archéologie à la dynastique' in *Dits et écrits I*, pp. 1273–84. Marx and Nietzsche theoretically dismantle the legal relations underpinning traditional idealism and the
idealism underpinning traditional legality; it still remains to formulate an alternative
idealism and legality that are informed by both of their critiques.

27 Absorption and the postulation of absolute alterity are two common instances of
non-dialectical epistemology referred to as identity thinking by critical theorists such
as Adorno. Identity thinking refers to a form of thought in which the object is classi-
fied in terms of the conceptual category it falls under, rather than understood in its
objective particularity. In its various expressions identity thinking is symptomatic of
a form of thought that achieves the (only apparently) paradoxical result of reification
through subjectification. To render the object commensurable with its concept by
either (1) absorbing it within a subjective conceptual scheme or (2) by designating it
as absolutely incommensurable with the subject is to think subjectively, however
objective the positivist methodology associated with (2) might seem to be. Against
reified forms of subjectivity (traditional idealism) and objectivity (positivism, functionalism) critical theory attempts to think what Adorno designates as 'Der Vorrang

des Objektes' (the priority of the object). See Adorno's essay 'Subject and Object' in Andrew Arato and Elsa Gebhardt, *The Frankfurt School Reader*, New York, Continuum, 1978. The implications of this attempt are considered below. One important point to keep in mind for now is that alterity as otherness is not an onto-logical condition of informal unknowing into which humans are 'cast', since this is merely a rhetorically radical response to the formal unknowing which marks the limits of reason and political authority in Kantian philosophy. Adorno shows that otherness in this sense is not a static or historicised given, but needs to be established by new forms of thought that acknowledge and allow space for the non-conceptual moment in thinking.

28 Hence Kant explains that we can think about God, 'unmoved movers' and other thought experiments pertaining to noumenal essences, but we can have knowledge only of the objective phenomena that appear to us in consciousness. One can see that according to this logic reason is largely instrumental, whilst thought is demoted to particular experience and arbitrary speculation. That Kant was evidently alarmed by this himself is suggested by the fact that he felt compelled to search for a less categor-ical separation between thinking and knowing in the *Critique of Judgement*.

29 On this point see Max Horkheimer's essay of 1942, 'Vernunft und Selbsterhaltung', in *Traditionelle und kritische Theorie. Fünf Aufsätze*, Frankfurt, Fischer, 1992, pp. 271–301. This essay, 'Reason and Self-preservation', is contained in Axel Honneth (ed.), *From Max Horkheimer*, London, Routledge, 1986. The relation between instru-mental reason and domination is the central theme of the essays collected in Hans Ebeling (ed.), *Subjektivität und Selbsterhaltung. Beiträge zur Diagnose der Moderne* (*Subjectivity and Self-preservation*), Frankfurt, Suhrkamp, 1996. That collection includes contributions from Hans Blumenberg and Dieter Henrich.

30 See Adorno, *Drei Studien zu Hegel* (*Hegel: Three Studies*), Frankfurt, Suhrkamp, 1963.

31 This becomes particularly evident in Kant's discussion of the transcendental deduc-tion in the second volume of the *Critique of Pure Reason* (1781). See Kant, *Kritik der reinen Vernunft* II, Frankfurt, Suhrkamp, 1968. Adorno develops this point in detail in his discussion of subject/object, the Kantian block and Kant's transcendental deduction in his lectures on Kant's *Critique of Pure Reason* at the University of Frankfurt in 1959. These have been published in German by Suhrkamp and translated into English by Rodney Livingstone and published by Stanford University Press in 2001. See Adorno, *Kants Kritik der reinen Vernunft* (*Critique of Pure Reason*), Frankfurt, Suhrkamp, 1995, chapters 10, 13, 16 and 19–21. For a brilliant discussion of this and other issues concerned with the relation between idealism and critical theory, see Simon Jarvis, *Adorno: A Critical Introduction*, Routledge, 1998, chapter 6.

32 The condition for the thinking mind to be able to accomplish this in traditional ideal-ism has already been indicated: it must limit the epistemological claims of reason to non-contradictory, synthetic functions, whereby non-contradictoriness is possible only if the thinking subject is transcendental and unitary. The resulting epistemology yields largely formal knowledge that is blocked off from knowledge of the things in themselves, and blocked off too from the distinctness of individual experience. This particular kind of rationality and this particular kind of insistence on non-contradic-tion backfires badly, in so far as it legislates forms of economy and polity into existence that render the transcendence of necessity and heteronomy impossible. Accordingly, traditional idealism must cede place to a form of critical idealism if the promise of freedom and transcendence first raised by traditional idealism is to be redeemed. Just as Kant's discussion of the transcendental deduction in the second edition of the *Critique of Pure Reason* indicates that the subject may indeed enjoy the

possibility of transcendence through reason, though not in the decidedly bourgeois way that Kant imagines this possibility, Freud's work also indicates that the unitary conception of the subject is untenable. This is a pathological condition for Freud because, like Kant, he is unable to imagine non-individualistic conditions of autonomy and knowledge. It is this inability to imagine such a possibility as real that is problematic.

33 See note 6 above on the political and aesthetic-epistemological possibility of closing that chasm. It is suggested that it is not a 'natural' or ontological separation, i.e. that the structure of experience can change, and, with it, the quality of objectivity.

34 In both régimes reason expresses a fetish relationship between the subject and survival, not a mimetic relationship between subject and object. One sees how legal-rational domination actually works: retaining legal enforcement whilst undermining the cognitive integrity of the individual citizen creates a political framework which abolishes the conditions of knowledge-producing experience. If one deconstructs the liberal democratic understanding of legality and legitimacy, one can see that the first issue to be addressed is how to legislate institutional conditions into existence in such a way that experience is allowed to become capable of generating knowledge of nature and the world instead of being forced to devise strategies for survival and domination. The discipline called political science which since the 1950s has focused on voting behaviour and party systems would have an entirely different scope and method as soon as the basis of legitimacy is framed as an epistemological matter rather than a technical question of governance. For an in-depth discussion of these issues from an epistemological perspective incorporating the ideas of Aristotle, Marx, Polanyi and others, see John O'Neill, *The Market: Ethics, Knowledge and Politics*, London, Routledge, 1998.

35 G. D. H. Cole, *Self-government in Industry*, London, Bell, 1917, *Guild Socialism Re-stated*, London, Parsons, 1920, and *Social Theory*, London, Methuen, 1920.

36 This is not to deny that there were and continue to be differences from one state socialist system to the next. For an analysis focusing on the former USSR and the planned economies in Eastern Europe covering some of the major reforms of the early 1980s, see Alec Nove, *The Economics of Feasible Socialism*, London, Allen & Unwin, 1983, and Branko Horvat, *The Political Economy of Socialism*, New York, Sharpe, 1982. For a detailed analytical and historical look back at the upheavals of 1989–91, see Janos Kornai, *The Socialist System: The Political Economy of Communism*, Princeton NJ, Princeton University Press, 1992.

37 For a more detailed exposition, see Darrow Schecter, *Radical Theories*, chapters 1 and 4, and Antony Black, *Guilds and Civil Society in European Political Thought from the Twelfth Century to the Present*, London, Methuen, 1984.

38 Cole, *Guild Socialism Re-stated*, pp. 117–37, A. J. Penty, *Old Worlds for New: A Study of the Post-industrial State*, London, Allen & Unwin, 1917, pp. 50–1, 76–82.

39 See Chris Wyatt, *G. D. H.Cole: Emancipatory Politics and Organisational Democracy*, in its entirety, and Darrow Schecter, *Radical Theories*, chapter 4. Some readers familiar with the qualified defence of guild socialism in *Radical Theories* may find it odd that the present author finds it necessary to return to that argument, however briefly. The argument in that book about the epistemological dimension of the labour process and human transformation of external nature is valid but remains incomplete as it stands without a larger framework addressing the issues of law, idealism and legitimacy taken up in the current project. The complexity of the argument in this chapter would have been compounded by additional stylistic clumsiness if all of the major points made about critical idealism were shown to have their place in libertarian

socialist praxis in a constant process of referring backwards and forwards in the text. Instead, the reader can reconstruct the overall argument by drawing out the implications of critical idealism, and by seeing how they correspond in general terms with libertarian socialist proposals, some of which clearly need updating since their original formulation in Cole's writings.

Chapter 5

Materialism, legitimacy
and reconciliation with human nature

IN the preceding chapter the five central strands of the theory of critical idealism articulated over the course of this book are woven together. The first
appears for the first time in the introduction. It is indicated there that the most
radical route to reconciliation between the various factions of humanity, and
hence to positive freedom for citizens, can be ascertained by comparing the
different forms of knowledge-yielding mediation between humanity and nature.
This is the somewhat paradoxical idea that the most direct path to understanding between humans is not to be sought by studying humanity's interaction with
other humanity in the currently existing forms of dialogue and political representation through which humanity talks to itself. It can be discovered instead by
analysing humanity's relation with external and human nature. Stated more
bluntly, the most direct path is indirect, and, to be more precise, conditioned by
reason and law. The second strand is that it is possible to know the conditions of
reconciliation and freedom not despite, but because of, the dynamic of systematic exclusion and coerced integration which structures reality in all social
ensembles to different degrees. This dynamic assumes a distinct institutional
profile according to the specific modalities of instrumental reason and law operative in each particular historical context. That is to say that, if the relationship
between forms of exclusion and forms of integration was arbitrary or hermetically distinct, there would be no way to understand society as the plastic form in
which the relation between humanity and nature in both senses is mediated, nor
could one analyse the relationship between legality and legitimacy except in
terms of apology and ideology. There is also a paradox implied by the second
strand, since a condition of knowledge (reconciliation) is put forward as a result
of the knowledge process (reconciliation)[1]. Restating this problem, which is
sometimes referred to in philosophy as the hermeneutic circle, helps clarify the
relation between epistemology and politics that is insistently pursued throughout these pages. It can be formulated as follows: how can one know something
without already knowing what knowledge is? From the standpoint defended in
preceding chapters, it is certain that there is knowledge, justice and freedom. Yet

it is also certain that a justice system can produce just decisions only on condition that one knows what justice is, because it already exists in the form of just procedure. In other words, justice cannot result as the casual by-product of a formal justice system. The same point can be made with regard to freedom. How can one know what freedom is unless one is already free? These questions point to the latest in a series of legitimation crises that have marked the entire history of liberal democracy. Legal practice today strongly suggests that either justice does not exist, or is largely punitive, or is conceivable only in another world without exploitation and aggression. Political practice confirms that the exercise of freedom is largely restricted to its commercial and contractual manifestations. Whilst early liberalism often attempts to resolve the problems connected with the hermeneutic circle anthropologically by attributing reason, knowledge, freedom and the capacity to do justice to humanity as part of the complex array of human rights and innate faculties, later liberal democratic thought resolves it systems-theoretically by arguing that political institutions and social structures guarantee freedom and achieve stability by spontaneously producing impartial systems of justice and functional order. Liberal democrats past and present typically ask, what is human about politics, what is natural about human rights, how is my liberty compatible with the liberty of everyone else, and, how is social order possible? The approach taken here radicalises the premises of the liberal democratic solution to the hermeneutic circle, and sets out to answer a slightly different set of questions. The main question asked in this study is, in what kind of society and through what kinds of mediation are forms of knowledge possible that would enable one to speak about epistemologically grounded legitimacy and political freedom beyond the narrow parameters defined by anthropological versus systemic perspectives?[2] The third strand is the related claim that, when considered in the broadest possible terms, the primary modes of knowledge-yielding mediation are reason and law rather than human essence or systemic autonomy, such that the legitimacy of law depends on the kinds of reason and law that are practised. This is to lay stress once again on the problematic character of individual and collective *self-legislation* and the arbitrariness of ascriptions of inherent rationality or republican virtue to a supposedly unitary entity labelled 'humanity'. The fourth and fifth strands take up the issues raised at the end of chapter 4, and form the central core of concerns in this final chapter. The fourth is that since the primary modes of mediation are conceptual as well as material, there is no plausible way to erect fixed boundaries separating idealism, legality and consciousness from materialism, legitimacy and institutions. Chapters 3 and 4 develop this point in detail by stressing the dialectical movement from law to idealism to new law, and by looking at the implications of this process of transformation for determinate relations of production and property ownership. The concluding pages of chapter 4 on libertarian socialism explicitly show why the organisation of the labour process represents a pivotal moment in framing the reciprocal relations between legality and legitimacy, and in deciding the regulatory or reconciliatory quality of knowledge. It is emphasised that when the division of labour is dismantled by decoupling income from consumer choice, and by institutionalising the input of individual and collective consumer values into the production process at the various stages of production, commodity production is made redundant by production for the transcendence of need.[3] Liberating the possibility of the transcendence of need from the perpetual satisfaction and renewal of need in its private capitalist and state socialist guises allows need to be transformed into an individual value able to shed light on the relation between humanity and human nature as it unfolds in the media of history and society. This frees the concept of value itself from the punitive and regulatory codes of morals and ethics that have dominated discussions of value for centuries. Reconciliation with external nature through libertarian socialism enables the expression of values to enter an aesthetic and cognitive dimension which is not possible when they are appropriated by organised religions or otherwise transformed into submissive practices of piety, propriety and duty. The fifth strand builds on the other four and brings this study to a conclusion. In stark contrast to virtually all conventional usage to date, it will be seen that, when disentangled from the instrumental practices of systematic exclusion and coerced reconciliation, legitimacy becomes a pluralist concept bearing upon the experience of individual citizens, as opposed to a collectivist concept related to the strategic unities forged by states and parties. Whilst the aesthetic and rational dimension of values is suppressed when they are conceived of as a function of ethics and morality, the epistemological dimension of legitimacy is blocked off when politics is conceived as a variety of techniques for producing social stability. Politics has been perennially concerned with striking some kind of pragmatic balance between freedom and equality or between freedom and authority, with the ultimate aim of securing order. It is possible to change the quality of freedom quite dramatically once it is no longer juxtaposed with authority, and that possibility becomes a reality when freedom is enacted as freedom to know. Reconsidered in the light of critical idealism, politics becomes an end in itself which is concerned with freedom and legitimacy in epistemological terms rather than with power and hegemony in disciplinary terms. Legitimacy can continue to be about order and authority, as it almost always has been, or it can be transformed into an art of experience and knowledge. The conditions for that transformation are analysed in preceding chapters and in what follows.[4]

Chapter 3 shows that the organisation of humanity's legal and technical relations with external nature on the basis of commodity production lays the groundwork for a form of liberal legality whose legitimacy is based on its supposed neutrality with regard to competing versions of legitimacy, but which is nonetheless empowered to legislate on what is legitimate. Chapter 2 indicates that the modes of exclusion and integration characteristic of the capitalist version of the commodity régime, as well as the forms of applied instrumental reason that it uses and enforces, are not so much dismantled as reorganised in state socialism. The reorganisation of humanity's relations with external nature under the direction of a single political party abolishes one kind of commodity production, though without seriously rethinking the problem of instrumental reason underpinning commodity production and political hierarchies. Perhaps it might have been possible to simply abolish instrumental forms of reason via state ownership if reason was the exclusive property of the epistemological subject, and if individual subjectivity could be organised collectively in the institutions of the party-state. But even in the case of more moderate models of legal reform pursued in the past by some social democratic governments, collectivisation tends to exacerbate epistemological subjectivism and instrumentality by uncritically accepting the supposition that rationality and legality are modalities of subjectivity. Like reason, law is an instance of mediation rather than an innate characteristic of the liberal democratic individual subject or the state socialist collective subject, which is why state socialism achieves a putsch that deforms liberalism rather than a revolution that transforms it. The critical idealism developed in this book suggests that one can rationally specify and create the conditions for the abolition of instrumental reason and reified consciousness. In the previous chapter it is seen that this can be accomplished through legal abolition of the division of labour, and the transcendence of property relations grounded in different notions of appropriation and reappropriation. The latter remain committed to individual and collective epistemologies claiming reason and law for an autonomous knower whose autonomy and knowledge are exercises in self-defence against nature. Self-defence against nature is bound to produce relations of hegemony and outright domination in society, since humanity is itself part of nature without being identical to it. The war against nature for the sake of human autonomy is never won, since even the most apparently successful battles eventually turn out to be negative victories for the vanquished that ricochet as hierarchies, bureaucracies, discrimination and other examples of oppressive social relations. This idea concerning the banning and unhappy return of human nature in repressive institutions runs from Nietzsche and Freud to critical theory and Foucault. It achieves particular clarity in the theses expounded by Horkheimer and Adorno in the *Dialectic of Enlightenment*. In this context Horkheimer and Adorno represent a kind of stand-off position between the insights of Nietzsche and Freud on humanity and human nature considered from the perspective of coerced integration, and those of Marx on humanity and external nature considered from the perspective of surplus value and systematic exploitation. A new constellation of materialist concepts capable of re-articulating the relation between epistemology and legitimacy is required in order to prevent that stand-off from becoming a permanent impasse. A

Nietzschean analysis of values, vital spontaneity and artistic impulse without a Marxist analysis of political economy and the division of labour is likely to be as inadequate as a theory of political economy with no place for individual expressions of life affirmation and aesthetic rationality.[5]

This analysis points to the conclusion that the key to reconciliation between humanity and other humanity are forms of mediation between humanity and nature which reconcile the beauty of spontaneity in all of nature, including humanity, with the capacity to transcend the more brutish aspects of natural spontaneity, such as illness and unnecessary death, that is offered by non-instrumental reason and non-instrumental law. The latter indicate a path beyond the *Dialectic of Enlightenment* by changing the bases of legitimacy from freedom of the will and a consideration of the conditions of unity and order to freedom to know and a consideration of the conditions of reconciliation. Consequently, a model of libertarian socialism based in broad outline on the central tenets of guild socialism is put forward in the previous chapter that offers the key to a theoretical and practical vision of humanity and external nature relations which will not give rise to liberal democratic hegemony in new guises. The libertarian socialist juncture marks the most important stage in the overall argument, since in identifying the conditions for the abolition of instrumental reason and reification one is no longer stuck in the hermeneutic circle, having to passively accept the validity of the liberal dichotomies, or already be knowledgeable and free in some theologically absolute sense that is never attained, in order to know what freedom consists in. Nor is one compelled to identify the proletariat, the people, the multitude, new social movements or some combination thereof as the successful unity of theory and praxis, and a particular example of subjectivity that can somehow be extended into a universal model of free social relations. From a critical idealist perspective, compulsion to identify a legitimation subject of this kind is an instance of coerced reconciliation, and as such, an unacceptable step back behind what is achieved at least in theoretical terms by the most advanced articulations of liberalism. The related argument is that the reproduction of separation as exclusion and connection as coerced integration in already existing as well as in new institutional configurations undermines the possibility of transcendence of necessity and, with it, the possibility of legitimate law in liberal democracies and other social ensembles that do not adequately challenge the premises of liberalism. The undermining of transcendence signals a failure to achieve basic Enlightenment aims implied by the traditional idealist conception of practical reason, and has far-reaching consequences for those theorists of communicative action and other proponents of post-metaphysics who want to jettison idealism whilst retaining a legal mode of legitimacy.[6] By not addressing the problem of instrumental reason state socialism fails in practice, but it does manage to pose fundamental questions concerning the links between humanity, external nature, transcendence and legitimacy. Social relations in contemporary liberal democracy, social democracy and state socialism indicate that all attempts to reconcile humanity and other humanity that are not accompanied by the legal revolution implied by libertarian socialism will fail. From this vantage point, one can proceed to show why this transformation in idealist thinking about legality, as well as the changes in political economy demanded by it, also signals a turn in materialist thinking about legitimacy.

Epistemological legitimacy contra instrumental reason and law: addressing the division of labour as the key to a critical idealist materialism

Whether manual, sensuous, intellectual, or all three, as in the case of art, production transforms nature and humanity, sustains life and is the basis of knowledge. Knowledge, however rudimentary in some instances, is the key factor in all production. Hence the important epistemological question is not which comes first, production or knowledge, but rather what kind of production and what kind of knowledge one is talking about. Whilst knowledge has to do with the way experience is organised into concepts, it has been seen that experience is a dialectical process of synthesis and mediation. Traditional idealism liberates epistemological theory from speculative discussions about the primacy of nature and experience versus humanity and consciousness. It demonstrates that all of reality is constituted by syntheses and mediation processes. Critical idealism, in its turn, highlights the different outcomes implied by instrumental as compared to non-instrumental modes of synthetic mediation. A libertarian politics of experience, if one may put it that way, starts with the demonstration that there is nothing inevitable or 'normal' about a specific form of mediation, and that the instrumental or non-instrumental quality of synthetic experience turns to a significant degree on the terms in which political legitimacy is understood and institutionalised. Critical idealism takes the discoveries of traditional idealism further by demonstrating that the blocks separating manual, sensuous and intellectual production are the cause and result of the primary modes of mediation, and that these hold the key to a praxis of unblocking capable of breaking down the political division between art and production corresponding to the theoretical separation of freedom and necessity. Defenders of historical materialism may well object that this aim is central to Marx's project, and they can select passages from the *1844 Manuscripts, The German Ideology* and *Capital* to show why. There is undoubtedly a great deal of evidence for this interpretation. Yet his more dogmatic defenders will have some difficulty explaining how one should read those texts today, in the light of the authoritarian turn of the Russian Revolution and the imminent collapse of the last bastions of state socialism. They are likely to have great difficulty in clearly defining Marxist politics as distinct from Leninist, syndicalist, anarchist, council communist, situationist and other currents of left politics. Liberal democratic critics defending the inevitability of the liberal dichotomies as well as traditional idealist critics who insist on the irreducibility of theory to history might say that Marxism is theory; Leninism and the others are examples of unsuccessful or totalitarian practice. Hence Marxism itself is theoretically flawed.[7] There are more pertinent criticisms, however. In his determination to stand Hegel on his feet and formulate a scientific theory of socialism, Marx prefers to speak of reason in history rather than reason in idealism and law. Thus for Marx the history of credible forms of idealism finishes with Hegel. From this perspective, any Kantian 'ought' which is set in opposition to the reality of the unfolding historical 'is' looks moralistic rather than moral, and in any case a hopeless metaphysical appeal to a world of ethical principles detached from the rationality of the real already discerned by Hegel. In distinguishing between political emancipation and human emancipation in his early writings, and then between base and superstructure in the more mature works, he implicitly relegates law, politics and aesthetics to the superstructure. It is unsurprising for a thinker of his epoch that the dialectics of mediation tend to cede place at times to images of the inexorable movement of progress and its economic motor. But it is not sufficiently clear to Marx's subsequent followers and critics that what is thereby obscured is the dialectics of a consistent and thoroughgoing politics of non-instrumental reason and law which is neither dependent on the appearance of a new revolutionary collective subject nor a theory of communicative action or some other compromise with liberal democracy and capitalism. What such a politics entails needs to be spelled out in more detail in the rest of this concluding chapter. But two of the final conclusions of this study can already be discerned at this stage. The first is that the critique of metaphysics and traditional idealism demands a politics of non-instrumental mediation between humanity and nature rather than the invocation of iron laws of history or a theory of communicative action in any shape or form. The second is that such a politics is the most appropriate for the creation of legitimate forms of legality.[8]

Obscuring the possibility of a politics of non-instrumental reason translates into the pernicious tendency to glorify the power of the party and the immediate legitimacy of the people reduced to its essence as a class subject in state socialist attempts to transcend liberal democracy. It is clearly not the case that Marx's writings sanction anything remotely similar to Bolshevik tyranny. There are nonetheless substantial differences between (1) scientific socialism based on theories of the laws of history, the falling rate of profit, the base and superstructure, etc., (2) state socialism based on the unchallenged authority of the party and (3) libertarian socialism based on the transcendence rather than the satisfaction of need. Each of these different socialisms proposes a unique alternative to capitalism and liberal democracy. Chapter 3 anticipates the specificities of the third alternative by drawing attention to the peculiarities of the role of the consumer in the Juggernaut of capitalism. It is observed that there is far more to this particular form of mediation with external nature than the fact that it legally transforms labour power into a commodity. Commodity production is totalised by transforming legitimate needs and creativity into goods that have to be bought and sold for the continued transformation of labour power into commodities. Hence what one is confronted with is more than a mode of production ordered by a system of legal norms. It is a mode of production–consumption within a constellation of ideologically legitimised legality. Theory and praxis are divorced in reified practice, thus reducing praxis to negative liberty and passive consumption rather than expanding praxis into an active model of cognition. Whether the theory of scientific socialism directly leads to state socialism is a matter of conjecture. What has been ascertained on more solid grounds, however, is that if capitalism and state socialism both satisfy need, albeit in very different ways and to a different extent, neither offers the possibility for the transcendence of need without which law is not legitimate.[9] This analysis points to the third discernible conclusion of this book: legitimate law for all transcends need in each by making it possible to transform individual need into an aesthetic value with cognitive content. Like the primary modes of mediation, the cognitive content of need already exists. This is a corollary of the point that it is possible to know the conditions of reconciliatory knowledge and positive freedom not despite but because of the dynamic of systematic exclusion and coerced integration. But the cognitive content of need requires a different kind of legality in order for its rationality to achieve more than merely instrumental epistemological validity. At this stage it is apparent that what is meant by a different kind of legality is not a more inclusive legality or an ostensibly more democratic legality. Nor is it a legality whose formalism is diluted by pragmatic concessions to maintaining an acceptable degree of social harmony. It is discussed at the end of chapter 4 in terms of a libertarian socialist legislation of mediation, as distinct from various legislations of appropriation. This requires further explanation and is elaborated below.

It has been observed that there are private capitalist, state socialist and other forms of commodity production, all of which are steeped to varying extents in instrumental reason. Commodity production institutionalises coercion, but not so much because it exploits the right to extract surplus value from productive labour in capitalism, or because it dictates that shopfloor workers must labour according to Taylorist rhythms and Stakhanovite incentives in state socialism.[10] More fundamental is that the commodity régime in its diverse manifestations is directly authorised to legislate on what is legitimate, and that this authorisation confers on the régime in question the legal right to attempt to manufacture unity and order in the name of stability, whilst ideologically obscuring the reality that the conditions of non-instrumental knowledge are never immediately given, but need to be created. The right to legislate on what is legitimate without creating those conditions is tantamount to the right to integrate without reconciling. Key for the critique of communicative action in this book is that in the first instance reconciliation means reconciliation between humanity and external nature. As such it implies forms of non-instrumental knowledge that are much more comprehensive and far-reaching than the kinds of agreements that temporarily reconcile speakers in a life-world that is supposedly detached from the subsystems of power and money. Whenever discourses and practices of reason and law are strategically enlisted for the purposes of re-establishing order and shoring up the social bases of authority, one can speak about the prevalence of instrumental mediation over other synthetic possibilities. The problems related to coerced reconciliation are especially difficult to pinpoint in liberal democratic legal systems, where authorisation is indirect and hegemony is more prevalent than outright force and propaganda. In these systems the law is empowered to legislate on what is legitimate despite claims that jurisdiction is defined by neutrality with competing conceptions of legitimacy. Regardless of the system under examination, however, the right to integrate without reconciling is symptomatic of instrumental mediation in the broadest sense. Rationality and legality become tools in the political programme of securing order, rather than the epistemological ends in themselves that reason and law are in a society in which the basis of legitimacy is reconciliation. This is not because reconciliation is recognition, communitarian or ethical, but because it denotes non-instrumental knowledge, that is, knowledge that transcends mechanical and biological necessity without needing recourse to hierarchies to suppress human nature so that external nature can be brought under control. A central claim of *Beyond Hegemony* is that the constellation constituted by the phenomena of exploitation–integration, instrumental mediation and ideological legitimacy that underpin legal forms of legitimacy enables one to outline the conditions of an alternative constellation in which a legitimate form of legality structures human experience of nature.

In the absence of reconciliation in both senses used here, hierarchies will be required to integrate, and they will need to be justified by the representatives of institutionalised power. This is not to say that the techniques required to secure order do not produce knowledge at all. Foucault and others convincingly show that they do produce knowledge – and legitimacy – of an instrumental kind. The crux is that integration without reconciliation inevitably results in hierarchy and the related phenomena of conformity, institutionalised fear and entrenched oligarchy. This analysis strongly suggests that neither the phenomena just mentioned nor reason and law can be consigned to the status of a separate sphere or any other secondary plane that one might associate with the notion of the superstructure or an autonomous system. The state socialist experiment indicates that hierarchy is compatible with the abolition of private property. It also shows that the abolition of private property is in no way synonymous with the abolition of commodities in particular and the transcendence of non-instrumental production in general. In other words, it is possible to rescind private property without abolishing the pernicious forms of mediation between humanity and external nature accompanying the division of labour. In so doing, one moves from an institutional ensemble in which exclusion and inequality are the most salient aspects of social life to one in which coerced integration becomes the greatest problem. The dialectic of separation and unity acquires a new profile, though without addressing the underlying question of instrumental versus non-instrumental mediation. One is once again falling behind theoretical terrain that has already been staked out by liberalism. This is why the liberal dichotomies analysed in chapter 1 are not merely ideological, and indeed why they are extremely difficult to overcome without settling for Pyrrhic victories secured by force or strategic compromise. Marx is correct to perceive the intimate links between capitalism and liberal democratic legality, and he is right to point out the centrality of the commodity in the capitalist mode of production. But his analysis largely stops there. He does not really explore the forms of instrumental reason which produce the commodity itself. This omission opens the door to the possibility of an unwieldy system of socialist commodity production that ends the revolution by limiting it to a change in property relations. Marx conflates the forms of legality operative in capitalism, and hence modern legality in more general terms, with an ordered framework for the organisation of commodity production. Understood in these terms, legality signifies reification and repression. It also signifies alienation, since the law stands between the workers and the commodity they have produced. One could interpret this to mean that the workers are free once they are empowered to reappropriate that product with the help of the party-state. At that point reification, repression and alienation cease to exist. This is an imprecision that has encouraged Marxists after Marx to conflate the abolition of private property with the end of commodity production and the beginning of the 'administration of things'. Although Marx formulates a cogent critique of commodity fetishism, reification, private property, the state and the division of labour, one might say that the critique of instrumental reason within the Marxist tradition begins with the fourth chapter of Lukács's *History and Class Consciousness* (1923), entitled 'Reification and Proletarian Consciousness'. A more persuasive argument, however, is that Lukács is beholden to Marx's central concepts in that seminal work, and that the critique of instrumental reason on the left (*History and Class Consciousness* had a major impact on Heidegger) really begins with Adorno and the first generation of critical theorists associated with the Frankfurt School. It is certainly true that the latter, and particularly Adorno, are not easily classifiable as Marxists. This is not simply a scholastic piece of academic or Marxist trivia, since without a critique of instrumental reason one cannot construct a theory and praxis of non-instrumental law. In the absence of the latter, the risk is that nature becomes a terrain for human exploitation in the name of scientific socialism, with all of the problems that this approach to mediation raises for society and nature that have been witnessed in places like Eastern Europe, Cuba and China.[11]

The main characteristics of the different kind of legality alluded to above can be gleaned from the critique of the right to integrate without reconciling that is sketched in condensed form in the preceding pages, and which occupies a central place in the critique of liberal democracy that runs throughout this book. In addition to being a legality that transcends need rather than satisfying it, it approaches the problem of reason in terms of political economy by calling for a form of libertarian socialism that is more centrally concerned with deconstructing the sovereign bases of instrumental legitimacy and superseding the division of labour than it is with abolishing private property. Perhaps most important, it denotes a form of mediation between humanity and external nature which does not legislate directly on matters touching humanity and human nature. It is thus a form of legality which allows the individual dimension of legitimacy to achieve epistemological expression, and, as such, it is a legitimate form of legality rather than a legal form of legitimacy. On this basis, legitimacy is no longer embodied by variously staged representations of a sovereign person or assembly, general will, unified foundation, unadulterated source, people's state or any other populist and metaphysical construct. When the cognitive dimension of legality is no longer juxtaposed to but becomes the basis of the cognitive dimension of legitimacy, legality ceases to be merely formally legal. Legality is legitimate as well, and integration ceases to be coerced.[12] From this perspective one can see that when the very concept of legitimate epistemology is dismissed and subordinated to the cognitive dimension of legality, legal epistemology is to a large extent limited to instrumental epistemology focused on the conditions of order rather than on the conditions of knowledge. Acknowledging the marked differences implied by arguments for knowledge and arguments for order would destabilise the hierarchies operative in liberal democratic society. Liberals are generally loath to admit that one cannot hold on to a praxis of law as knowledge at the same time that one enforces the institutions needed to secure negative forms of freedom linked with the dictates of private interest and a will that has been declared innately free and rational. If pushed this far, they are likely to say that knowledge is intellectual and scientifically usable, or it is not really epistemologically relevant at all. Hence whilst for most liberals non-instrumental reason and knowledge do not exist in political terms, artistic production is sensuous and expressive rather than intellectual or rational. Thus non-instrumental knowledge of all kinds, and especially in political economy and aesthetics, is potentially subversive of the existing forms of hierarchical order that help reduce knowledge to criteria of utilisation within an economic system that employs labour power to produce commodities for passive consumers with no real representation or recourse to protest beyond the highly ineffective strategy of the boycott.[13] Where legal epistemology is instrumental epistemology rooted in paradigms of regulatory authority and power, the conditions of knowledge are either annexed to the knowing subject, declared irrelevant or declared unknowable. The corollary is that legitimacy is understood in monolithic, decisionistic and non-negotiable terms. In modern democratic societies based on various liberal and socialist conceptions of the people's will, such epistemologies tend to produce totalised forms of social organisation. It has been seen in the course of this study that this is a problem that is not limited to state socialism and fascism. Carl Schmitt famously remarks in the opening lines of *Political Theology* (1922) that sovereign is he who decides a state of exception. Such an approach can deflect attention from the fact that liberal democracies function on the basis of a legal system that gives no one a choice in the matter of being a citizen if they are born within the borders of the sovereign state, and then restricts the scope of citizenship to the enforcement of negative freedom and contractually mediated forms of damage limitation. Schmitt's apocalyptic tone is highly misleading insofar as it conjures up an image of the autonomy of the decision and its political transparency, as well as the resolution of the collective will that stands behind it. The mode of production–consumption that transforms legitimate needs into commodities that have to be bought and sold for the perpetual transformation of labour power into commodity quietly outlaws transparency from the decision-making process. Far from being pluralist and open, as is often claimed by its apologists, the legal form of legitimacy that sustains liberal democracy and capitalism is highly centralised and bureaucratic. It offers an example of an instance of legal form that has to be consciously taken apart and deconstructed rather than collectivised or reappropriated on the basis of crude forms of materialism or various discourses of inclusiveness and democratic legitimacy looked at in chapter 2.[14]

The pathos of Schmitt's authoritarian defence of politics against the intrusions of the economy and other interests he seems to consider mundane is banal and melodramatic. It is thus a bit puzzling that there has been a rediscovery of his writings in recent years. It may be that his emphasis on 'the political' looks like a salutary republican response to the threat to national sovereignty posed by globalised capitalism. Like Arendt, Habermas and many other thinkers attempting to rethink the foundations of politics in light of the questions raised by Marx, Schmitt proposes a concept of transcendence directed against the marked tendency in capitalist societies with liberal and social democratic governments to reduce political questions to economic and technical ones. Yet one can invoke the state, civil society, sovereignty, the political, communication, the public sphere, being, community, republicanism and a variety of other palliating remedies against the workings of the capitalist economy and the demise of politics. The weaknesses in the respective arguments in question indicate that a theory of transcendence that does not also offer a critique of the legality and idealism underpinning liberalism and capitalism quickly evolves toward an implicit apology of a form of political economy that institutionalises instrumental reason at all levels of society, regardless of its property relations. That is to say that one can critique liberal democracy and capitalism from positions that can be described as Marxist or non-Marxist. But such critique falls flat if it does not address the kinds of idealism that yield instrumental reason and law in conjunction with correspondingly authoritarian populist practices of legitimacy. There is no plausible way to transcend the symbolic and real violence of capitalism by relying on the supposed autonomy of systems, humanist republican virtue, or a universal class or multitude assigned with the task of abolishing all classes and the basis of legality along with them.[15] A critique of instrumental reason that does not offer a critique of the division of labour as well as existing forms of legitimacy is problematic on grounds which include the fact that, albeit in very different ways, state socialism relies on instrumental reason, commodity production, hierarchy and coerced integration as much as liberal democracy does. The implications are not limited to the fall of the Soviet Union. It suggests instead that the state socialist victory over idealism, like the ontological, communicative action, post-structural and postmodern victories to follow it, is precipitate. The end of idealism is the end of a coherent politics of non-instrumental reason. It is the end of a dialectical mediation between humanity and nature, i.e. the demise of a dialectic of separation and unity that anticipates reconciliation by specifying its two material conditions. The fact that these conditions can be known by way of critical idealism constitutes the fourth conclusion in the overall argument developed in *Beyond Hegemony*. There is thus a political response to the problems posed by the hermeneutic circle that does not entail an affirmation of the liberal dichotomies or passive acceptance of traditional and negative versions of idealism.[16] The abandonment of idealism amounts to a retreat to either some guise of humanism or identity politics, some variant of positivism and systems theory, or an unhappy combination thereof. One might say that the association of liberal democracy and traditional idealism should not taint idealism as such any more than the association of state socialism with Marx should be allowed to invalidate what is still very much alive in the latter. That is also why it is conservative and pedantic to insist on the purity of idealism or Marx by not linking the re-evaluation of idealism and Marxism with a re-evaluation of the mediating instances of reason and law. Commodity production can be maintained without private property. But it cannot withstand the breakdown of the division of labour and the combined epistemologies of manual, sensuous and intellectual production when these are not pitted against each other by disciplinary and regulatory legal forms. It is explained in the previous chapter why production for direct use co-ordinated with consumer representation in local, regional, national and eventually international consumer councils annuls the direction of production by capital and private property, though without resurrecting the problem of private capital in the institutions of state capital and party dictatorship. It is shown that a legally mediated reconciliation with external nature of the kind offered by libertarian socialism is capable of addressing the phenomena of separation and unity connected with liberal democratic legal systems without recreating them as flagrantly statist examples of coerced integration. Socialist libertarianism does this because it is a form of reconciliation with external nature that does not oppress the capacity for knowledge in human nature. By dismantling the hierarchies needed to sustain the divisions between different aspects of the knowledge and production processes, the real bases of passive conformity and fear are laid bare. A couple of concluding remarks on this subject introduce the themes of the final section.

On the basis of the foregoing arguments one can see that, contrary to naturalistic, psychological, anthropological, ontological and other claims to the contrary, phenomena such as conformity and fear have a materialist basis in the hierarchies created by the dichotomisation of the labour process into its material-sensuous and ideal-creative dimensions. It is historically verifiable that resistance against these epistemological and political dichotomies has engendered a variety of movements striving for the elimination or a celebration of the distance between humanity and nature. Whilst romanticism offers a paradigm example of the former, futurism offers a good example of the latter, though of course the romantics and some of their right-wing progeny generally do not attribute the nature–humanity divide to the separation of mental and manual production and knowledge. In any case, many of the movements seeking to eliminate the distance try to recover a sense of original or primordial unity with nature that they believe was lost in the successive stages of the industrial revolution and distinctly modern forms of social stratification. This is an extremely complicated issue, because it is a little bit misleading to say that the division of labour *creates* a distance between humanity and nature which inflicts violence on each in distinct and overlapping ways. It is true that violence is present and its exercise is distinct and nonetheless overlapping because of humanity's unique position, which consists of being part of as well as distinct from nature. Movements with a vaguely romantic lineage articulating visions of an archaic unity characterised by authoritarian and totalitarian practices of legitimacy have indeed arisen and continue to flourish. It has moreover been observed that ideas about unconditional origins and unanimous consensus are not limited to overtly authoritarian political forms. They can be found at the foundations of liberal and democratic notions of sovereignty, the state of nature and the general will as well. But the explanations of fear and conformity are not to be sought in the mere fact of distance, since a certain qualified distance between humanity and nature always obtains, owing to the reality of mediation and post-metaphysical conceptual form. Being part of as well as distinct from nature is a key factor in explaining the distinct and yet overlapping character of the violence inflicted on humanity and on nature by dividing the labour process into its constituent parts. Changing regulatory practices of law and the labour process will not abolish humanity's paradoxical location, but it will change the way it is experienced and known. Hegel's traditional idealism offers a closed totality of humanity–nature relations in which thought eventually becomes one with nature in harmonious reconciliation. Adorno's negative idealism counters with a theory of a deferred totality in which non-reified knowledge is indeed recognisable as the reality of a harmonious totality, but that totality of harmonious relations is visible only in the traces of its manifest absence, or, if one prefers, visible in the concrete examples of decidedly unharmonious forms of nature–humanity relations that characterise the historical process from Odysseus to Auschwitz and Hiroshima, and beyond to the totally administered society. Readers will decide whether the critical idealism developed here carries these debates forward in any significant way.[17]

Although capitalism intensifies the distance between humanity, nature and objects, the gulf is not created by capitalism or by any other mode of production. The eventual transcendence of the dichotomisation in its existing form is a possibility inscribed in the primary mediation processes that constitute the conditions governing the production of knowledge, for it is these which determine whether or not humanity experiences distance as proximity that illuminates or isolation that terrifies. The theory of reconciliation as proximity in this book would almost certainly signify a return to traditional idealism or a sociologically informed idealist reversal of the base–superstructure undertaken by Weber, if it was not accompanied by the argument for libertarian socialism that follows from the first claim of critical idealism concerning the conditions of both knowledge and legitimate law. This is a philosophical demonstration with political implications, not a statement of political allegiance in search of legitimating rationalisations. In the *Protestant Ethic* Weber is at pains to reiterate that he shares Marx's penchant for empirical and materialist analysis against philosophy and abstraction, and that he by no means denies the reality of social classes and differential life-chances in market-oriented societies. He insists nonetheless that religious views can be as important in affecting the structure of the economy as the economy is in producing religious forms of escapism from what Marx refers to as the dull compulsion of economic life. Historical research has been amassed by Weber, Marx and others making convincing cases for both approaches, with the result that an impasse has been reached. This reinforces the point that the question is not so much the relative independence of the base from the superstructure or the determination of the latter by the base. The question is really an epistemological one about the division of labour, instrumental reason and law, the causes of hierarchy and the bases of legitimate political authority. When the base is declared determinant, as in state socialism, an ideological meta-status is conferred on the economy, so that those in charge of its functioning are able to form an oligarchic leadership clique. The supposed autonomy of law and the state from the economy that are enforced as part of the definition of liberal democracy enforces a system of systematic production–consumption and functionalist integration whose workings have already been analysed in detail.[18]

Perhaps the first step toward the realisation of a politics of non-instrumental reason and a praxis of legitimate law entails disentangling the conditions of knowledge from the definition of humanity, without abandoning the idealist insight that knowledge is mediated by human subjectivity. This may enable humanity in its present form to transcend itself instead of redefining the essence of the human and the political in new combinations. In order to change the experience of distance from isolation to proximity and thereby change the structure of experience and knowledge itself, a libertarian socialist change in legality of the kind specified in the last chapter and reiterated above is required. Like the invocation of transcendence on the basis of existing law, the invocation of unity within the institutions of the current state remains ideological, as are all forms of transcendence and unity short of reconciliation of humanity and nature. Once the conditions of non-instrumental reconciliation have been specified, concrete steps toward praxis are possible without relying on some notion of unmediated unity of humanity and nature underlying most democratic discourses of legitimacy (metaphysics as anthropology, looked at in chapter 2), a notion of permanent separation underlying liberal discourses of legality (metaphysics as residual theology, examined in chapter 1), or the ungainly liberal democratic hybrid that is now increasingly upheld as the only viable model of social and political organisation.

Aesthetic rationality beyond the fact/values dichotomy

If the populist and metaphysical bases of legitimacy are conspicuous in the presence of a legitimation subject, metaphysics and populism are not dispensed with when values are subordinated to liberal democratic practices of highly questionable objectivity, spurious juridical neutrality and the supposedly general norms regulating contractual exchange. The attempt to limit the influence of values on the legal system to a generic set of constitutional articles of faith boomerangs in the flourishing of fetishes, cults and a variety of other indications of potential for rapid mobilisation. This mobilisation potential is particularly striking amongst relatively wealthy populations whose physical and creative needs have been channelled into economic and administrative systems of planned satisfaction. The role of the legal enforcement of the division of labour in perpetuating the spiral of unsatisfying satisfaction and the symbolic violence that this entails require no further elaboration. It is a violence that consists in the refusal to acknowledge that within the structure of need there is a rational and epistemological dimension that is suppressed when the labour process is parcelled up, consumption is privatised and fetishised, and need is packaged and sold rather than transformed into an individual value and transcended. Thought about reason and law that is prohibited from integrating normative and aesthetic considerations is legally authorised to classify and order without being allowed to pronounce on the validity of classificatory hierarchies except in terms of the so-called inevitable inequalities that result from the vast range of talents and luck that compete in complex societies. To talk about the transcendence of need and the creation of values in conjunction with reconciliation might appear like a romantic argument seeking to recuperate a radical origin or lost unity between humanity and nature, words and the things they represent, intellect and emotion, thought and being, etc. It is rather a philosophical and a political argument for an institutional constellation in which the relationship between art, production and knowledge is articulated in a way that has not yet existed in actual praxis. The location of humanity as part of and separate from nature can be looked at as a materialist paradox rather than the liberal democratic tautology positing the inherently rational and juridical essence of human nature. If it is romantic in a reactionary sense to seek to abolish humanity's location inside and outside of nature, it is not at all romantic to change the way it is explored and known. On the contrary, one might say that herein lies the chance of thinking about different ways of conceptualising freedom beyond the impoverished choice between liberal-juridical negative liberty versus democratic-authoritarian positive liberty. The explanation why it is not possible to recuperate an untouched origin uniting thought and being is not systemic complexity or ontological difference. It is that the encounter between humanity and human nature is unique for each person, such that the resulting knowledge is also individual. In order for the particularity of each instance of knowledge to be freed from systematic reduction to the idiosyncratic intuitions of the coarse majority and dubious exaltation of scientific innovation and artistic expression on the part of the sublime few, the structures of mediation between humanity and nature must be changed, so that the aesthetic dimension of rationality can become the basis of the new form of legality that is outlined in very broad lines in this chapter and at the end of the previous one. It has been seen why a new form of legality, as distinct from a more inclusive or ostensibly more democratic legality, is needed to re-articulate the supra-individual, dialectical conditions of knowledge outside of the framework provided by the anthropological annexation of those conditions initially offered by liberalism, and it has been seen why attempts to democratise and collectivise liberal legal anthropology by a variety of parties and movements have generally tended to fail. This re-articulation is a necessary step in the process of thinking about the possibilities of transcendence in opposition to the subjectivist dialectic of annexation and reappropriation. By disentangling the idea of transcendence from tautological definitions of essence, one can think about and legislate the conditions under which production and creation become more than instances of the individual and collective affirmation of already existing identities.

The liberal dichotomies looked at in the first chapter are of great aid here, since they stipulate that reconciliation between citizens that is not based on knowledge and rationality is coerced reconciliation and integration, i.e. illegitimate, but they do so within a constellation in which the basis of legitimacy is unity and order. The subjugation of reason to the manufacture of integration and order yields decidedly instrumental forms of reason and law. The latter subordinate the creation of the socio-political conditions of knowledge to the hierarchy-demanding imperatives of functionalist conceptions of stability that stem from fear of the uncontrollability of nature in humanity and the external world. It has been seen that liberal democracy's answer to the conditions of knowledge consists in variously unstable combinations of anthropology and agnosticism that vacillate between the postulation of the autonomy of individuals and the autonomy of systems. These combinations are in crisis once one accepts that law that is not based on knowledge produces illegitimate forms of unity, since tying the legitimacy of law to epistemological criteria points beyond the instrumental versions of law, reason and politics that sustain liberal democratic governments. It is moreover possible to see that law will always be illegitimate as long as it is an instrument in the project of securing the bases of order, since knowledge, like artistic creation, is not subordinate to other means, but is an end in itself. This leads to the fifth conclusion of this book. That is that *the knowledge of each person*, both cognitive and aesthetic, pertaining to external as well as internal nature, is the only possible basis for a legitimate form of law. Otherwise the knowledge and aesthetic values of some citizens are allowed to stand in as a general model of cognition that simultaneously marginalises and integrates what other citizens know. This typically occurs in a series of processes of exclusion and appropriation that culminates in oligarchic articulations of monolithic legitimacy, i.e. forms of populism from the political right to left which manipulate and mobilise need through ideological discourses of national unity and the proliferation of leadership cults. Populist forms of coerced integration offer examples of a mode of political appropriation that is in many instances compatible with the economic appropriation of labour power and knowledge of external nature in the form of surplus value. Although the mechanisms of surplus value can be studied in terms of class analysis and wage labour, the more general mechanisms of appropriation at work when reason is largely instrumental and legitimacy is collectivist are not limited to the extraction of surplus value. Political appropriation can be regarded in more global terms as a modality of instrumental mediation. The systematic appropriation of the knowledge of human nature of some citizens by others can be described as an appropriation of individual aesthetic value. Appropriation of surplus value and aesthetic value is appropriation of knowledge relating to discrete yet related dynamics of legality–legitimacy dialectics corresponding to humanity's paradoxical location in the world. The issue is not one person's knowledge versus another's, but finding a mode of production of knowledge that lets both coexist on the basis of a mode of material production that does not punish the attempt to transcend necessity by making conformity and fear the price for guaranteed survival.[19]

When individual need is allowed to break out of the endless cycle constituted by new models of satisfaction and the successive stages of their imposition and replacement, it expresses something about each person's encounter with human nature that is cognitive–sensuous as well as intellectual–emotional. This is because human need is rarely strictly cognitive, biological or emotional in some supposedly one-dimensional way, just as what is referred to as genius is never narrowly aesthetic or scientific. There is thus an aspect of need that cuts across the boundaries of the division of labour and currently existing epistemological boundaries. It is a supra-individual yet non-collectivist, in other words, a transcendental dimension that also casts existing legality–legitimacy dialectics and fact–value dichotomies in a new light.[20] The links between production, need, knowledge and aesthetics form a key part of the idea of value developed here, which can be stated as follows. It has been established that the knowledge of each person – not the fabricated unities constituted by the nation, state or general will – is the only possible basis for a legitimate form of law, and that need in each person is a decisive factor in knowledge processes that are structured by nature–humanity mediations and the labour process in a way that is simultaneously ideal and material. By implicitly undermining the division of labour and existing epistemological boundaries, the phenomenon of need raises questions about monolithic versus pluralist conceptions of legitimacy. Production for need undertaken against a background of epistemological legitimacy is a form of production that brings out the individually aesthetic component of the knowledge process without which production is commodified and legitimacy is instrumental. The liberation of production from commodification and the emancipation of legitimacy from instrumental reason and law signal the possibility of an aesthetic and cognitive praxis of value creation, where value refers to an individual discovery about the interaction of nature and society at every specific historical juncture. From that moment on, it is no longer plausible to juxtapose irrational values with objective facts. Instead of focusing in the first instance on the question of private versus public property, the libertarian socialist revolution of legality deconstructs the collectivist bases of legitimacy, so that the critique of systematic exclusion is at the same time a critique of populism and oligarchy in its liberal democratic, authoritarian corporatist and state socialist guises. It is on this basis that a revolution of existing values could take place, where revolution implies a change in the way the condition of being part of and separate from nature is explored. This opens up the possibility of a change in the structure of experience in general and the experience of the hermeneutic circle in particular, and with this change, the potential transformation of need into a cognitive-aesthetic value on the part of individuals who have been freed from scarcity. Within the terms used in this book, this constitutes the reconciliation of humanity and human nature and the second condition of legitimate law.

The theory that there is a mode of appropriation of experience that includes but is not reducible to the appropriation of surplus value complements the idea that there is far more to the phenomenon of instrumental mediation than systematic economic exploitation. It has been seen that instrumental mediation also integrates, with the consequence that the spontaneity of human nature is suppressed. In terms of an analytical description of the systemic features of a legal system that legislates on matters of legitimacy despite pretended neutrality and objectivity, one can say that the appropriation of external nature for purposes of accumulation works in tandem with the appropriation of human nature for the purposes of order, so that there is no single cause or origin that can explain them both. Hence it is not sufficient for critique to be radical in the sense of going to a metaphorical root or source of the problem of appropriated experience and reified consciousness. The dynamics that shape them are plural in a way that defies reappropriation by a unified epistemological subject acting as a unanimous collective. Moreover, there is no non-authoritarian way to seize the epistemological processes of mediation between humanity and nature. Although humanity participates decisively in determining whether they are structured in a regulatory or reconciliatory manner, these are dialectical processes of contact with objectivity that do not belong to humanity in any meaningful sense. If there is a link between the imperatives of regulatory legality, accumulation, exclusion, exploitation, inequality and appropriation of external nature, on the one hand, and populist legitimacy, hierarchy, integration, the suppression of spontaneity and the appropriation of human nature, on the other, it is the phenomenon of instrumentality and the political appropriation of individual experience in the broadest sense. The argument for a new philosophy of legitimacy is an argument for the superseding of instrumental reason at its pivotal point of contact with nature, i.e. in law, and a re-evaluation of the concepts of idealism, experience and need. It is emphatically not an argument for communicative action, systemic differentiation and autonomy or the postmodern rejection of grand narratives. With regard to the re-evaluation of experience and need, it is not so much the liberal dichotomies as the idealist theory of practical reason that is of great service, since practical reason specifies that it is the legally and rationally mediated transcendence of necessity that distinguishes the political freedom of humanity from the mechanical freedom of falling objects and the predatory freedom of animals. A consistent and thoroughgoing legally mediated transcendence of necessity implies a form of law which, like the particular means of expression chosen by every artist and independent worker, is not merely an instrumental means to stability and order. The means are part of the process of creation itself, in which order is established without sacrificing spontaneity and freedom. For example, a beautiful building is aesthetically pleasing because it combines materials won from labour upon stone, bricks, wood, iron, steel, etc., so that structure and order are created by transforming the natural materials involved beyond recognition without destroying them. In cases where architects and the workers achieve real excellence, the edifice in question appears to incorporate the spontaneous existence of the constitutive elements to such an extent that it almost seems to move whilst being stationary. The living quality of the various architectural means has been respected in such an imaginative way that the resulting construction not only provides shelter and serves a wide range of purposes. It continues to exhibit a life of its own in a new form shaped by the productive and aesthetic values of its producers. In the process, and as a result, human life in society is transformed by the protection against inclement weather offered by a work of art that is itself alive, and so to speak breathing. The imagination of the architects and workers has managed to imitate the dynamism of nature by making contact with a dimension of objectivity that is shared by humanity and nature in qualitatively different ways, even though humanity is part of nature. Insofar as what is imitated does not have an original it is not a thing. When looking at original forms of production and art, one is observing the imitation of a form of non-reified knowledge concerning mediations in which the dialectics of separation and contact between humanity and nature appear to meet, overlap and divide again. Thus the imitation of a dimension that has no original may subsequently assume form as an aesthetic object or even an ordinary thing that expresses some aspect about the reality of the existence of knowledge as a condition of knowledge and an aspect of the knowledge process itself, but the dimension of objectivity in which the conditions of knowledge are known is not reducible to the object in question. [21] What is referred to as aesthetic value in this chapter has the quality of a surplus which, like surplus value, cannot be appropriated without legally mediated, illegitimate violence. Whilst surplus value is extracted and invested in the accumulation process, aesthetic value is marginalised and suppressed by the social institutions of coerced reconciliation and populist practices of legitimacy. But it cannot be eliminated in even the most totalitarian societies. This does not mean that where there is appropriation there are automatically forms of resistance. The mechanisms of integration in liberal democracies have been very effective in securing high levels of hierarchy, conformity and fear. Moreover, the appropriation of aesthetic value can induce passivity and illness instead of an articulate political and aesthetic response.

Hence it is important to demonstrate that only the knowledge of each citizen can provide the basis of a legitimate form of law. It is the marginalisation of that knowledge that blunts spontaneity, dulls the imagination and helps cause aggression. The irreducibility of productive and aesthetic objects to their formal properties is related to the fact that, owing to the epistemological surplus that it carries, aesthetic value helps to create a reality in which the work of art always exceeds what one can say about it. This is why original art offers a legitimate, i.e. a more than merely formal, form of knowledge. It is a form of knowledge that is potentially subversive of instrumental law and reason in that it confronts knowledge as strategy in today's society with knowledge as reconciliation in a society whose conditions of existence are inscribed as a possibility within the present one.[22]

By being part of nature, but not synonymous with it, humanity has the chance to transcend mechanical and predatory modes of action without having to renounce vital affirmation. Affirmation is, however, not an end in itself, since affirmation that does not reconcile practical reason and individual vitality tends to amount in most instances to mendacious self-assertion and aggression. Affirmations of freedom of the will are likely to be expressions of the freedom to dominate rather than instances of genuine autonomy. These are affirmations of general models of freedom and cognition that imply general models of legitimacy which do violence to the particularity of every individual nature in humanity in the name of 'human nature'. Aggression is not only allowed, it is encouraged because it is claimed to be natural; it supposedly keeps one fit in the struggle for survival and equipped in one's dealings with competitors. The attempt to master nature in the external world and in humanity can be seen as a project to eventually eliminate all differences between humanity and nature. The plan to eliminate that difference constitutes a preparatory step toward the destruction of the living nature in the humanity of those who are being integrated, and an appropriation of their individual aesthetic value. [23] Since life, objectivity and the conditions of knowledge are in constant (though not random) flux, so too are the relations between legality and legitimacy. This means that the project of reconciliation entails a constant search for new epistemological, social and aesthetic forms. In contradistinction to the notion of the mediated identity between humanity–nature and thought–being found in Hegel and a number of other traditional idealists, the qualitative difference between the ways in which humanity and nature participate in objectivity can be understood conceptually in terms of *mediated non-identity*. Moreover, the concept of mediated non-identity between humanity and human nature lends some clarity to the idea of imitating what has no original. Mimetic imitation does not imitate reality, strictly speaking. It interrogates the transcendental conditions constituting the objectivity of objects and knowledge, and thereby allows reality to become visible or audible in the process of production and the work of art.

Mimesis thus helps create reality in a non-arbitrary or purely subjective way. Since reality is not one-sidedly human or natural, but rather synthetic, mimetic rationality sounds out the possibilities of non-oppressive syntheses that respect the mediated non-identity between reason in humanity and nature in humanity. In so doing it sounds out the possibilities and conditions of non-oppressive realities. In conjunction with critical idealism, mimetic forms of materialism suggest that the possibilities for non-oppressive syntheses and realities are bound up with a libertarian union of intellect and feeling, planning and spontaneity, i.e. with the end of the division of labour and the union of social production and individual aesthetics. To think of political-aesthetic experience in this way is not to say that it is irrational or romantic. It is a way of giving expression to the idea that when sensuous and intellectual human labour encounters nature, the changing contours of a third and highly unpredictable dimension of objectivity are revealed that is playful, somewhat mysterious (not mystical) and in any event open-ended. Values related to beauty, movement, mediation and form are created in that dimension, i.e. in a space that belongs to no one and which transcends individuals and institutional divisions between aesthetics, epistemology, economics and politics. It is here that it is possible to visualise spontaneous forms of order in which the transcendence of necessity for the entire citizenry is achieved not despite but because of the freedom to know on the part of each citizen. In any society one can do what one likes, provided that it is within the limits of the law – liberal democratic society is not the first or only one in which people are free. Where the law is legitimate and not just legal, freedom is not based on the right to buy what others have produced in order to reaffirm what one is by satisfying basic needs, calculated according to the income that one has earned by working for someone else. It is the freedom to overcome what one is and what one needs by producing to create new forms of non-instrumental objectivity on the basis of aesthetic rationality. These are forms of objectivity that include the subject but do not reduce reality to a pale reflection of subjectivity by reducing subjectivity to the one-dimensional notion of competence needed to sustain commodity production and consumption. It is clear from the preceding that the reduction of subjectivity to competence is an ostensibly value-neutral technique for measuring efficiency and success. In reality it privileges the instrumental knowledge and strategic values of some citizens over the knowledge of external and human nature of others.[24]

Fulfilling the second condition of legitimate law thus turns on the possibility of enlarging and expanding the diverse instances of aesthetic rationality against the general appropriation of experience, and thereby opposing existing separations between production and art, facts and values, reason and aesthetics. Aesthetic rationality undermines instrumentality by incorporating individual aesthetic values into the production process so that production creates a basis for the transcendence of necessity without suppressing human nature with various forms of hierarchy. The superseding of commodity production and the simultaneous decollectivisation of legitimacy can be regarded as parallel processes in the construction of a form of law that achieves reconciliation beyond stability and order. Decoupling consumer choice from income and initiating a direct producer–consumer dialogue interrupt the commodification of need, whilst marking the possible transformation of needs into diverse instances of non-instrumental knowledge and non-relativist value. Identifying the socio-economic conditions under which need could become non-reified knowledge instead of perpetually satisfied need is an important step in the transition beyond the liberal democratic dichotomies to a mediated form of theoretical–practical unity that one can legitimately call praxis. The dismantling of the division of labour breaks down the rigid demarcations between production, consumption, planning and execution, such that the abolition of surplus value and other methods of exploitation is achieved in conjunction with the end of consumer passivity. It is not difficult to see that in this context consumer passivity and citizen passivity are not unrelated phenomena. They are also not temporary deviations that can be put right with infusions of communicative action, communitarian spirit or the republican virtue called for by many established academics and moderate activists who claim to be alarmed by the depoliticising effects of global neo-liberalism. The causes of passivity and conformity have to be addressed more rigorously by analysing the forms of mediation which determine whether or not the aesthetic values of each citizen acting in the third dimension alluded to above are able to achieve active visible and audible expression, or if such knowledge and movement are going to be suppressed. The suppression of the spontaneity and creativity of the worker, consumer and citizen in commodity régimes finds its complement in the reduction of the role of the artist to a faithful imitator of outmoded canons or a subordinate to new commercial trends. If one can say that it is insufficient for critique to be radical in the sense of going to a unified metaphorical root or source of the problem of appropriated experience and reified consciousness, it is also the case that contemporary resistance on the part of producers, consumers and citizens of all kinds, including artists, eludes easy designation according to conventional categories of identity and struggle.[25]

Notes

1 In framing the matter in this way, more apparent paradoxes arise, some of which will not be paradoxical to those broadly familiar with the postulates of historical materialism and the main lines of critical theory. One is that fields of inquiry and practical intervention such as political economy and aesthetics are in a very real sense more politically relevant than political parties, constitutions and parliamentary elections have been for some time now. It is apparent from what has been argued so far that this is not the preamble to an attempt to update the mechanical materialism suggested

by the base–superstructure model, or to revise the negative theology and negative idealism that sometimes seem to inform Adorno's work.

2 The converse of the liberal democratic hermeneutic circle is often referred to as the paradox of freedom, which holds that freedom must be curtailed by the state in order for everyone's negative freedom to be protected. In this way an argument about the limits of knowledge is articulated with parallel arguments about the limits of freedom and the collectivist character of legitimacy: everyone is a citizen whether they want to be or not, yet citizenship is not empowered to correct the mechanisms of exclusion codified in the legal system. Contemporary apologists of liberal legal form are now wont to say that political projects aiming at correction of this kind are underpinned by the metaphysical assumptions of the philosophy of consciousness, and have been invalidated theoretically by the reality of communication and historically by the fall of state socialism. Alternatively, it is argued that such correction violates the reality of systemic differentiation, and is therefore impossible in non-authoritarian terms. It is easy to see that these arguments complement one another quite effectively at the same time that they dismiss the possibility of reconciliation in the mediating sense in which that term is used here.

3 Whilst this epistemological understanding of the labour process and need first emerges in the works of Hegel, Marx, Morris, Ruskin and Cole, it reappears in a wide variety of practical and theoretical contexts thereafter. The anarchist and anarcho-syndicalist collectives in the Spanish Civil War provide one good example. For an analysis of the theoretical implications of those struggles, see Darrow Schecter, *Radical Theories: Paths beyond Marxism and Social Democracy*, Manchester, Manchester University Press, 1994, chapter 2. The autonomist groups and writers in Italy in the 1970s offer another. For a very good summary of the Italian scene in those years, see Steve Wright, *Storming Heaven: Class Composition and Struggle in Italian Autonomist Marxism*, London, Pluto Press, 2002.

4 Arendt demonstrates that revolutionary situations are the great exception to the reduction of politics to day-to-day administration. See *On Revolution*, New York, Penguin, 1963. In that book she makes the point that what distinguishes the revolutionary situation from the normally prevailing modes of bureaucratic management is not the possible or actual transfer of power that the revolution in question signifies. It is the opening up of a public sphere which indicates something about the architecture of space between individual citizens in their capacity as conscious, world-transforming actors.

5 A brilliant attempt to take up the questions raised by Marx and Nietzsche from a decidedly non-idealist and non-juridical perspective can be found in the works of Deleuze and Guattari, a number of which are cited in previous chapters.

6 A number of prominent theorists of the Marburg School such as Cohen and Natorp, as well as some Austro-Marxists, have already made the point that practical reason and democracy are incompatible with the workings of capitalism, such that the implementation of genuinely democratic laws demands the reorganisation of the economy along socialist lines. The obvious problem is that it is difficult to see how the socialism they advocate is very different from Karl Kautsky's (1854–1938) or some other brand of collectivist statism. Lenin remarks that the Marxist says yes to democracy but asks, for what class? Posing the question of legitimacy in this way eventually allows him to regard the dictatorship of the proletariat as a democratic dictatorship. In order to refute Lenin without capitulating to liberal or social democracy, a theorist of legitimacy is likely to say yes to socialist mediation between humanity and external nature but ask, what kind of institutions make a non-oligarchic form of socialism possible?

This way of asking the question illustrates the point that it is not the choice between democracy and communism or democracy and fundamentalism that is at issue. The question is whether legitimacy is going to be oligarchic and populist, or if it will be epistemological and pluralist.

7 The most prominent traditional idealist after Hegel is probably Benedetto Croce (1866–1952). Croce is best known for his influence on Gramsci's attempt to enrich historical materialism with key idealist ideas. Croce had an inestimable impact on Gramsci, Gentile and more recent Italian thinkers such as Norberto Bobbio (1909–2004). Interested readers should consult Richard Bellamy, *Modern Italian Social Theory*, Stanford CA: Stanford University Press, chapters 5–8. Students with an interest in other traditional idealists such as T. H. Green (1836–82) can obtain useful information in Bellamy, *Liberalism and Modern Society: an Historical Argument*, Cambridge, Polity Press, 1992 chapter 1. Bellamy observes that the relations between liberalism and idealism are much more problematic in countries such as Germany and Italy that experienced a fascist interlude than in England, thus raising an interesting issue. It has proven to be extremely difficult to harmonise the idealist conception of transcendence with the demands of organised private interests on legality and democracy, except in highly unusual circumstances that are incapable of being reproduced on order. In the English case, these include a comparatively early and easy separation of church and state, and a completely different form of feudalism, if one can even call it that, than the forms of feudalism that were typical in continental Europe. This fascinated Montesquieu about the English constitution, as is well known, along with more recent scholars. See for example G. M. Trevelyan, *English Social History: A Survey of Six Centuries, Chaucer to Queen Victoria*, London, World Books, 1944.

8 Hence there is a path beyond the *Dialectic of Enlightenment* which does not embark upon the path of creeping (Habermas) or flagrant (Luhmann) functionalism. To put the matter slightly differently, there is a way to argue with Adorno against Adorno's tendency toward negative idealism and negative theology which does not embrace functionalism. That is by insisting that the bases of legitimate law are epistemological rather than procedural-pragmatic or systemically isolated from the sites of social exploitation and political conflict.

9 All propaganda and Cold War victories notwithstanding, it is not of terribly great consequence whether the products in question are manufactured by state-managed enterprises, competing private firms or some kind of hybrid like the market socialism operative in Tito's Yugoslavia. Nor does it make a great deal of difference if planners or advertising firms decide in central committees or in corporate boardrooms how need is to be administered from above. For an analysis of the problems with the Yugoslav experiment in self-management and market socialism in general, see Darrow Schecter, *Radical Theories*, chapter 5. That book points out that whilst market socialism might be regarded as the most liberal variant of state socialism, social democracy can be seen as the most socialist variant of capitalism. Market socialism and social democracy thus offer very inconclusive solutions to the problems of liberal democracy and capitalism.

10 In 1935 Alexis Stakhanov produced 102 tons of coal in a single six-hour shift in a Soviet mine. He quickly became a national hero and the emblem of Stakhanovism, which entitled particularly productive workers to extra pay, free holidays and subsidised visits to the Kremlin to receive the Order of Lenin. John Robottom remarks that for every successful Stakhanovite worker there were hundreds whose rate of pay actually dropped and who suffered from exhaustion and Communist Party

harassment. See John Robottom, *Modern Russia*, second edition, Harlow, Longman, 1972, chapter 8.

11 It is moreover difficult to find a theory of non-instrumental law in either first or second-generation critical theory. Telling in this context is the virtual absence of references to Adorno in the works of Kirchheimer and Neumann, and the evident lack of interest in law on the part of the author of *Negative Dialectics* and *Aesthetic Theory*.

12 Once again, those keen to preserve the distance between the legacy of the founder of scientific socialism and the history of failed revolutions may well say that Marx means nothing other than this in the *Critique of the Gotha Programme* (1875), where he states that the principle of the future communist society will be 'from each according to his ability, to each according to his needs'. The approach developed here shares this conclusion. It is moreover of no great consequence whether one refers to such a society as communist or libertarian socialist. But it remains to be shown how the division of labour is to be abolished, since oppressive forms of state manifestly do not wither away of their own accord or by dint of the laws of history, whatever these might actually be. To indicate how the division of labour is to be transcended one needs to formulate a theory of critical idealism, a critique of instrumental reason and law, as well as a theory of reconciliation. The theories of scientific socialism, historical materialism and base and superstructure are inadequate for these tasks. See Marx, the *Critique of the Gotha Programme*, in Robert C. Tucker (ed.), *The Marx–Engels Reader*, London, Norton, 1978, pp. 525–41, and especially p. 531.

13 One of the master strokes of liberal democratic ideology is the widely held belief that capitalist forms of commodity production are highly efficient because firms that do not adequately respond to consumer demand have the choice of changing their marketing strategies and product line or going out of business. Would it not be far more efficient to make consumer representation a part of the production process and the aggregation of demand rather than waiting for a product to fail or be boycotted?

14 Carl Schmitt, *Politische Theologie*, Berlin, Duncker & Humblot, 1996, p. 1.

15 Whilst the orthodox Marxist critique of instrumental reason that does not want to bother with legality and idealism degenerates into some version of 'class politics' that is usurped by a vanguard, the non-Marxist critique that is detached from questions of idealism and the division of labour ends up defending the Kant–Aristotle synthesis discussed in the introduction, though it might throw in a bit of systems theory as a concession to social complexity. It is now clear that both of these positions are unsatisfactory.

16 A third perspective which has not been directly discussed might be described as a radical hermeneutical position which suggests that it is possible to break out of the constraints of temporal linearity by remembering the future. Thinkers such as Walter Benjamin (1892–1940) attempt to combine the ideas of Proust, Bergson and some of the surrealists to argue that there are epistemological structures in dreams, language and memory that can liberate humanity from the continuum of time and thereby open up revolutionary possibilities for social change. Benjamin implies that the past could be irretrievably gone only if the future was also in some real sense already determined. On this reading, the future is open and the past can be redeemed from suffering and injustice. He intimates that a tiger's leap into the past, the spontaneous intervention of blood-sparing divine justice, as well as the coming of what he calls the messiah are all political possibilities that can never be excluded. But there is little that can be excluded on *a priori* grounds, and there is really no way of knowing how Benjamin's vision of revolutionary waking out of the slumber of reified consciousness could ever come to fruition. This is a poetic but very vague alternative to the prob-

lems connected with the vanguard and party state, on the one hand, and negative idealism/theology, on the other. Despite its poetic overtones, the hermeneutic position he represents does not sufficiently come to grips with the problems of radical humanism discussed in chapter 2. See the essays collected in *Illuminationen* (*Illuminations*), Frankfurt, Suhrkamp, 1977, and *Angelus Novus*, Frankfurt, Suhrkamp, 1988. Both works are available in English.

17 For an in-depth discussion of the respective positions of Hegel and Adorno on these issues, see Jan Weyand, *Adornos kritische Theorie des Subjekts*, Lüneberg, Zu Klampen, 2001, Part I. Adorno convincingly demonstrates that philosophy (and social science) becomes ideological apology if it does not address the effects of the division of labour and instrumental reason on the knowledge process, i.e. that the critique of knowledge is a critique of society and vice versa. Yet philosophy is not limited to those concerns, and indeed, philosophy that limits itself in this way turns into an apology of domination in its turn. Adorno's contribution marks the end of traditional modes of philosophising and social scientific investigation, though not, as Marx suggests in the *Theses on Feuerbach*, because philosophy and inquiry will one day be made redundant by revolutionary praxis. What is still needed is an interdisciplinary approach to humanity–nature and legality–legitimacy relations that carries theory and praxis forward beyond Adorno. There is no doubt that Foucault and Deleuze and Guattari have done this brilliantly as regards the former. The present book attempts to build on their analyses in relation to the latter.

18 Max Weber, *The Protestant Ethic and the Spirit of Capitalism* (1906), London, Collins, 1991. The point about the identity and simultaneous non-identity of humanity and nature indicates that the dialectic of idealism and materialism has to be reconsidered beyond the sociological frameworks of Marx and Weber, and beyond conventional epistemological paradigms generally. It is clear from the foregoing discussion that the theory of determination in the last instance (Marx and Engels) is as problematic as the notion of elective affinities (Weber) between material conflicts and intellectual representations.

19 Punishing the transcendence of necessity by enforcing passivity and conformity may be part of the reason why *all* law in modern industrial societies seems oppressive in relation to the marginalised and integrated forms of reason and cognition that are subsumed under the strictures of the general model. It is perhaps ironic that whilst certain Marxist theorists are notorious for invoking the notion of *false consciousness* to explain the persistence of consensus amidst palpable exploitation, the imposition of the general model invokes something similar *vis-à-vis* other models as long as the bases of legitimacy are instrumental, and anything that challenges uniformity can be perceived as a threat to the established order.

20 A corollary to the point that the central issue in politics is legality–legitimacy relations rather than the optimality of negative versus positive liberty, value relativity versus positivism, or the primacy of the base versus the primacy of the superstructure, is that the division of countries in the world according to the classification of democratic and non-democratic governments is specious. In most instances the term democratic designates metaphysical and populist legitimacy rather than a form of real self-government organised by autonomous citizens acting together. The division has moreover revealed itself as a pretext for imperialist interventions all over the globe that did not stop with the end of the Cold War, as the recent wars in Afghanistan and Iraq demonstrate.

21 It will rightly be objected that one example drawn from architecture hardly suffices to show how necessity can be transcended through the production of aesthetic-cognitive

values. But one could illustrate the point with a great variety of examples taken from all kinds of artistic praxis. There is not enough space to make a convincing case for libertarian socialism and the abolition of the division of labour, critical idealism, reconciliation, a legitimate form of law as well as an elaborate theory of political aesthetics in a single book, since the latter demands a study in its own right. What is argued in this chapter in terms of values and aesthetics does form part of the overall argument, however. Readers are asked to excuse the brevity of exposition.

22 There will no doubt be considerable disagreement about what constitutes aesthetic excellence and originality. If the preceding analysis regarding the conditions of legit- imate law is accurate, however, it is reasonable to believe that there could be as many different forms of original artistic expression as there are different citizens in whom the encounter with human nature is unique.

23 Humanism is thus a mistaken response to the problems associated with liberalism, metaphysics and Enlightenment. Adorno makes a similar point in a passage that has often been misinterpreted as flippant. He remarks that the inmates of the concentra- tion camps in the Second World War were murdered as standardised copies of an individual (Exemplare) rather than as individuals. The obvious point that absolute integration is a prelude to murder should not obscure the more profound thesis developed over his entire *oeuvre*, which is that coerced reconciliation is at work wher- ever instrumental reason and subjectivism prevail over aesthetic reason and dialectical objectivity. See the third section of *Negative Dialectics* entitled 'Meditations on Metaphysics'.

24 Hence the theories of reconciliation and legitimate law do not rely on a theory of freedom based on the idea of sublimation any more than they rely on notions of reappropriated essence. They analyse the question of the conditions of freedom first raised by traditional idealism without locating these in an *a priori* theory of individ- ual experience or dissolving particular forms of individual knowledge in the overarching march of history, and they point to the conclusion that the only credible forms of transcendence are ones which abolish the institutionalisation of instrumen- tal reason. The resulting critique attempts to go beyond hackneyed denunciations of capitalism in order to articulate a more encompassing critique of appropriation and all forms of populist legitimacy.

25 This is borne out by the emergence of ATTAC and other instances of global anti-capi- talist protest. The long-term success of such movements will depend on their capacity to articulate a juridical alternative to liberal democratic legislations of appropriation.

Conclusion

CHAPTER 5 shows why nature in humanity is both human and non-human, and that understanding the mediated non-identity between the human and the natural non-human is the legitimate epistemological and political alternative to humanist appropriation of nature and/or positivist distance from nature in systems-theoretical or other guises. It is not difficult to discern that humanist appropriation and positivist distance are in fact two sides of the same reified coin. In this context reification is broadly synonymous with subjectification and incomprehension of otherness in humanity, nature and objects. Liberal democratic and radical modernist attempts to realise the promise of Enlightenment by liberating humanity from the danger and unpredictability of nature have given rise to considerably different strategies to make an increasingly homogeneous conception of humanity the measure of all of reality in the name of a uniform 'human nature', and have succeeded in creating authoritarian and totalitarian political régimes relying on a wide range of techniques of legitimation. The varying degrees of success attained by these projects to establish hegemony through legal forms of legitimacy is fairly easy to measure if one equates relative prosperity and stability with the uncoerced reconciliation characteristic of a political community whose institutions are structured by legitimate forms of law. That is an ideological equation perpetuated by the victorious liberal democratic heirs of the Enlightenment. The most recent expression of this particular line of interpretation is the allegedly post-metaphysical thinking of theorists of communicative action and recognition, who provide arguments in support of the currently dominant models of democratic humanism and coerced reconciliation which continue to be enforced in Europe and North America. The urgency of relaunching the Enlightenment project on new bases seems especially urgent today, when the oil and arms clique in charge of the government of the United States at the time of this writing seems to be determined to impose unstable versions of these models on the rest of the world as a feeble-minded response to its own failures in global and domestic politics since the fall of the Soviet state socialist alternative to liberal democracy. The contribution to the relaunching of that project that is attempted in this book is summarised very briefly below.

At the end of the introduction it is stated that the four principal sources guiding the formulation of the main arguments in this study are libertarian socialism, a drastically modified form of idealism, critical theory and legal theory. The four sources are synthesised in order to articulate four theories intended to project thinking about political legitimacy beyond the restatements of Kant and the sociologically reconstructed versions of Aristotle which in various combinations continue to dominate mainstream social and political thought. What emerges is (1) a theory of reconciliation between humanity and external nature derived from libertarian socialism and legal theory, (2) a theory of reconciliation between humanity and human nature worked out on the basis of selected readings in traditional idealism, critical theory and modern art, (3) a theory of epistemological legitimacy in contrast to collectivist legitimacy, where epistemological legitimacy is defended as the basis of a legitimate form of law, and (4) a tentative sketch of the aesthetic dimension of reason stemming from a radicalisation of the premises of liberalism and traditional idealism. It is seen in chapter 5 that when analysed in conjunction with critical idealist arguments for the abolition of commodity production and the dismantling of the division of labour, aesthetic reason provides key arguments for a critique of instrumental reason and law. Starting with chapter 1, the point of departure for the theories of reconciliation and critical idealism in *Beyond Hegemony* is a reconsideration of the method and aims of traditional idealism. The imaginative power of traditional idealism taken up by a number of liberal thinkers such as Kant lies in the discovery that the transcendence of necessity is contingent upon factors which are external to and internal to humanity. The processes through which the mediation of the human and non-human unfold help forge the protean boundaries of rationality and are decisive in determining the antagonistic or reconciled quality of reality. Chapter 2 illustrates that, in attempting to radicalise the internal factors alone, movements which are ostensibly in opposition to liberalism succeed in the main merely in reproducing the liberal conception of humanity in a non-liberal idiom, when in fact the possibility of materialist transcendence of scarcity and fear depends on humanity making non-instrumental contact with the objective otherness of nature in nature and humanity. Chapter 3 shows that all modes of thought which imagine the conditions of freedom as the transcendence of necessity in juridical terms are idealist whether or not they style themselves as post-metaphysical, pragmatic or communicative. By combining the arguments in the first four chapters it becomes clear that the legalised instantiation of freedom which raises the possibility of transcendence but which refuses to acknowledge the overcoming of need in juridical terms is compelled to institutionalise two complementary forms of regulation. It is compelled to theorise freedom in terms of boundaries, restrictions and negation, and it is compelled to dismiss the epistemological dimension of need and the possible transformation of needs into non-relativist values. Rather than remaining consistently committed to the boundaries they establish by saying that legality is one thing and legitimacy is another, liberal theory generally tends to vacillate between the position that legality is one thing and legitimacy is another, on the one hand, and affirmations that legality is also the basis of legitimacy, on the other. With the second step liberalism collapses what already exists with all that is real and knowable, and indiscriminately bans everything that is not reconcilable with negative freedom to the pursuit of private happiness. This creates a fecund tension within liberalism, since the best liberal thinkers from Kant to Rawls imply that there is always a literally utopian moment in thought beyond the here and now of linearity that is not entirely speculative. In general, however, the liberal democratic way to argue for the legitimacy of law in epistemological terms without taking up the epistemological dimension of need is in effect a way of saying that what is legally known is always a limit, and that freedom consists in the non-infringement of that limit.[1] But for pragmatic reasons concerning the necessity of order, some kind of collective concept of legitimacy is needed to produce an argument for the legitimacy of legality beyond negative limitation. That is the coercive, integrating moment in liberal hegemony. Many of liberalism's opponents are wont to mistakenly identify what appears to be the unspoken alliance between apocryphal tolerance, strategic rationality and legality as the key to liberal democratic hegemony, and to reject the possibility of a juridical theory of political freedom as a consequence. Contrary to what these critics say, however, it is the complex array of integrating mechanisms which manufacture ideological legitimacy that make liberal democratic reality particularly antagonistic and regulatory. It is in any case reason and law that open up the possibility of a transition from ideology and regulation to reconciliation and genuine legitimacy.

A closing remark about the implications of critical idealism and epistemological legitimacy may be in order. If reconciliation between humanity and external nature as the first condition of legitimate legality can be roughly designated by the term libertarian socialism, there is as yet no term to designate the second condition, which is the reconciliation of humanity and human nature. The issue is discussed in this book in relation to the creation of individual values in an extra-moral sense and aesthetic rationality, but it is clear that much more work needs to be done on this subject. In light of some of the things that have transpired in the name of socialism, the absence of a label might well prove to be salutary for political thought. Besides, the forms of knowledge that this second form of reconciliation will produce are bound to be plural to such an extent that an overarching category may not be possible or even desirable. With the help of Marx, Ruskin and Morris, Cole has managed to sketch such a clear vision of libertarian socialism that it now needs to be legislated, with a number of modifications, not invented. Praxis anticipating reconciliation between humanity and human nature is awaiting a similar boost.

Note

1 Most liberal democrats implicitly concede that the terrain beyond, the terrain of epistemological legitimacy and positive freedom, is surely there. But it cannot be *rationally* known, and as such it is a matter of subjective preference. One must

Conclusion

renounce knowledge of it because humanity is allegedly not born with the faculties that would make its discovery possible. Liberal democracy attempts to base law on knowledge and legitimacy on the transcendence of necessity. On this issue liberalism is evidently revolutionary, since the possibility of realising the promise of Enlightenment turns on the possibility of locating a constellation of political institutions in which legitimate law and objective knowledge frame the terms of transcendence. Liberal democracy accepts this idealist concept and makes it the cornerstone of its understanding and practice of legitimacy. But the social interests which steer the liberal machine can hold on to negative and mainly contractual practices of liberty only at the price of institutionalising regulatory law and reified knowledge. According to the logic of liberal democratic argument itself, this marks the end of liberal democratic legitimacy. This is because the path of argument that produces a cogent defence of legal legitimacy enables another constellation of possibilities to achieve visibility as the institutions of legitimate legality.

Bibliography

Adorno, T. W. *Minima Moralia. Reflexionen aus dem beschädigten Leben* (1951), Frankfurt: Suhrkamp, 1997.

Adorno, T. W. *Zur Metakritik der Erkenntnistheorie. Studien über Husserl und die phänomenologischen Antinomien* (1956), Frankfurt: Suhrkamp, 1990.

Adorno, T. W. *Drei Studien zu Hegel*, Frankfurt: Suhrkamp, 1963.

Adorno, T. W. *Negative Dialektik* (1966), Frankfurt: Suhrkamp, 1992.

Adorno, T. W. *Stichworte. Kritische Modelle 2*, Frankfurt: Suhrkamp, 1969.

Adorno, T. W. *Ästhetische Theorie*, Frankfurt: Suhrkamp, 1970.

Adorno, T. W. *Soziologische Schriften* I, Frankfurt: Suhrkamp, 1979.

Adorno, T. W. *Noten zur Literatur*, Frankfurt: Suhrkamp, 1981.

Adorno, T. W. *Kant's Critique of Pure Reason*, Stanford CA: Stanford University Press, 2001.

Adorno, T. W. *Vorlesung über Negative Dialektik*, Frankfurt: Suhrkamp, 2003.

Agamben, Giorgio. *Homo sacer: il potere sovrano e la nuda vita*, Turin: Einaudi, 1995.

Agamben, Giorgio. *Homo sacer II: lo stato di eccezione*, Turin: Boringhieri, 2003.

Allison, Henry E. *Kant's Transcendental Idealism: An Interpretation and Defence*, New Haven CT: Yale University Press, 1983.

Always, Joan. *Critical Theory and Political Possibilities: Conceptions of Emancipatory Politics in the Works of Horkheimer, Adorno, Marcuse, and Habermas*, Boston MA: Greenwood Press, 1995.

Andrle, Vladimir. *A Social History of Twentieth Century Russia*, London: Arnold, 1994.

Arato, Andrew and Gebhardt, Eike (eds), *The Frankfurt School Reader*, New York: Continuum, 1982.

Arendt, Hannah. *The Origins of Totalitarianism*, New York: Faber, 1951.

Arendt, Hannah. *On Revolution*, New York: Penguin, 1963.

Aron, Raymond. *Les Étapes de la pensée sociologique*, Paris: Gallimard, 1967.

Avinieri, Schlomo. *Hegel's Theory of the Modern State*, Cambridge, Cambridge University Press, 1972.

Avrich, Paul. *Kronstadt, 1921*, New York: Columbia University Press, 1970.

Baudelaire, Charles. *Les Plus Belles Pages de Charles Baudelaire*, edited by Jacques Crepet, Paris: Éditions Messein, 1950.

Baudelaire, Charles. *L'Art romantique*, Paris: Flammarion, 1968.

Beck, Ulrich. *Risikogesellschaft. Auf dem Weg in eine andere Moderne*, Frankfurt: Suhrkamp, 1986.

Bibliography

Bellamy, Richard. *Modern Italian Social Theory*, Stanford CA: Stanford University Press, 1987.

Bellamy, Richard. *Liberalism and Modern Society: An Historical Argument*, Cambridge: Polity Press, 1992.

Benhabib, Seyla, Bonss, Wolfgang, and McCole, John (eds). *On Max Horkheimer*, Cambridge MA: MIT Press, 1993.

Benhabib, Seyla. 'Toward a Deliberative Model of Democratic Legitimacy', in Benhabib, Seyla (ed.), *Democracy and Difference: Contesting the Boundaries of the Political*, Princeton NJ: Princeton University Press, 1996.

Benjamin, Walter. *Illuminationen*, Frankfurt: Suhrkamp, 1977.

Benjamin, Walter. *Angelus Novus*, Frankfurt: Suhrkamp, 1988.

Berman, Harold J. *Law and Revolution: The Formation of the Western Legal Tradition*, Cambridge MA: Harvard University Press, 1983.

Bernstein, Richard. *Beyond Objectivism and Relativism: Science, Hermeneutics and Praxis*, Philadelphia: University of Philadelphia Press, 1983.

Best, Steven, and Kellner, Douglas. *Postmodern Theory: Critical Interrogations*, London: Macmillan, 1991.

Bhaskar, Roy. *Scientific Realism and Human Emancipation*, London: Verso, 1986.

Bhaskar, Roy. *Dialectic: The Pulse of Freedom*, London: Verso, 1993.

Black, Antony. *Guilds and Civil Society from the Twelfth Century to the Present*, London: Methuen, 1984.

Bloch, Ernst. *Das Prinzip Hoffnung* (1959), Frankfurt: Suhrkamp, 1998.

Blumenberg, Hans. *Die Legitimität der Neuzeit* (1966), third edition, Frankfurt, Suhrkamp, 1997.

Bobbio, Norberto. *Quale socialismo?*, Turin: Einaudi, 1976.

Bobbio, Norberto. *Teoria generale della politica*, Turin: Einaudi, 1999.

Bollack, Jean. *Poesie der Fremdheit*, Frankfurt: Suhrkamp, 2002.

Braudel, Fernand. *Civilisation matérielle, économie et capitalisme*, Paris: Colin, 1979.

Castoriadis, Cornelius. *L'Institution imaginaire de la société*, Paris: Seuil, 1975.

Caygill, Howard. *A Kant Dictionary*, Oxford: Blackwell, 1995.

Cohen, Hermann. *Ethik des reinen Willens*, Berlin: Cassirer, 1904.

Cohen, Hermann. *Kants Theorie der Erfahrung*, Berlin: Cassirer, 1919.

Cole, G. D. H. *The World of Labour*, London: Bell, 1913.

Cole, G. D. H. *Self-government in Industry*, London: Bell, 1917.

Cole, G. D. H. *Guild Socialism Re-stated*, London: Parsons, 1920.

Cole, G. D. H. *Social Theory*, London: Methuen, 1920.

Coole, Diana. *Negativity and Politics: Dionysus and Dialectics from Kant to Poststructuralism*, London: Routledge, 2000.

Copleston, Frederick. *A History of Philosophy VII, Eighteenth and Nineteenth Century German Philosophy* (1986), London: Continuum, 2003.

Dangerfield, George. *The Strange Death of Liberal England*, London: Constable, 1936.

Deleuze, Gilles, and Guattari, Félix. *Nietzsche et la philosophie*, Paris: Presses Universitaires de France, 1962.

Deleuze, Gilles, and Guattari, Félix. *La Philosophie critique de Kant*, Paris: Presses Universitaires de France, 1963.

Deleuze, Gilles, and Guattari, Félix. *Capitalisme et schizophrénie : l'anti-Oedipe*, Paris: Minuit, 1973.

Deleuze, Gilles, and Guattari, Félix. *Kafka : pour une literature mineure*, Paris: Minuit, 1975.

Deleuze, Gilles, and Guattari, Félix. *Qu'est-ce que la philosophie?* Paris: Minuit, 1975.

Derrida, Jacques. *L'Écriture et la différence*, Paris: Seuil, 1967.

Dyzenhaus, David. *Legality and Legitimacy: Carl Schmitt, Hans Kelsen and Hermann Heller in Weimar*, Oxford: Oxford University Press, 1997.

Ebeling, Hans (ed.). *Subjektivität und Selbsterhaltung. Beiträge zur Diagnose der Moderne*, Frankfurt: Suhrkamp, 1996.

Eckersley, Robyn. *Environmentalism and Political Theory: An Ecocentric Approach*, London: UCL Press, 1992.

Elias, Norbert. *Über den Zivilisationsprozess*, Frankfurt: Suhrkamp, 1997.

Fetscher, Iring (ed.). *Karl Marx und Friedrich Engels. Studienausgabe* IV, Frankfurt: Fischer, 1990.

Fetscher, Iring, and Schmidt, Alfred (eds). *Emanzipation als Versöhnung*, Frankfurt: Neue Kritik, 2002.

Fitzpatrick, Sheila. *Stalin's Peasants: Resistance and Survival in the Russian Village after Collectivization*, Oxford: Oxford University Press, 1994.

Fitzpatrick, Sheila. *The Russian Revolution*, second edition, Oxford: Oxford University Press, 1994.

Foucault, Michel. *Les Mots et les choses : une archéologie des sciences humaines*, Paris: Gallimard, 1966.

Foucault, Michel. *L'Archéologie du savoir*, Paris: Gallimard, 1969.

Foucault, Michel. *L'Ordre du discours*, Paris: Gallimard, 1971.

Foucault, Michel. *Surveiller et punir : la naissance de la prison*, Paris: Gallimard, 1975.

Foucault, Michel. *Dits et écrits 1954–1975*, Paris: Gallimard, 2001.

Freud, Sigmund. *Zur Psychopathologie des Alltaglebens. Über Vergessen, Versprechen, Vergreifen und Irrtum* (1904), Frankfurt: Fischer, 1998.

Freud, Sigmund. *Der Moses des Michelangelo* (1914), Frankfurt: Fischer, 1999.

Freud, Sigmund. *Das Unbehagen in der Kultur* (1930), Frankfurt: Fischer, 2000.

Friedeburg, Ludwig von, and Habermas, Jürgen (eds). *Adorno-Konferenz, 1983*, Frankfurt: Suhrkamp, 1983.

Frisby, David. *Fragments of Modernity*, Cambridge MA: MIT Press, 1986.

Fromm, Erich. *Beyond the Chains of Illusion*, New York: Trident, 1962.

Fromm, Erich. *Analytische Sozialpsychologie und Gesellschaftstheorie*, Frankfurt: Suhrkamp, 1970.

Fromm, Erich. *Greatness and Limitations of Freud's Thought*, London: Harper & Row, 1980.

Genet, Jean. *Journal du voleur*, Paris: Gallimard, 1949.

Geuss, Raymond. *The Idea of a Critical Theory*, Cambridge: Cambridge University Press, 1981.

Giddens, Antony. *Beyond Left and Right*, Cambridge: Polity Press, 1994.

Gobetti, Piero. *On Liberal Revolution*, New Haven CT: Yale University Press, 2000.

Gödde, Christoph. *Theodor W. Adorno und Alfred Sohn-Rethel. Briefwechsel 1936–1969*, Munich: text + kritik, 1991.

Gramsci, Antonio. *Il Risorgimento*, Rome: Riuniti, 1979.

Gripp, Helga. *Theodor W. Adorno*, Paderborn: UTB, 1986.

Habermas, Jürgen. *Strukturwandel der Öffentlichkeit* (1962), Frankfurt: Suhrkamp, 1990.

Habermas, Jürgen. *Legitimationsprobleme im Spätkapitalismus*, Frankfurt: Suhrkamp, 1973.

Habermas, Jürgen. *Theorie und Praxis. Soziologische Studien.* Frankfurt: Suhrkamp, 1978.

Habermas, Jürgen. *Faktizität und Geltung. Beiträge zur Diskurstheorie des Rechts und des demokratischen Rechtsstaats*, Frankfurt: Suhrkamp, 1992.

Habermas, Jürgen. 'Three Normative Models of Democracy', in Benhabib, Seyla (ed.), *Democracy and Difference*, Princeton NJ: Princeton University Press, 1996.

Hegel, G. W. F. *Frühe Schriften*, third edition, Frankfurt: Suhrkamp, 1994.

Hegel, G. W. F. *Differenz des Fichteschen und Schellingschen Systems der Philosophie* (1801), Stuttgart: Reclam, 1982.

Hegel, G. W. F. *Phänomenologie des Geistes* (1807), Stuttgart: Reclam, 1987.

Hegel, G. W. F. *Grundlinien der Philosophie des Rechts* (1821), Frankfurt: Suhrkamp, 1986.

Heidegger, Martin. *Sein und Zeit*, Tübingen: Niemeyer, 1993.

Heidegger, Martin. *Nietzsche* I (1961), Stuttgart: Neske, 1998.

Held, David. *Introduction to Critical Theory: Horkheimer to Habermas*. London: Hutchinson, 1980.

Henry, Michel. *Marx* I, *Une philosophie de la réalité*, Paris: Gallimard, 1976.

Henry, Michel. *Marx* II, *Une philosophie de l'économie*, Paris: Gallimard, 1976.

Hobsbawm, E. J. *Industry and Empire*, London: Penguin, 1968.

Holzhey, Helmut (ed.). *Ethischer Sozialismus. Zur politischen Philosophie des Neukantianismus*, Frankfurt: Suhrkamp, 1994.

Honneth, Axel. *Die soziale Welt des Sozialen*, Frankfurt: Suhrkamp, 1990.

Bibliography

Horkheimer, Max. *Traditionelle und kritische Theorie. Fünf Aufsätze*, Frankfurt: Fischer, 1992.

Horkheimer, Max, and Adorno, Theodor W. *Die Dialektik der Aufklärung* (1947), Frankfurt: Fischer, 1988.

Horvac, Branko. *The Political Economy of Socialism*, New York: Sharpe, 1982.

Hosking, Geoffrey. *A History of the Soviet Union*, final edition, London: Fontana, 1992.

Hosking, Geoffrey. *The First Socialist Society: A History of the Soviet Union from Within*, Cambridge MA: Harvard University Press, 1993.

Husserl, Edmund. *Die Krisis der europäischen Wissenschaften und die transzendentale Phänomenologie* (1936), Hamburg: Meiner, 1992.

Jäger, Andreas. *Was ist Ökonomie? Zur Formulierung eines wissenschaftlichen Problems im 19. Jahrhundert*, Marburg: Metropolis, 1999.

Jarvis, Simon. *Adorno: A Critical Introduction*, London: Routledge, 1998.

Jaspers, Karl. *Die grossen Philosophen*, Munich: Piper, 1988.

Kant, Immanuel. *Kritik der reinen Vernunft* (1781), two volumes, Frankfurt: Suhrkamp, 1968.

Kant, Immanuel. *Metaphysische Anfangsgründe der Rechtslehre* (1785), Hamburg: Meiner, 1963.

Kant, Immanuel. *Kritik der praktischen Vernunft* (1787), Frankfurt: Suhrkamp, 1982.

Kant, Immanuel. *Kritik der Urteilskraft* (1790), Stuttgart: Reclam, 1963.

Kelly, Erin (ed.). *John Rawls: Justice as Fairness, a Restatement*, Cambridge MA: Bellknap Press, 2000.

Kelsen, Hans. *Was ist Gerechtigkeit?* (1953), Stuttgart: Reclam, 2000.

Kervégan, Jean François, and Marmasse, Gilles. *Hegel : penseur du droit*, Paris: Éditions CNRS du droit, 2004.

Kirchheimer, Otto. *Politik und Verfassung*, Frankfurt: Suhrkamp, 1964.

Kirchheimer, Otto. *Politische Herrschaft. Fünf Beiträge*, Frankfurt: Suhrkamp, 1967.

Kirchheimer, Otto. *Funktionen des Staats und der Verfassung. Zehn Analysen*, Frankfurt: Suhrkamp, 1972.

Kirchheimer, Otto. *Von der Weimarer Republik zum Faschismus. Die Auflösung der demokratischen Rechtsordnung*, Frankfurt: Suhrkamp, 1976.

Köhnke, Christian. *Entstehung des Neukantianismus*, Frankfurt: Suhrkamp, 1993.

Kornas, Janos. *The Socialist System: The Political Economy of Communism*, Princeton NJ: Princeton University Press, 1992.

Krakauer, Siegfried. *Das Ornament der Masse*, Frankfurt: Suhrkamp, 1963.

Leck, Ralph M. *Georg Simmel and Avant-garde Sociology: The Birth of Modernity, 1880–1920*, New York: Humanity Books, 2000.

Lenin, Vladimir. *Collected Works XXVII*, Moscow: Progress Publishers, 1975.

Lester, Jeremy. *Modern Tsars and Princes: The Struggle for Hegemony in Russia*,

London: Verso, 1995.

Löwith, Karl. *Nietzsches Lehre von der ewigen Wiederkehr des Gleichen*, Stuttgart: Klett-Cotta, 1958.

Luhmann, Niklas. *Legitimation durch Verfahren* (1969), Frankfurt: 1983.

Luhmann, Niklas. *Rechtssoziologie*, Opladen: Westdeutscher Verlag, 1980.

Luhmann, Niklas. *Ausdifferenzierung des Rechts. Beiträge zur Rechtssoziologie und Rechtstheorie*, Frankfurt: Suhrkamp, 1984.

Luhmann, Niklas. *Soziale Systeme. Grundriss einer allgemeinen Theorie*, Frankfurt: Suhrkamp, 1984.

Luhmann, Niklas. *Das Recht der Gesellschaft*, Frankfurt: Suhrkamp, 1993.

Lukács, Georg. *Geschichte und Klassenbewusstsein. Studien über marxistische Dialektik* (1923), Amsterdam: De Munter, 1967.

Lyotard, Jean-François. *La Condition postmoderne*, Paris: Minuit, 1979.

Manent, Pierre. *Les Libéraux*, Paris: Gallimard, 2001.

Marcuse, Herbert. *Reason and Revolution: Hegel and the Rise of Social Theory*, London: Routledge, 1955.

Marcuse, Herbert. *Soviet Marxism*, New York: Columbia University Press, 1958.

Marcuse, Herbert. *Eros and Civilisation: A Philosophical Inquiry into Freud*, New York: Vintage, 1962.

Marcuse, Herbert. *One-dimensional Man: Studies in the Ideology of Advanced Industrial Society*, Boston MA: Beacon Press, 1964.

Marcuse, Herbert. *Negations: Essays in Critical Theory*, London: Penguin, 1968.

Marcuse, Herbert. *An Essay on Liberation*, London: Allen Lane, 1969.

Marcuse, Herbert (ed.). *Aggression und Anpassung in der Industriegesellschaft*, Frankfurt: Suhrkamp, 1972.

Marcuse, Herbert. *The Aesthetic Dimension: Toward a Critique of Marxist Aesthetics*, Boston MA: Beacon Press, 1978.

Marcuse, Herbert. *Nachgelassene Schriften*, II, *Kunst und Befreiung*, Lüneburg: Zu Klampen, 2000.

Marx, Karl. *Ökonomisch-philosophische Manuskripte vom Jahre 1844*, Leipzig: Reclam, 1988.

Marx, Karl. *Der achtzehnte Brumaire des Louis Bonaparte* (1852), in Iring Fischer (ed.). *Karl Marx und Friedrich Engels. Studienausgabe* IV, Frankfurt, Fischer, 1990.

Marx, Karl. *Grundrisse der Kritik der politischen Ökonomie* (1858), Frankfurt and Vienna: Europäische Verlagsanstalt, 1972.

Marx, Karl. *Das Kapital* I (1867), Berlin: Dietz, 1998.

Marx, Karl. *Der Bürgerkrieg in Frankreich* (1871), *Werke* XXIV, Berlin: Dietz, 1963.

Marx, Karl. 'Critique of the Gotha Programme' (1875) in Robert C. Tucker (ed.), *The Marx and Engels Reader*, New York and London: Norton, 1978.

McCauley, Martin. *Russia since 1914*, London: Longman, 1998.

McCauley, Mary. *Bread and Justice: State and Society in Petrograd, 1917–1922*, Oxford: Clarendon Press, 1991.

McClellan, David. *Marxism after Marx*, Boston MA: Houghton Mifflin, 1979.

Montesquieu (Charles de Secondat). *L'Ésprit des lois* (1748), Paris: Gallimard, 1982.

Mouffe, Chantal. *The Return of the Political*, London: Routledge, 1993

Müller, Christoph, and Staff, Ilse (eds). *Staatslehre in der Weimarer Republik*, Frankfurt: Suhrkamp, 1985.

Neumann, Franz. *Demokratischer und autoritärer Staat*, edited by Herbert Marcuse, Frankfurt: Fischer, 1986.

Nove, Alec. *The Economy of Feasible Socialism*, London: Allen & Unwin, 1983.

O'Neill, John. *The Market: Ethics, Knowledge and Politics*, London: Routledge, 1998.

Outhwaite, William. *Understanding Social Life* (1975), second edition, Lewes: Schroud & Pateman, 1986.

Outhwaite, William. *Concept Formation in Social Science*, London: Routledge, 1983.

Outhwaite, William. *New Philosophies of Social Science: Realism, Hermeneutics and Critical Theory*, Basingstoke: Macmillan, 1987.

Pasolini, Pier Paolo. *La divina mimesis*, Turin: Einaudi, 1975.

Pazanin, Ante. 'Die Überwindung des Gegensatzes von Idealismus und Materialismus bei Husserl und Marx', in Waldenfels, Bernard *et al.* (eds), *Phänomenologie und Marxismus*, I, *Konzepte und Methoden*, Frankfurt: Suhrkamp, 1977.

Pears, David. *Wittgenstein*, London: Fontana, 1971.

Penty, A. J. *Old Worlds for New: A Study of the Post-industrial State*, London: Allen & Unwin, 1917.

Pippin, Robert B. *Kant's Theory of Form: An Essay on the Critique of Pure Reason*, New Haven CT: Yale University Press, 1982.

Preuss, Ulrich. *Legalität und Pluralismus. Beiträge zum Verfassungsrecht in der Bundesrepublik Deutschland*, Frankfurt: Suhrkamp, 1973.

Proust, Marcel. *Contre Sainte-Beuve* (1912), Paris: Gallimard, 1954.

Proust, Marcel. *À la recherche du temps perdu* (1913–27), Paris: Gallimard, 1954.

Pugliese, Stanislao G. *Carlo Rosselli: Socialist Heretic and Antifascist Exile*, Cambridge MA: Havard University Press, 1999.

Rawls, John. *A Theory of Justice*, Cambridge MA: Harvard University Press, 1971.

Rawls, John. 'Justice as Fairness: Political not Metaphysical', *Philosophy and Public Affairs*, 14 (1985).

Rawls, John. *Political Liberalism*, New York: Columbia University Press, 1993.

Reiss, Hans (ed.). *Kant: Political Writings*, Cambridge: Cambridge University Press, 1970.

Robottom, John. *Modern Russia*, second edition, Harlow: Longman, 1972.

Bibliography

Schecter, Darrow. *Radical Theories: Paths beyond Marxism and Social Democracy*, Manchester: Manchester University Press, 1994.

Schecter, Darrow. *Sovereign States or Political Communities? Civil Society and Contemporary Politics*, Manchester: Manchester University Press, 2000.

Schelling, F. W. J. *Zur Geschichte der neuen Philosophie* (1854), Leipzig: Reclam, 1984.

Scheueman, William. *Between the Norm and the Exception: The Frankfurt School and the Rule of Law*, Cambridge MA: MIT Press, 1994.

Scheueman, William. *The Rule of Law under Siege: Selected Essays by Franz Neumann and Otto Kirchheimer*, Berkeley CA: University of California Press, 1996.

Schmidt, Alfred. *Der Begriff der Natur in der Lehre von Marx*, Frankfurt: Europäische Verlagsanstalt, 1962.

Schmitt, Carl. *Politische Theologie* (1922), Berlin: Duncker & Humboldt, 1996.

Schmitt, Carl. *Legalität und Legitimität* (1932), Berlin: Duncker & Humboldt, 1993.

Schnädelbach, Herbert. *Philosophie in Deutschland 1831–1933*, Frankfurt: Suhrkamp, 1983.

Schnädelbach, Herbert. *Hegels praktische Philosophie. Ein Kommentar der Texte in der Reihenfolge ihrer Entstehung*, Frankfurt: Suhrkamp, 2000.

Scott, Alan. *Ideology and New Social Movements*, London: Routledge, 1999.

Service, Robert. *A History of Twentieth-Century Russia*, London: Penguin, 1997.

Shaw, Martin (ed.). *Understanding Globalisation: Knowledge, Ethics and Agency*, London: Routledge, 1999.

Siep, Ludwig. *Praktische Philosophie im deutschen Idealismus*, Frankfurt: Suhrkamp, 1992.

Simmel, Georg. *Schriften zur Soziologie*, Frankfurt: Suhrkamp, 1983.

Spriano, Paolo. *Gramsci e Gobetti*, Turin: Einaudi, 1977.

Tarrow, Sidney. *Power in Movement: Social Movements, Collective Action and Politics*, Cambridge: Cambridge University Press, 1984.

Theunissen, Michael. 'Negativität bei Adorno', in Friedeburg, Ludwig von, and Habermas, Jürgen (eds), *Adorno-Konferenz 1983*, Frankfurt: Suhrkamp, 1983.

Thornhill, Chris. *Political Theory in Modern Germany: An Introduction*, Cambridge: Polity Press, 2000.

Thornhill, Chris. *Karl Jaspers: Politics and Metaphysics*, London: Routledge, 2002.

Thornhill, Chris. 'Systems Theory and Legal Theory: Luhmann, Heidegger and the False Ends of Metaphysics', *Radical Philosophy*, 116 (2002).

Thornhill, Chris. 'Adorno Reading Kant', *Prague Literary Review*, 2 (2004).

Tilly, Charles. *Coercion, Capital and European States, AD 900–1992*, Oxford: Blackwell, 1992.

Bibliography

Tocqueville, Alexis de. *De la démocratie en Amerique* (1835), two volumes, Paris: Gallimard, 1978.

Trevelyan, G. M. *English Social History: a Survey of Six Centuries, Chaucer to Queen Victoria*, London: World Books, 1944.

Tucker, Robert C. (ed.). *The Marx and Engels Reader*, New York and London: Norton, 1978.

Vico, Giambattista. *La scienza nuova* (1744), Milan: Garzanti, 1983.

Wade, Rex A. *The Russian Revolution, 1917*, Cambridge: Cambridge University Press, 2000.

Waldenfels, Bernhard, Broekman, Jana, and Pazanin, Ante (eds). *Phänomenologie und Marxismus* I, *Konzepte und Methoden*, Frankfurt: Suhrkamp, 1977.

Walicki, Andrzej. *A History of Russian Thought from the Enlightenment to Marxism*, Stanford CA: Stanford University Press, 1979.

Ward, Chris. *Stalin's Russia*, London: Arnold, 1993.

Weber, Max. *The Protestant Ethic and the Spirit of Capitalism* (1906), London: Collins, 1991.

Weber, Max. *Wirtschaft und Gesellschaft* (1921), Tübingen: Mohr, 1980.

Weber, Max. *Gesammelte Aufsätze zur Religionssoziologie*, three volumes, Tübingen: Mohr, 1934.

Weber, Max. *Gesammelte politische Schriften*, ed. Johannes Winkelmann, Tübingen: Mohr, 1988.

Weyand, Jan. *Adornos kritische Theorie des Subjekts*, Lüneburg: Zu Klampen, 2001.

Wiggershaus, Rolf. *The Frankfurt School*, Cambridge MA: MIT Press, 1999.

Wittgenstein, Ludwig. *Tractatus logico-philosophicus* (1921), Frankfurt: Suhrkamp, 1984.

Wright, Steve. *Storming Heaven: Class Composition and Struggle in Italian Autonomous Marxism*, London: Pluto, 2002.

Wyatt, Chris. 'G. D. H. Cole: Emancipatory Politics and Organisational Democracy', DPhil, University of Sussex, 2004.

Index

Note: n. after a page reference indicates the number of a note on that page.

Index